Praise

For the Love of Babies

"Dr. Hall expertly and compassionately shares the courage, love and determination that can be found in a NICU. Each story is a testimony to the power of medical science and to the fighting spirit of even the smallest baby. At its core, *For the Love of Babies* is about hope for each little survivor and their family, for increased understanding through research, and especially, hope for the day when fewer parents find themselves in the foreign, frightening world of NICUs as more babies are born full-term and healthy."

--Dr. Jennifer Howse,
President of the March of Dimes Foundation

"*For the Love of Babies* is a remarkable, moving and incredible piece of writing, not to mention a true addition to the literature we really need on the subject of NICUs, babies, doctors and parents."

--Vicki Forman,
Author of *This Lovely Life* (Mariner Books)

"From beginning to end, Dr. Hall speaks the language of the NICU with refreshing honesty. She provides insight into the neonatologist's world while describing dilemmas faced daily by those caring for our youngest and most fragile children. Writing with great empathy and power in every word of these stories about babies and their families, Dr. Hall shows readers that although life is not always fair, it is how you approach life that matters most."

--Deb Discenza,
Co-Author of *The Preemie Parent's Survival Guide to the NICU*
(Seahill Press)

"The short stories in this book are the essence of human compassion. The Neonatal Intensive Care environment is intense, frightening, intimidating and even overwhelming, steeped in emotions of fear, anger, frustration, incomprehension, blame, and loss. However, at the same time, it is filled with understanding, love, hopefulness, and professionalism.

It is very clear that Dr. Hall (no relation) feels all of these emotions and has captured them in these pages.

Who should read this book? Everyone interested in neonatal intensive care, parents, supportive friends and relatives, nurses, medical students and residents, neonatologists, and other members of the supporting staff. These stories convey the love and compassion which Dr. Hall experiences and wishes to transmit to her readers."

--Robert T. Hall, MD,
Emeritus Professor of Pediatrics,
University of Missouri Kansas City School of Medicine,
former Chief, Division of Human Development, Children's
Mercy Hospital, Kansas City, MO.

"*For the Love of Babies* is a heartfelt collection of stories that every parent should read. This life-changing book is not only for those who are expecting children but for those who have been blessed with them. Although each story is profoundly different, I was touched by the love and agony and eventual hope that each parent found for her baby. When I read *For the Love of Babies,* I learned that life is not measured by the materials we possess, but rather, by the moments that help us grow by helping others."

--Sandy Puc,
Co-Founder of Now I Lay Me Down to Sleep Foundation

About the Cover Photo

It wasn't easy for the quadruplets on the front cover to get to where they are today. The babies were born ten weeks early to Angela and Anthony Decker, after Angela went into preterm labor. All of the babies faced their own challenges during their journeys through the Neonatal Intensive Care Unit.

The baby on the far left was the largest at birth, weighing two-pounds fourteen-ounces. On the third day of life, he experienced a life-threatening complication from a PICC line (peripherally inserted central catheter). Fluid from the intravenous line leaked into the sac around his heart (the pericardial sac) and interfered with the heart's normal function. During a Code Pink, the neonatologist on duty inserted a needle into the pericardial sac to remove this fluid, saving the baby's life. This quadruplet was in the NICU for forty-seven days, and weighed five-pounds four-ounces when he was discharged in excellent condition.

The next baby, the only girl of the group, weighed two-pounds eight-ounces at birth. She stayed in the NICU for fifty-one days, and left weighing five-pounds four-ounces. She required orthopedic consultation and casts on both legs after her discharge to correct her feet—turned inward as a result of intrauterine crowding.

The smallest quadruplet weighed just two-pounds four-ounces when born. He developed a bowel obstruction after birth and underwent surgery on the twenty-third day of life. Of the four babies, he remained in the NICU for the longest, at fifty-four days. At the time of discharge, he was gaining weight steadily, and had reached four-pounds six-ounces.

The baby on the far right had a birth weight of two-pounds eleven-ounces. His NICU course was the least complicated of all the quads, but he still required assistance with his breathing (nasal continuous positive airway pressure and then nasal cannula) for twenty days, as well as a PICC line for nutritional support for seventeen days. He was the first to go home, weighing five-pounds seven-ounces, after a NICU stay of forty-four days.

Photo Credit: Kathryn Baird,
www.kathrynbairdphotography.com

Credit for photo of Dr. Hall on the back cover: Stephen Smith, www.stephensmithimages.com.

FOR THE LOVE OF BABIES

One Doctor's Stories
About Life in the Neonatal Intensive Care Unit

By Sue L. Hall, M.D.

WorldMaker Media
www.worldmakermedia.com

This book is dedicated to my own two babies, Katie and Hillary, who had to share me with countless other babies as they were growing up.
I love you both.

ISBN: 978-0-9828273-7-6
Library of Congress Control Number: 2011930145

WorldMaker Media
P.O. Box 610383
Newton, MA 02461
www.worldmakermedia.com

Cover Design by Amy Rooney

Preface

The stories of my experience as a doctor in the Neonatal Intensive Care Unit are all true. I have woven together, blended, and even partially fictionalized some stories from a variety of my experiences with patients and their families, as well as with my professional colleagues. I have altered the timeline of when events occurred in some instances, as well. My goal is to protect the privacy and confidentiality of those with whom I have worked: first and foremost, patients and their families, and then doctors and other medical staff. I have changed all names for this reason.

Contents

Part One: Starting Out in California

Part Two: A New NICU in the Midwest

Part One

Starting Out in California

Chapter 1

The Resurrection of Charlie Nash

"Where's the kiddo?" I asked.

"Hi, Dr. Hall. He's right over here." Carrying her clipboard of papers, Dr. Tanya Runyon crossed the Neonatal Intensive Care Unit ahead of me and stopped in front of a baby as orange as a pumpkin.

Wrong holiday, I thought, when I saw the baby. It was the night before Easter—nowhere near Halloween.

"Hey, baby," I said, preparing to examine the baby that lay stretched out on an open bed in front of me. "My hands may be a little bit cold."

"Do you always talk to babies?" Dr. Runyon asked. "They can't talk back."

"Yes, I always let them know what's coming, especially if it's my cold hands."

The baby lay under a triple bank of phototherapy lights, which radiated an eerie blue glow. Wearing a black mask over his eyes for protection, he looked as though he were enjoying his own personal tanning booth. He appeared sturdy and healthy except for his orange skin, a sign of jaundice. As I put a stethoscope over his chest, he pushed it away with his hand. How is a newborn capable of such intentional action, I wondered. Did he know what was coming?

After I examined the baby, I told Dr. Runyon, "If we're going to do an exchange transfusion, we need to get consent from his parents. Do you have the paperwork ready?"

***

Late that afternoon I had received a call at home just as my preschool daughters and I finished dipping hard-boiled eggs into cups of pastel-colored water in preparation for Easter. As a newly minted neonatologist taking calls about patients from home instead of staying overnight in the hospital, I felt frustrated at being pulled away from an annual tradition my daughters and I enjoyed together. Balancing motherhood and work created an uncomfortable tension in my life that was not easily resolved, especially when my daughters protested my departure, as they did on this afternoon.

As I left my children to drive to the hospital, I thought about how the task awaiting me there would take several hours. I arrived just as the sun washed the color out of the horizon; the forest of pine trees dotting the hill behind the hospital lost its form and would soon be swallowed by the dark.

By contrast, when I entered the brightly lit neonatal intensive care unit, known as the NICU, a change of shift was underway. Nurses grouped in twosomes chatted noisily by babies' bedsides, while the resident doctor stood watch over all twenty babies lined up in bassinets and isolettes around the perimeter of the large room.

Dr. Runyon greeted me: "The bilirubin level on that kid with Rh incompatibility is now high enough that he's going to need an exchange transfusion."

When Charlie Nash was born, my medical team diagnosed Rh incompatibility. His mother had O-negative blood, and Charlie had O-positive blood. When Charlie's O-positive red blood cells seeped into his mother's bloodstream, her O-negative cells reacted to his positive cells as foreign invaders. She produced antibodies that crossed the placenta, and then attacked and destroyed his blood cells, causing anemia. As dangerous as anemia can be, the breakdown product of the ruptured red blood cells (bilirubin) has the potential to cause even greater harm. Bilirubin, which gives the skin its characteristic orange color, can cross the blood-brain barrier and cause permanent brain damage—if the level rises high enough.

From the details Dr. Runyon told me, I agreed that it was time to perform an exchange transfusion on Charlie to prevent his bilirubin from reaching a level that might injure his brain. During an exchange transfusion, we would slowly remove an amount of blood equal to twice his blood volume, and replace it using blood with a normal bilirubin level. I made sure Dr. Runyon specifically ordered a whole unit of blood (500 ml.) for the procedure, and of a blood type that would not adversely react with his mother's antibodies.

The disease caused by Rh incompatibility is rarely seen anymore in this country, thanks to the advent of the RhoGAM® shots given to women with O-negative blood type in the twenty-eighth week of pregnancy. RhoGAM prevents the mother's body from forming antibodies, which can threaten babies she might carry in the future. In the United States, each year, only a few women and their babies develop the full-blown syndrome, but Charlotte and Charlie Nash were among those unfortunate few.

"This will be my first exchange transfusion," the resident said when I reached her. "I can't wait."

And this will be my first exchange transfusion to supervise, without someone supervising me, I thought.

One of the stranger conundrums about practicing medicine is how excited some doctors become when they take care of very sick patients, or perform invasive procedures. The more technically challenging and the riskier the procedure or operation, the greater the thrill of achievement. Although both Dr. Runyon and I were looking forward to adding to our skill set with this procedure, I was thinking I would rather it could take place any time other than this Saturday night. It would be so much more fun to be home preparing Easter baskets with my daughters.

It was 1989, and I had recently completed the ten years of training (medical school, residency in pediatrics, and fellowship in neonatology) required to become completely and solely responsible for the patients under my care. As a junior faculty member in the Department of Pediatrics at one of the local medical schools, I supervised Dr. Runyon and many other resident physicians at the county hospital's NICU. The residents came here on a training rotation from their base at the university hospital. The resident doctors—recruits fresh from medical school—provided the daily "hands-on" care for all babies, stayed to tend them at night, and ran to emergency deliveries—if they were needed. While they were adjusting to their increased responsibilities since graduating from medical school, I was still trying to become comfortable in my new role as the final decision-maker for every baby's care.

I then turned my attention fully to the baby before me. "Before we begin, let's review all the baby's labs," I suggested to Dr. Runyon. "Make sure this is really necessary. What is his bilirubin now?"

"Eighteen. When the baby was born twenty-four hours ago, it was six."

"Aieee," I exclaimed. It had jumped far too high, far too fast. I noticed that the build-up of bilirubin in Charlie's body had indeed turned his skin orange.

We sat down at a desk with a computer and pulled up the baby's labs on the screen in front of us. Together we scanned them: hematocrit 26 percent, reticulocyte count 18 percent, and the number for sodium was 142, potassium was 4.1, and on and on. In less than five minutes, we had reduced the baby's plight to a series of numbers from which we would develop a complex mathematical equation. Within hours, the bilirubin was certain to exceed twenty—the level at which we had to be concerned about possible brain damage occurring—and it would rise further if we did nothing.

"The blood just arrived from the blood bank," announced Marti, the charge nurse. "We'll get it set up while you guys get consent."

Dr. Runyon led me to Charlotte Nash's room. She was resting in bed while her husband, Jim, sat next to her in a plastic chair. Half-eaten hamburgers, wilting French fries, and nearly empty shakes from the ever-popular Southern California institution, In-N-Out Burger, were strewn on the table that stretched across her bed. A pile of thick books with a yellow legal pad balanced on top leaned precariously from the seat of a chair next to Jim.

This couple did not fit the profile for county patients. While most of our patients were from other countries—Mexico, Guatemala, El Salvador, Columbia, Russia, Ethiopia—this couple were clearly from Main Street, U.S.A.

"Are you all celebrating?" I asked. "Congratulations on Charlie's birth."

"Thanks," they replied in concert.

"What's with all the books?" I asked. "That's a scary stack."

"I just finished law school in December, and I'm studying for the Bar exam. I'm not working right now, so my wife had to get Medicaid to cover her prenatal care. That's why we're here at the county hospital," Jim explained.

"Well, good luck with your exams. I don't envy you. I've taken enough of those killer exams to never want to go through that again." I could define my life over the previous ten years by measuring the intervals between major qualifying exams in medicine.

"Dr. Runyon and I came to get your consent for a procedure called 'an exchange transfusion,'" I continued. "It's unusual that your baby has such significant jaundice. Didn't you get RhoGAM with your previous pregnancies?"

"I was in a fender-bender during my last pregnancy," Charlotte said. "I didn't think I'd been hurt, so I didn't go to the doctor. My doctor later found I'd produced antibodies to Rh-positive blood, meaning that I had had some internal bleeding from my placenta at the time of the accident. He told me if I'd come in and gotten RhoGAM within seventy-two hours of the accident, this might not have happened."

"Oh, that's too bad. And once your body produces those antibodies, it remembers, and the next time you're pregnant, you produce even more." I finished the story for her. "That is why we are here now.

"So, in an exchange transfusion," I continued, "we take your baby's blood out, and put new blood back into him. This does several things: it takes out his blood cells that are marked as 'different' from yours, so they won't break down; it removes your dangerous antibodies from his bloodstream; it gives him new blood cells that will not be broken up; and it cleans the bilirubin out of his blood."

"Whew," said Jim. "That is a lot."

"Yes, it is complicated. But without doing the procedure, his bilirubin level will go higher, and he could develop brain damage."

I did not tell them about the time I had seen a baby with this same condition in Nicaragua. In the small town I visited on a medical mission, blood was not available for transfusion. The doctors had no treatment to offer, other than standard phototherapy, which we were now using with

Charlie. The baby demonstrated all the signs of impending brain injury, including arching his back so far behind him while stiffening his arms that he looked like a circus contortionist.

In the village's clinic later that same week, I examined another child, a six-year-old with signs she had suffered through this same complication as a newborn. Brought in by wheelchair, her arms writhed uncontrollably while she drooled into a bib tied around her neck. In the developed world, this is a preventable complication.

"What are the risks?" Charlotte asked.

"There's a 1 percent risk of death. Some of the blood chemistries get out of whack, but usually, things go well."

I could not help thinking about the time I had had to sign a consent form to have a medical procedure done under general anesthesia. When the surgeon told me there was a chance I could die as a result of the anesthesia or as a complication of the procedure, I balked at signing. "I'm not going to give you permission to kill me," I said.

"Look, it is just a standard consent form," he said. "I have to tell you the risks."

Knowing I needed the operation, I had no choice but to sign. That was the position in which I had just placed Charlie's parents. As a physician, I knew that his parents should expect to hear my opinion on why the procedure was necessary, what the risks and benefits of the procedure were, and what alternatives there were to performing the procedure. I also knew that the risks, however frightening, should never be glossed over or minimized, in the event that they actually might occur.

"Can we see him before you start the transfusion?" Jim asked, after Charlotte watched him scrawl his signature on the consent form.

"Sure. It will take a couple of hours once we get started, so come now."

Dr. Runyon and I returned to the NICU with the consent form and got everything ready while the parents shared a brief visit with their baby. "I love you. I love you. I love you," said Jim, grasping his son's tiny fingers. "Do you think he'll still be able to get into Yale Law School?" he asked me while I donned my sterile garb. "I've got high hopes for this boy."

As I tied my surgical mask across my face, I said, "I don't see why not."

Dr. Runyon tucked her ponytail under her gauzy blue paper hat, and we were ready to start, both of us wearing floor-length blue-paper gowns and sterile gloves. We had created our own "mini-operating room without walls" right in the middle of the NICU.

The procedure started slowly and then picked up speed. First, Dr. Runyon used a large syringe to draw blood out of one of Charlie's umbilical IV lines and then expel it into a "waste" bag that hung at the bedside. Simultaneously, I pushed red cells supplied by the blood bank into the baby's bloodstream through the other umbilical line. With both of us working on the baby, we could cut the time it usually takes—often several hours—in half.

Stevie Wonder's voice soared over the NICU as we worked, and since it was quiet, I could actually hear the words of "I Just Called to Say I Love You" across the din of the room:

"Ya hear that, Charlie?" I asked. "I heard your daddy tell you he loves you, and now Stevie Wonder is singing to the whole world about it."

"Man, it's so hot under this gown," I complained about forty minutes into the procedure.

Just then Marti said, "Dr. Hall, the monitor looks weird."

I glanced up, and sure enough, the little up-down-up line that regularly marked each heartbeat in red, like a visual metronome, had transformed into an unruly squiggle.

"What's going on?" I asked. Fear seized me. My breathing quickened. I flushed and felt hotter still under all my paper garments. "Let's stop for a minute," I said.

"Looks like V-fib," said Dr. Runyon.

I did not want to agree with her, but I had to. "Sure does," I muttered.

Ventricular fibrillation—V-fib for short—occurs when the heart stops beating and starts to tremble chaotically. Instead of contracting forcefully to propel the blood out of the heart, no blood is ejected. V-fib is a life-threatening emergency: a quivering heart cannot supply blood to the brain, and an oxygen-deprived brain can ruin an otherwise promising life in five minutes.

"Draw a blood gas," I instructed.

Dr. Runyon pulled back on the syringe and red blood flowed easily into it. A respiratory therapist appeared at her side to pick up the sample.

The therapist was gone before I even finished saying "*Stat!*"

Moments later, he reappeared with the results. "The pH is low enough to qualify as a panic value," he said.

What had happened? Since I had reviewed the baby's blood tests before we started, I knew the acid-base balance in his body was now significantly abnormal; his current blood pH of 6.9 showed a frightening difference from the normal value of 7.4. My thoughts did not want to go forward; my brain froze. I willed myself to think logically.

Aha, I thought after a moment. *The heart is protesting because it is being bathed in acidic blood, instead of blood with the usual normal pH of 7.4.* I knew stored blood was acidic, but I had never seen it cause a problem like this before. *What had I done differently to cause this?*

'Let's send a sample from the blood we're infusing. Run it quick," I begged. I handed the specimen to the therapist, who dashed off to the lab once again. "Draw up six milliequivalents of sodium bicarbonate, Marti. Please," I added as an afterthought.

I fixed my eyes on the baby's monitor screen. The squiggle taunted me. My breath still felt frozen inside of me, but I had to shake it loose so I could inhale. I would need all my breath to outrun the freight train I felt barreling up behind me. *Get the baby off the track*, I thought.

"Can you feel a pulse?" I asked Dr. Runyon.

She slipped her index finger down under the green cloth drapes where we had hidden Charlie when we created our sterile field. Placing her finger on his neck, she felt for the soft flicker over his carotid artery.

"I'm not sure," she said, her face a jumble of emotions: fear, confusion, uncertainty—the same emotions I was feeling. Then she added, "It's there, just weak and irregular."

I glanced from the monitor to Charlie—what I could see of him. He was still pink and breathing easily, and his eyes peered out above the green towels that covered his body from belly to chin. *Not too bad... yet,* I thought.

Marti handed the syringe containing sodium bicarbonate to Dr. Runyon, who infused it promptly. The therapist returned with the tiny slip of paper containing results of the most recent test. "The blood sent up from the blood bank has a pH of 6.5."

I felt my stomach climb into my mouth.

Blood stored in the blood bank for a number of days degrades to an acidic state. This rarely presents a problem, since most transfusions are small in proportion to a person's blood volume. The bit of acid-tinged blood is quickly diluted in the recipient's bloodstream. Even in an exchange transfusion such as we were doing, it is not recommended to check or adjust the pH of the blood being infused. I could only surmise we had done the exchange—taking out large volumes of Charlie's blood with its normal pH and replacing it with blood with an acid pH— too fast, faster than Charlie's body was able to adjust. Charlie's heart was in full rebellion. We had upset its precise electrochemical balance.

Dr. Runyon and I stood like matching statues over Charlie's body. "What else can we do?" she asked.

Call the attending, I thought. *Oh, that's me now. This is my emergency to handle on my own. I've got the diplomas and certificates to prove it.*

"Yeah, what are you going to do?" asked Marti, the nurse helping us. "Jeez, you've got to do something." Marti's voice was several decibels higher than her usual already-loud register.

"Marti, we *are* doing something. We're giving bicarb. But, get the Code Pink cart close by, just in case we need more meds," I replied. "And be ready to start CPR at any moment." I could not let Marti's anxieties exacerbate my own. My challenge was to remain calm, so I could think clearly. Clear thinking while working under pressure is an important skill for every doctor to master, but especially for those working in high-stress areas of the hospital, such as in intensive care units, operating rooms, and emergency departments.

Marti bustled behind us, pulled the cart into position, and opened several drawers to remove syringes and needles, boxes with small vials of medication, and equipment to intubate the baby should his breathing cease. Her movements were frantic, loud, jarring. They reflected the anxiety I felt, but tried hard not to show.

"Standard treatment for V-fib is to shock the baby," I told Dr. Runyon. "But it's not likely to work if we don't correct the acidosis first." Giving the baby a jolt of electrical current from large paddles applied to his chest would give his heart a chance to 'reset' and resume its normal rhythm. I did not want to do it unless it had a better chance of working. "Let's give more bicarb."

A crowd of nurses gathered around Charlie's bedside, all eyes trained on his monitor. They looked as if they were watching a slow-motion replay of a car crash to understand exactly how one car had careened into another. I noticed two others who sat feeding babies on their laps on the opposite side of the room; my guess was that they did not want to be anywhere near the fear on Charlie's side.

Soon the bicarb was in, followed by a bolus of normal saline, a dose of calcium, and a shot of glucose. Occasionally, the crowd cheered when a normal-appearing beat moved randomly across the monitor screen. But just as quickly, their elation turned back to terror when the beat disappeared.

"Hey, come on, Charlie," I pleaded. "We're trying to help you." Since he was still alert, I thought he must be getting enough blood to his brain in spite of the irregular heart rhythm.

"Shall I call cardiology?" Dr. Runyon asked. Sweat beaded her forehead just below her blue-paper hat.

"Be my guest." *Why hadn't I thought of that?* During my short tenure at the county hospital, I had already learned that practicing medicine there was a bit like practicing in a third-world country. Many of our patients were from the third world, resources were generally scarce, and we had no highfalutin consultants like they did at the university hospital. We were out in the boonies by ourselves, improvising with what we had. One of the things we did have was a telephone.

It took a few long minutes for the page operator to locate the cardiologist on call. Finally, Dr. Runyon spoke to him. "He recommends lidocaine," she yelled across the room to me.

"Lidocaine? I haven't given that in forever. I have no idea what the dose is." *Why can't a cardiologist just be here with us?* I thought. I could use the moral support.

"What's the dose?" she asked into the phone.

Once she had her instructions, Dr. Runyon whipped out a calculator and figured the concentration and drip rate of the medication. "Will someone run this down to pharmacy?" she asked after scratching her results on an order sheet. "We need it *stat.*"

"Yeah, right," said the respiratory therapist. He was the only one in the room who acted as if nothing were happening. He continued to make his rounds, examining the other babies and checking their ventilator settings and oxygen-saturation probes, while a nurse picked up the order and slipped out of the NICU to take it to the pharmacy.

My eyes flitted back and forth between Charlie and his monitor. He remained pink with his orange undertones. If he did not get enough oxygen, what color would he be? Blue plus orange equals what?

"At what point do we start CPR, Dr. Hall?" Marti asked.

My stomach flipped over. The minutes ticked by; I had no idea how many had passed.

"If he loses consciousness or stops breathing, or his color goes bad, we'll start CPR." *Will that be too late? Won't those be signs he's already slipped over to the other side?* Since he didn't seem worse, I was optimistic his blood pH was improving and we were nearing our mark.

In the background, the radio blared. The night shift always turned the volume up loudly, or maybe it just seemed loud because a hush had fallen over the NICU. Emergencies could either be tumultuous and chaotic as we struggled to bring a baby back to life, or they could be deathly silent as we pondered what intervention to try next.

"Dr. Hall, don't you think you ought to talk with the baby's parents?" Marti interrupted my thoughts.

"Good idea. Yes, can someone go get them?" I dreaded this conversation, but I knew it was better to give them a warning than to walk in unexpectedly, some minutes later, to announce their son had departed this Earth.

"Will do," she agreed.

Seconds passed before Charlotte and Jim stood at the door of the NICU. I pulled away from Charlie's bedside, took off my mask, hat, and gown, wadded them up, and threw them in the trash. I was not going to continue the exchange transfusion tonight, no matter what happened.

"I'm having trouble with Charlie," I told them. "His heart isn't beating regularly. It's just sort of quivering. His acid-base balance was upset by the transfusion, and we're trying to fix it."

Looking as if he had been punched in the gut, Jim sucked in a slow, deep breath.

"It's not like he could die or anything, is it?" Charlotte asked.

"I sure hope not. I'm working as hard as I can to get his heartbeat back on track. Please don't abandon hope, but I should get back to him now."

"Let's go back to the room, honey," Jim said, wrapping his arm around his wife. Looking back at me, he added, "Call us when we can see our baby."

I wished I had the luxury to spend more time talking with Charlie's parents about his tenuous condition, but I was grateful to be left alone to focus on helping him survive this emergency. How could I have taken a baby who was in perfect health—except for his blood group incompatibility—

and brought him to the brink of death? Although I had not given the baby the condition that required the exchange transfusion, I had likely performed the transfusion too quickly, thereby jeopardizing his life. I thought about the statistics I quoted to Charlie's parents. "A 1 percent risk of death," I'd said. Had I even believed that was possible? One is a pretty big number when it is you or your baby experiencing the complication, especially when the complication is death.

When I returned to Charlie's bedside, Marti was hanging a small, clear plastic bag containing the lidocaine. As it dripped through the baby's IV, I held my breath. *Faster, faster*, I thought. *Please, please, please*, I prayed, *let this work.*

"One more blood gas," I said. "Let's see if we're making progress."

Shortly, the results returned. "Doin' better," exclaimed the respiratory therapist, a surprised smile on his face. "Doin' better."

Normal blips punctuated the monitor screen more frequently now. Then, almost as mysteriously as the squiggle appeared, it faded and was replaced by the usual reassuring pattern.

"Yay!" cried Marti.

"Hey, we don't call it 'intensive care' for nothing," I said. *Thank God the medications worked*, I thought.

"Whew," exclaimed Dr. Runyon. "That was a close one. I thought I liked intensive care, but after tonight, I'm not so sure."

"Well, we've learned a lot tonight, haven't we?" I said. "If we need to repeat an exchange transfusion tomorrow, since we didn't even get halfway through this one, we'll do it more s-l-o-w-l-y and add some bicarbonate to the blood before transfusing it." *You can't be too careful*, I thought, *if you intend to meet that highest standard of practicing medicine, Do No Harm.*

We took the sterile drapes off Charlie, checked his lab values, and continued his phototherapy. I went to his mother's room, where Charlotte and Jim greeted me with tense faces. "He's okay. Things are back to normal," I said. "Thank God."

I was ready to leave the NICU for home, but first I stopped to talk with several of the nurses. "What do you think happened?" one of them asked. I knew I should help them understand what had transpired in case they needed the knowledge in the future.

"Just don't be in a rush during exchange transfusions, like I was," I said. "Time *is* of the essence, but not in the way you usually think it is. Slower is safer." After explaining my thoughts, I headed for the door.

"Keep everyone safe, Dr. Runyon," I said as I walked out. "And Happy Easter to all." I was glad Charlie would get to see Easter as well, and I was still amazed and mystified by how he seemed to pull through in good shape.

I had left my career as a social worker to enter medicine both so I could find out how children with developmental disabilities I had previously worked with had "gotten that way," and to be in a position to do something concrete to help them get better. I hoped I had not just created another disabled child in Charlie Nash.

Several days later, after another exchange transfusion successfully cleared Charlie's jaundice, we did a CAT scan of his brain, to make sure he had not suffered any ill effects from the long time his heart beat was irregular. The radiologist read it as normal.

"He's still got that chance at Yale," I told his Dad. "Go for it!"

Notes:

Rh isoimmunization, the condition for which Charlie was being treated, rarely leads to the need for exchange transfusion in the United States anymore, due to the advent of the Rh Immunoglobulin shot (RhoGAM®), which prevents mothers from developing antibodies to the Rh factor. An excellent patient-education pamphlet explaining the Rh factor, and how sensitization occurs during pregnancy in women who have Rh-negative blood type, is on the website of the American Congress of Obstetricians and Gynecologists: (http://www.acog.org/publications/patient_education/bp027.cfm).

The incidence of kernicterus and long-term brain damage resulting from hyperbilirubinemia of any cause diminished markedly during the 1980s when conservative guidelines were in place detailing when doctors should perform exchange transfusions. These guidelines were relaxed somewhat in the 1990s, primarily for babies whose jaundice was the result of breastfeeding, usually occurring after discharge from the hospital. Coincident with relaxation of standards for exchange transfusion, "early discharge" from the hospital after birth became the norm, with "drive-through" deliveries occurring and babies allowed to go home with mothers after periods as short as six-to-twelve hours after birth. Subsequently, researchers documented a resurgence in cases of kernicterus. (American Academy of Pediatrics Subcommittee on Hyperbilirubinemia. 2004. "Management of Hyperbilirubinemia in the Newborn Infant 35 or More Weeks of Gestation." *Pediatrics 114*(1): 297-316.)

Prevention of kernicterus is now a patient-safety goal mandated by The Joint Commission (http://www.jointcommission.org), the organization that accredits hospitals and other health care facilities. Recommendations for how doctors should evaluate and follow-up each baby's risk for jaundice within the first few days after birth are in The Joint Commission's *Sentinel Event Alert,* August 31, 2004. (http://www.jointcommission.org/sentinel_event_alert_issue_31_revised_guidance_to_help_prevent_kernicterus/.)

Physicians in all fifty states have both an ethical obligation and a legal requirement to obtain informed consent before performing any invasive procedure on a patient. The goal is to enable patients (or their parents, in Charlie's case) to make educated decisions after learning about all the different treatment options. The process of obtaining informed consent is much more than simply asking a patient or his or her proxy to sign a piece of paper. It involves communication between doctor and patient or in the case of babies, their parents, about the patient's condition, why a particular procedure is being recommended, what the risks and benefits of the procedure are, as well as alternatives to the proposed procedure including the risks and benefits of the alternatives.

The patient or his or her representative—including parents—should also be told the risks and benefits of not having the procedure done. It is the physician's obligation to have these discussions using terms that laypeople can understand, and to allow adequate opportunity for patients or their representatives to have all their questions answered. See the website of the American Medical Association to read more about this process: (http://www.ama-assn.org/ama/pub/physician-resources/legal-topics/patient-physician-relationship-topics/informed-consent.shtml).

Chapter 2

The Long and Winding Road to Med School

In 1973, I entered the real world armed with my undergraduate degree, a double major in psychology and human biology, and great curiosity about children. In my first job as a teacher's aide in a school for what were then called "emotionally disturbed" preschoolers, I had plenty of opportunities to contemplate how the hapless children in my charge had developed their disabilities.

One afternoon, I kept an eye on Claire, as she inched her way across the top of the jungle gym. Earlier, I had watched with sympathy as she struggled to bend her stiff limbs into a crouch low enough to grasp the rail. At four-years-old, she was as thin as she was pale, with wispy hair and vacant eyes. Her strange wails touched my heart, and I wanted to understand their cause. At that moment, though, I simply tried to ensure she did not tumble off the jungle gym.

The sun was high during our mid-afternoon recess, and a light breeze kept me from feeling scorched as Claire struggled forward. Once she completed her crossing, I knew she would celebrate her accomplishment by running awkwardly across the yard, flapping her hands and rocking her body. If I could get her to make eye contact and connect with me emotionally during our recess, I would consider the afternoon a success.

I inhaled the soothing scent of the eucalyptus trees growing on the edge of the schoolyard, as I kept track of five-year-old Sammy, a chubby black boy. Out of the corner of my eye, I saw him on the other side of the playground. Sammy darted from the swings to the slide to the sandbox, never stopping to play for more than a minute at any location. He often knitted his eyebrows and looked into the sky, pausing to emit random noises that sounded as though they were from outer space. Sometimes I thought he might be, too. His diagnosis was childhood schizophrenia.

Nicholas, another one of my charges on the playground, wore his trademark ear-to-ear grin; he was having a good day. On bad days, we found him on the ground crying and pounding his fists, or having a seizure. None of the other children noticed the seizures, during which his left arm and leg jerked repetitively and his mouth became frothy. They were each too absorbed in their own alternative worlds.

Having just learned to walk, Nicholas seemed much younger than his four years. Since he still wore diapers, I hoped for his mom's sake that he would grow up faster. In our diagnostic conferences, I learned that a medical condition caused his problems. Was the bright red birthmark covering the right side of his forehead and his right eyelid a part of this?

How did these children get this way, I wondered. What were the biological underpinnings of their behavior? How were their parents able to cope with the children's complex issues, and how did they maintain hope for their improvement?

Traditional theories about how "refrigerator mothers"—mothers who were emotionally cold and distant—caused schizophrenia and other emotional problems in their children just did not sit right with me. Most people in the helping professions still interpreted children's strange behaviors on the basis of psychological theories, but a few were starting to recognize the importance of biology. Behaviors we did not understand might be wired into the recently discovered thing called DNA, and might not be the result of emotional neglect or maltreatment by insensitive parents. Many medical conditions causing profound developmental delay had not yet been identified. We simply did not have the tools in the 1970s to understand the causes underlying our very young students' problems.

Chatting with the mothers of these children at the white picket fence in front of the small school, it did not seem possible that they somehow caused their children's odd behaviors. How could a mother be emotionally cold enough (as cold as a refrigerator?) to cause severe mental illness by age four or five in one child, and at the same time be so warm and loving to her others? These mothers fit my definition of "normal." They were each concerned, caring, appropriate—and heartbroken. I refused to believe that they alone were to blame for the label their children were stuck with: "emotionally disturbed."

My desire to understand the biological basis of behavioral disturbances and mental illness began during my undergraduate study of psychobiology. When I could not fit this class into my schedule, the psychiatry professor who taught it, Dr. Keith Brodie (his real name), offered to privately tutor me for independent study credit. I crossed the sandstone plazas of the university on my bike weekly, arriving at his imposing private office in the medical school—weighted down by my bag of thick textbooks.

During our hour-long meetings, we discussed various chapters that poked holes in long-held beliefs about the causes of mental illness, from refrigerator mothers to Freudian repression. Dr. Brodie delighted in introducing me to clues about the biological underpinnings of behavior in our fascinating and thought-provoking conversations. When the semester came to an end, he asked me if I wanted to attend medical school. He would be willing to sponsor my application, if I were interested.

Medical school? I did not know if I would be able to handle the time demands of medical school, much less the long hours required of those pursuing a career in medicine. I had seen my pre-med friends studying from dawn to dusk and listened to them complain about their impossible exams.

I told Dr. Brodie, "No thanks" to med school. Instead, I completed a major in human biology, and then added a second major in psychology during my senior year because of the excitement I felt about my work with Dr. Brodie.

After several years of teaching children with developmental problems, I attended a master's degree program in social work. Because I already knew something about biology and psychology, learning about the social milieus in which people functioned would add another important piece to my understanding of them. I wanted to see how people outside my own insular experience in white middle class America lived, to find out what goes on in other cultures, in other peoples' homes and in their heads.

After completing my social work degree, I counseled families in homes where parents were suspected of abusing or neglecting their children. One father, deeply absorbed in mourning his wife's recent death, had no energy to feed or bathe either his six-year-old daughter or himself. An unemployed single mother with a drinking problem disciplined her hyperactive four-year-old son by whacking him on the butt hard enough to leave bruises. A pair of siblings were failing in school because their mother, whose mental functioning was limited by a head injury suffered years before, could not get them to class reliably. A two-year-old girl who lived in a run-down inner city apartment with her schizophrenic mother could hardly talk. A toddler who had been born prematurely was burned in a scalding bath by a father with a short fuse.

The connection between social environment and psychological outcome became abundantly clear to me. Yet, I still wondered, *how did these children get that way?* How did the four-year-old boy become so hyperactive? How did the head injury affect the mother's functioning? Would her children grow up normally, given her limitations? Was there some physical reason the two-year-old could not talk? Why was the toddler born prematurely? What complications did she have in the newborn period to make her cry so shrilly that her own father snapped while listening to her?

After being immersed in the fields of education, psychology, and sociology for seven years since graduation from college, I was eager to get back into biology. I wanted to see and understand how kids started out in life, and to give them the best possible chance at making their start a healthy one. I knew this would require not only providing them with excellent medical care, but also providing their families with generous doses of both emotional support and hope.

I entered medical school at age twenty-seven with a goal of becoming a neonatologist, a specialist in newborn intensive care. Ten years later, after completing the requisite education and training, I was finally ready to enter practice.

***

Since then, as a baby doctor—a neonatologist—it has been easy to fall in love with every one of my patients. They are innocent of everything. Completely vulnerable and dependent, their need for care and nurturing speaks to me. Their newness and freshness inspires so many possibilities for the future, so many opportunities to bring happiness and love into the world. They could become anything; they could become everything. These are among the sentiments that convinced me to become a neonatologist, a pediatrician with advanced training in the care of sick, premature, and other high-risk newborns. A *neonate* is a newborn child, or one in its first twenty-eight days of life: *neo* means *new* and *natus* is a form of the Latin verb *to be born.*

Many positive changes in the care of pregnant women and their babies have resulted in improved survival among newborns since I began my career in neonatology in 1989. Maternal steroids are now routinely given to mothers who deliver prematurely to hasten the development of their babies' lungs. Surfactant, the substance produced in the lung's tiny air sacs, or alveoli, can now be given as a medication directly into babies' lungs if need be. Ventilators and all types of specialized equipment have been developed, further engineered and refined to enhance the care of smaller and smaller babies. Doctors have learned much more about how to deliver adequate nutrition, prevent infection, and minimize harm as they shepherd tiny babies toward their futures.

And yet, babies still die in the neonatal intensive care unit, though not nearly as often as in the past. Currently, survival in United States' NICUs approximates 98 percent. But when you are the parent of a premature or ill newborn, the statistics are 100 percent or zero: your baby either survives or does not.

The neonatal intensive care unit is not a place for the faint of heart, either for parents or for healthcare workers. Parents who enter the NICU usually have no choice in the matter: a doctor has found their child to be in need of specialized, intensive, around-the-clock, high-tech care. Parents in the NICU are usually in shock and frequently terrified at having no choice but to enter this unknown world, and face struggles no one should ever have to face.

The first is to grieve the loss of what they dreamed and hoped their newborn's experience—and even their own experience as a parent—would be. Their shattered dreams could have been in the making for far longer than the short months of a mother's pregnancy. They could even have been the dream of a lifetime. The second difficult thing a NICU mother must do is to leave her precious newborn behind when she is discharged from the hospital. That, in itself, is enough to break anyone's heart.

The challenges rise in intensity after that. Some parents have to contemplate giving consent for their infant to have major surgery for a life-threatening condition. Some have to grapple with understanding and accepting a difficult diagnosis, one that may change the arc of their child's life forever, and their lives, too. A few even have to face the unthinkable: saying goodbye to their newborn for all time.

The most important task for parents is to find and sustain hope: hope that their baby will survive and do well. Similarly, the most important task for doctors is to help parents find and sustain this optimism, which is so vital to healing.

The stories that follow, collected during my twenty years as a neonatologist, are those that have touched my heart in some way and represent a range of human emotion as well as an array of conditions that have propelled babies into the NICU setting. The multiple threads of caring for the babies—by me, by other doctors, and the entire NICU staff, as well as the babies' parents—are woven together in each story. The reader's understanding of each story may be enhanced by reading the "Notes" section at the end of each chapter. These notes provide background information and explanations about the diagnosis or condition discussed in the chapter, and other resources for readers who wish to learn more.

All parents with babies in a NICU are challenged; how they rise to the challenge varies widely, and has the potential to impact their baby's ultimate development. Some are particularly courageous, loving, resilient, and strong; others are conflicted, confused, and overwhelmed. Sometimes they are a bundle of all those things simultaneously. All are in need of emotional support.

I have worked in a dozen NICUs, moving between county hospitals, university hospitals, and community hospitals. Readers will journey among these hospitals, none of which is identified except generically. Readers will also meet many doctors who worked tirelessly alongside of me. I have given each of them a fictitious name. The NICUs in the stories are more similar than they are different; each is full of babies and parents in crisis, and families on their own particular journeys through life.

***

Notes

Following in the Freudian tradition, which postulates that all behavior can be explained by an experience of childhood trauma, psychiatrist Dr. Leo Kanner, who first named "autism," published a paper in 1949 attributing its occurrence to "refrigerator mothers." Throughout the 1950s and 1960s, Dr. Bruno Bettelheim acted as a further proponent of Kanner's theories that maternal coldness somehow produced this condition in children, even though most children with autism had unaffected siblings. Not until 1964 did Dr. Bernard Rimland, a psychologist with an autistic son, challenge this theory in his book, *Infantile Autism: The Syndrome and its Implications for a Neural Theory of Behavior* (1964. New York: Appleton-Century-Crofts). Experts now believe that autism results from a combination of genetic and environmental influences, although debate still rages about what the environmental influences are.

Chapter 3

Josi's Song: Josi Sanchez

Sara Sanchez urged Josi, the small girl clinging to her skirts, to sing to me.

Watching them, I shook my head in amazement and remembered the day I had recommended that Josi's mother and father turn off their baby's life support. Josi was then just two-days-old and weighed one and a half pounds. She had been delivered to save her mother's life at twenty-four weeks out of the normal forty weeks gestation.

***

When Sara Sanchez's dangerously high blood pressure failed to respond to medication, she was on the brink of developing seizures or a stroke, the result of pregnancy-associated toxemia. Her doctor's only recourse was to deliver the not-yet-developed fetus that was somehow responsible for accelerating Sara's hypertension into a life-threatening state.

The baby born to save her mother's life was now in danger of losing her own battle for life. Sara's baby was suffering from low blood pressure and breathing problems.

When I first saw Sara standing by Josi's bed just hours after giving birth, I almost mistook her for the baby's grandmother—instead of her mother. Deep lines creased her weathered face. A thick braid with streaks of grey hung from the nape of her neck and tickled her waist. Her skirt brushed her bare ankles, and since she wore sandals, I could see the thickened and calloused soles of her feet. She seemed weary, but possessed of an inner calm. The resident's admission note in Josi's chart identified her mother as an "elderly multigravida," meaning she was more than forty-years of age and already had several children—all teenagers, I later found out.

Her husband looked like a cowpoke from a dusty Mexican desert. When he joined Sara at Josi's bedside, he held a battered straw hat in his leathery hands. His thin black hair was slicked straight back to cover the beginnings of a bald spot on the crown of his head. I guessed by looking at him and his wife that they did not have more than a few dollars in their possession.

I looked at the fragile form that lay in front of them. She should have been swimming in a sea of warm, salty amniotic fluid. Yet, here she was, nearly lost in a sea of medical equipment. She was barely recognizable as a human baby, and her hold on life was tenuous at best.

My medical Spanish was rudimentary, so I had a translator help me tell Sara and Josef about Josi's tough start in life and her complex medical problems. Trying to break down the medical explanations into words and concepts they could understand, I enumerated all the possible complications Josi could experience in stark terms. I wanted them to know every risk she faced, no matter how traumatizing it might be for them to hear. In my mind, it was not fair to force medical care on their baby if they did not understand the potential long-term consequences. I did not want to hand them a baby they were not prepared for and could not manage at the end of a lengthy hospital stay; yet, at the same time, I did not want to create a sense of despair.

"Things don't look good," I told Josi's parents, as one of the pediatric residents stood by my side; we tried to prepare them for the possibility that she might die in the next twenty-four hours. I worried that if she survived, she would have brain damage, mental retardation, or cerebral palsy. She could also become blind or deaf. If they feared disability more than death, if they could not accept a baby who might have these problems in her future, I informed them, they could decide to discontinue her treatment. She might, however, be one of the lucky ones to come through what was shaping up to be a long hospitalization relatively unscathed.

In the early 1990s, when Josi was born, few neonatologists even tried to save the lives of babies born at less than twenty-four out of the normal forty weeks of pregnancy. Such tiny babies were considered incapable of survival. Therefore, parents of babies born at twenty-four and even twenty-five weeks were routinely asked whether they wanted their babies resuscitated at delivery, given the nearly insurmountable odds to survival they faced.

If parents chose resuscitation in the beginning, they were told their decision could always be reconsidered if the baby were doing poorly. Life support could be discontinued if it looked as though the baby would not survive.

The pendulum has swung both ways on the topic of resuscitating extremely low birth-weight babies—those weighing less than two pounds at birth. In the 1960s and 1970s, the early days of neonatology, doctors made unilateral, arbitrary decisions that some babies were "just too small" to survive. No attempts were made to save them, as neonatologists believed that treatment would be futile, leading only to pain and suffering for the baby. Their beliefs were likely influenced by their perceptions of the future quality-of-life these extremely premature babies would experience. As technology improved, this began to change.

The pendulum veered rapidly to the other side in the 1980s and 1990s. Neonatologists took it upon themselves to aggressively intervene and "save" every baby who could possibly be saved, often regardless of the parents' wishes. "Because we can, we should" save these babies, many doctors argued. Gradually, survival of smaller and less mature babies increased.

Inevitably, a backlash occurred. A contingent of parents became quite vocal on the national stage, questioning what gave doctors the right to play God. How dare doctors usurp the power to make critical decisions for a baby from the people given that right by Mother Nature—the baby's family? How could doctors insist on continuing medical care for their child, if it meant he or she would be blind, deaf, retarded, unable to speak, or even move? Doctors were not the ones taking these profoundly impaired children home with them. Was all of this highly sophisticated intensive care truly in the family's best interests? Or the child's?

***

Josi's parents listened patiently while the translator communicated my thoughts to them. No, they were *muy contentes*, just fine, with us continuing to provide her care.

"She's in God's hands," Sara explained through the interpreter, although I got the drift of her sentiment when I recognized the word "*Dios*."

Josi was very sick with complications from prematurity for a very long time, as predicted for such a tiny baby. For weeks she needed the assistance of a ventilator to help her breathe. She had trouble digesting milk and more trouble taking it from a bottle. Hours stretched into days, and days into weeks, and weeks into months until she was deemed a survivor. When Josi went home, I felt as though we were releasing a rehabilitated baby condor back into the wilds.

Had Josi grown strong enough to withstand the world outside of the NICU? Would she be able to fly? To soar?

Josi would go home a "technology-dependent" infant. The length of time she had spent on the ventilator had damaged her lungs, and she would need oxygen. She would be attached to a monitor to alert her parents with a noxious beep in case either her heart rate or breathing slowed to a dangerous level. The lung damage made her breathe faster than normal and struggle for air; this left her unable to take a bottle or nurse. A feeding tube surgically inserted into her stomach would be her only way to get nourishment for the foreseeable future. An electronic pump that whirred and clacked, not a mother's soft, warm breast, would have the nighttime duty of feeding Josi.

Just one thing remained to be done before Josi's discharge: She needed to have her eyes examined. The procedure had been put off several times because she was deemed too sick to withstand it. When the ophthalmologist finally dilated her eyes and had a look, he rushed her into emergency laser eye surgery the same day.

The normal process of blood vessel growth from the center of Josi's retina out to its edge had gone awry, as it does in many premature infants, in a disease process known as retinopathy of prematurity. A scar that formed on the retina threatened to pull it away from its attachment to the back of the eyeball. If the retina detached completely, Josi would lose the sight in that eye. And in Josi's case, both eyes were affected.

In the operating room, the eye surgeon wore a piece of headgear that looked like an updated version of a miner's light with its central disc in the middle of his forehead. A thick black cable snaked from the apparatus down his back to the floor, where it was plugged into a grounded power outlet. He controlled its output by tapping his foot on a pedal on the floor. As he did so, the laser beam burst forth from the contraption on his forehead.

The ophthalmologist guided the beam into Josi's eyes by moving his head ever so slightly; he hoped his efforts would enable him to salvage some of her sight. When he lost his focus and looked up from his work, the red beam bounced eerily around the darkened room like a saber on a battlefield in a *Star Wars* movie. Since everyone in the operating room except Josi wore special thick protective goggles to shield our eyes, we were safe from the laser's dangerous effects.

When Josi left the hospital, it was too early to predict the ultimate outcome of her visual development or to know what she could see. After all, for the first couple of months, babies can only distinguish light and dark, and can see general outlines of faces from a distance of about eight-to-twelve inches. But based on his exams after surgery, the ophthalmologist was not very optimistic that she would have much, if any, vision.

Since I would be following Josi in our outpatient clinic, I would get an opportunity to find out if his pessimism were warranted.

***

Usually, neonatologists do not have contact with their patients for a period longer than several months, from birth until discharge from the NICU. But seeing patients in the follow-up clinic gave me the opportunity to follow patients for as long as I chose. I took pleasure in the time I spent building relationships with families over the several years I took care of their children.

Sara was one of the mothers I came to enjoy, although our working relationship was difficult at first. Sara did not understand anything I said to her in English and never even tried to learn a word of English. Realizing that our visits would simply take too long if I had to depend on the services of a translator to help me, I was forced to learn Spanish quickly.

Sara listened as I posed questions in rudimentary Spanish. She revealed only a hint of impatience occasionally, if I asked her to repeat herself when I had trouble understanding her answers. At these times, her replies were more emphatic than usual, so I would not mistake what she was trying to tell me, or so she must have thought.

Josi's medical condition remained complicated. Her breathing was slow to improve because of the many respiratory infections she contracted during her first year of life. She took multiple medications that needed constant adjustment, and she was not gaining weight well.

Josi's psychological condition concerned me as much as her medical condition because she seemed so fearful and so difficult to comfort. During her early visits to the clinic, she cried incessantly except when she was clinging to Sara's chest. Her little fingers burrowed into Sara's blouse and her head rested against her breast. I could not pry her away from Sara to examine her. When I tried to touch her, she flailed at my hands with a vengeance, and then grabbed her mother even tighter. I hoped Josi's clinging to her mother provided her with a feeling of security, and did not portend a future in which she would forever seem anxious, frightened, and disturbed.

During our visits, I decided to focus on acclimating Josi—first to my voice, then to my touch. I did not feel it necessary to torture this young child, who had already survived months of being poked, prodded, and pricked, by tearing her away from the one comfort she had found in her life, especially when I was not sure she could see me.

I made appointments for Sara to bring Josi to the clinic every few weeks. Her condition was still tenuous, but I thought that if Sara and I worked closely on a regular basis, we might be able to keep Josi out of the hospital.

As Josi's eyes gradually became smaller, I sadly realized she would never be able to see our clinic's red wagon. Her mother still took pleasure in treating her to a ride in it from the waiting room to the examining room; the motion soothed her crying briefly. It was infinitely easier, too, for Sara to get Josi around the clinic that way. Josi lay in the wagon on her tattered white blanket with her heavy green oxygen cylinder at her side. Her apnea monitor, the size of a small laptop computer, sat up against the edge of the wagon, always threatening to emit a shrill beep or two. It would alert her mother if she stopped breathing (apnea) or if her heart rate dropped below normal (bradycardia).

During the winter, our visits went from bad to worse. Once, Sara brought one-year-old Josi in with a dreadful cold. Gooey green snot clogged up the oxygen tubing in her nose and I heard her wheezing across the room. She thrashed about miserably, fighting off all my attempts to examine her, and Sara's report depressed me even more. Josi was now lashing out, biting, and scratching not only her parents and sisters, but also herself.

"Mira," said Sara. "Look." She pulled up Josi's shirtsleeves to show me the scratch marks and scabs that lined her child's arms.

This was exactly the type of life I had feared Josi would be living: technology-dependent, chronically ill, and most unhappy. I felt as if the NICU team and I had failed Josi and her family. I remembered, though, that Josi's parents had placed her life in God's hands. Josi was undeniably well-loved and well-cared for. That counted for a lot.

Sara was an unwavering and unflappable presence in Josi's life—always calm, always deliberate, always loving. Since she did not drive, her husband brought her to every appointment, although he usually waited outside in their beat-up car. Together they never missed a single appointment and were always on time. In spite of her limited formal education, Sara was quite competent and demonstrated proficiency in managing the medical aspects of Josi's care.

Sara also found a wonderful balance to encourage Josi's independent development, neither babying, overprotecting, nor neglecting Josi. As Josi grew out of her wild animal stage over the next year, I realized that Sara was the perfect mother for her. *No*, I thought; *she was the only mother for this child.*

Here we were in a city of thirteen million, a high-pressure city where people honked if you did not get your car off the mark within a millisecond of a streetlight turning green; where people thought nothing of driving—or sitting in traffic—for an hour and a half just to get to a minimum-wage job. In this area, people noisily demanded instant service wherever they went. Yet, this woman floated serenely through the chaos of the waiting room of our busy clinic as if she were taking an afternoon stroll down the dusty streets of a remote Mexican village.

She reminded me of the women I had seen during my medical missions to rural towns in Nicaragua and Mexico. I was awed by the way these women seemed to maintain inner peace and to be contented with the simplest things in life, in spite of the obvious hardships they faced. I could envision Sara walking down one of those sun-streaked, dusty roads, her baby wrapped in a sling that held her between her breasts, her long braid swaying behind her. But if Sara still lived in that remote village, her baby would not have survived more than an hour. And she may not have survived either.

One day, I entered the clinic's examining room to find Sara sitting on its single molded plastic chair, two-year-old Josi standing beside her, holding on with one hand. I squatted down so my face would be at Josi's level.

"Holá, Josi. Como estás?"

"Doctora? Doctora?" Josi said in her lilting voice.

She reached in my direction with her free hand, searching for my stethoscope. She followed my voice to my face, since by then she knew my stethoscope was always just under my chin. When her teeny hands located my face, they patted downward until she found the instrument where it lay around my neck. I took it off and handed her the end with the round bell. She pulled it greedily into her hands and put it first on her cheek, then on her chest. I took advantage of the opportunity, popped the earpieces in, and listened to her chest as she breathed. All clear; not a single wheeze.

"Bueno, Josi! Bueno. Y muchas gracias."

"Camina (walk), Josi!" her mother commanded with excitement in her voice.

Sara picked Josi up and deposited her on the other side of the small room then went back to her chair. I remained crouched between the two of them. From her side of the room, Sara called to Josi. Josi stood with her hands out at her sides for balance, her head cocked over toward her right shoulder.

I extended my hand to my little patient. She grasped my fingers and allowed me to steady and guide her, as she picked up her feet and set them carefully down in front of her with each step. She doggedly crossed the room to reach her mother's voice, and Sara beamed triumphantly when Josi once again clutched her skirts. I was as thrilled as if I had just watched my own child take her first tentative steps.

Maybe I had been wrong about Josi's prognosis all this time.

Josi heard my keys jangle in the pocket of my white coat, and her hands dove right in after the sound. I let her pull the keys out to play with them while Sara and I talked like old friends. Lately, our visits were much easier since Josi was doing so well; we did not have as many complicated medical details to cover. It helped, too, that I had graduated from speaking pidgin Spanish and developed much greater fluency.

My weekly practice sessions with Sara helped cement my newfound knowledge. Whenever I got stuck while speaking, I could now ask her, "Qué es la palabra?" ("What is the word?") Sara seemed to take almost as much pride in teaching me Spanish as she did in teaching Josi how to walk.

I rarely kept any patients older than one year of age in my clinic. New ones just kept coming after their release from the NICU, and I had to make room for them in my one-afternoon-a-week schedule. Josi was already two-years-old. She was now breathing well without her oxygen, and she no longer needed her apnea monitor. She had finally learned to take food by mouth, and even enjoy it, after a very long time of being fed exclusively through the tube into her stomach. She had not required rehospitalization since leaving the NICU—a minor miracle in itself. It was time to discharge her from my clinic.

I broached the subject with Sara. "Josi's doing well enough that she can go to a regular doctor now," I said, confident in my Spanish.

"No, doctorá. No," was her plaintive plea. "Por favor, no!"

Josi *was* one of my favorite patients. Now that our visits were monthly instead of weekly, I did not need to spend as much time with her as I used to. I smiled as I watched her toddle across the examining room in her pink and purple pastel sundress and white leather sandals, jangling my keys as she went.

I agreed to keep seeing her.

***

Shortly after Josi turned three, she entered a preschool for blind children. To attend this school, Josi, along with other visually impaired children, took a lengthy bus ride on the freeway three times a week. She had cried a bit the first day or two, but now she seemed to enjoy her time at school. With her busy schedule, Josi had even less time for clinic visits. Fortunately, she remained healthy, so we cut them back to every three months.

Toward the end of her first year of school, it was time for another check-up. Josi made her way down the hall of the clinic all by herself, one hand lightly grazing the wall as she marched along like a toy soldier. By this time, Josi was a popular figure, and nurses called out to her, some in English, some in Spanish, as she walked forward fearlessly. Sara trailed behind her carrying a satchel full of snacks. Once in the examining room, four-year-old Josi was in constant motion. She opened and closed the drawers on the examining table and turned the water off and on time and again. While Sara told me in Spanish how things were going, Josi chattered non-stop and peppered me with questions in English.

"What's this? Water? Hot? Cold?" she asked, as I handed her paper towel after paper towel to dry her hands.

It was then that Sara asked Josi to sing for me.

"Old MacDonald had a farm…E-I-E-I-O. And on his farm he had some ducks." Josi's ebullient voice carried out the open door and into the hall.

The clinic nurses, resident physicians, and other staff pediatricians gathered in the hallway outside our room and clapped and cheered when Josi concluded her bravura performance.

It was then I knew beyond a shadow of a doubt that I had been 100 percent wrong about Josi's prognosis. I could not have been happier.

***

Notes:

Neonatologists have long struggled with how to approach infants who are born, as Josi was, at the "edge of viability." As long ago as 1900, Dr. Pierre Budin—recognized as the first who attempted to save tiny babies with a consistent care approach—opined that the "natural limit of viability" was a one kilogram (approximately two pounds) birth weight. (Budin P. 1907. *The Nursling*. London, England: Caxton Publishing Co.) This limit has been lowered repeatedly, as technological advances have gradually enabled survival of smaller and smaller babies.

Regarding the notion that "because we can, we should" resuscitate tiny babies, Dr. William Silverman, one of neonatology's pioneering doctors, related such an episode from his experience. (Silverman W. 1992. "Overtreatment of Neonates? A Personal Retrospective." *Pediatrics 90*(6): 971-976.) He was dumbstruck by the actions of a new chief of obstetric anesthesia who was called to attend a delivery of a 500-gram infant born at twenty-three weeks of gestation.

When the anesthesiologist determined the newborn was not breathing and had no pulse, he used a scalpel to slice open the baby's chest, and then began performing open-chest cardiac massage in an attempt to "save" the baby. The baby died a few hours later, long before anyone attending the delivery had recovered from the shock of this extreme intervention performed "on behalf of" the baby. Open-chest cardiac massage is not a procedure routinely used to resuscitate newborns, although it is sometimes used to resuscitate babies whose hearts fail after open-heart surgery.

In the same article, Dr. Silverman addresses the issue of "overtreatment of seriously compromised neonates with life-prolonging hardware" stating that it "is, in the end, a weighing of values—a moral judgment." He also states his belief that "unrestrained intensive treatment of the smallest and most severely malformed babies is unreviewed and unlegislated social policy."

In a more recent paper with the provocative title, "Nobody likes Premies: The Relative Value of Patients' Lives," the authors found that doctors were less likely to consider resuscitating micro-premies, those with extremely low birth weights, than older children and adults with poorer prognoses. They question why this is so. (Janvier A., I. Leblanc, K. K. J. Barrington. 2009. "Nobody Likes Premies: The Relative Value of Patients' Lives." *Journal of Perinatology 28*(12): 821-826.)

Another recent discussion probes the moral dilemmas in the field of neonatology, and focuses on the question of when to resuscitate infants born at the "edge of viability." (Meadow W. and J. Lantos. 2009. "Moral Reflections on Neonatal Intensive Care." *Pediatrics 123*(2): 595-597.)

Currently, although clear-cut, well-agreed-upon national guidelines indicating which babies at twenty-three and twenty-four weeks gestation should be resuscitated do not exist. The position of the American Academy of Pediatrics is that parents should be involved in making decisions surrounding their infants' resuscitation and, if indicated, withdrawal of life support. (Committee on Fetus and

Newborn. 2007. "AAP Policy Statement: Noninitiation or Withdrawal of Intensive Care for High-Risk Newborns." *Pediatrics 119*(2): 401-403. *See* also Committee on Fetus and Newborn. 2009. "Clinical Report—Antenatal Counseling Regarding Resuscitation at an Extremely Low Gestational Age." *Pediatrics 124*(1): 422-427.)

Optimally, treatment decisions should be discussed prior to the infant's birth and should be individualized to the extent it is possible, given available information about the fetus. Tyson evaluated factors favoring survival for extremely low-birth-weight infants based on their individual characteristics, in an attempt to enable doctors to move away from using population-based statistics when counseling parents about to deliver an extremely premature infant. Survival is increased in females, babies whose mothers have been treated with antenatal steroids, and those who have a heavier weight for gestational age at birth. (Tyson J. E., N. A. Parikh, J. Langer et al. "Intensive Care for Extreme Prematurity—Moving Beyond Gestational Age." 2008. *The New England Journal of Medicine 358*(16): 1672-1681.)

The information in Tyson's article has been configured into a "calculator" by the Neonatal Research Network of the National Institute of Child Health and Human Development. This computerized program provides a range of possible outcomes (survival with or without various degrees of neurodevelopmental impairment) for individual infants based on their birth characteristics. This tool can be found online at http://www.nichd.nih.gov/about/org/cdbpm/pp/prog_ep bo/epbo_case.cfm.

Josi developed retinopathy of prematurity (ROP), a condition linked to premature birth in which normal development of blood vessels in the retina is interrupted, leading to aberrant growth of vessels and, in some cases, scarring and retinal detachment. Formerly known as retrolental fibroplasia, ROP used to be the main cause of blindness in children in the 1940s and 1950s; it now causes blindness in 500-700 infants in the United States each year. Its occurs primarily in infants born less than thirty-two weeks and less than 1,500 grams at birth, and its incidence is highest in the smallest and sickest babies. Laser surgery intended to prevent retinal detachment is the primary treatment for advanced cases. Even if blindness is avoided, babies who have had ROP may develop other visual problems including myopia and strabismus. (Bashour M., J. Menassa, C. Gerontis. 2011. "Retinopathy of Prematurity." eMedicine at http://emedicine.medscape.com/article/1225022-overview. Also, American Academy of Pediatrics. 2006. "Screening Examination of Premature Infants for Retinopathy of Prematurity." *Pediatrics 117*(2): 572-576.)

A new potential treatment that may ultimately replace laser surgery for ROP is on the horizon. A medication called Bevacizumab, when injected into the vitreous of the eyes of infants with significant ROP, has shown promise in small clinical trials. Use of the medication allowed continued development of blood vessels in the periphery of the retina, while laser surgery permanently destroys parts of the peripheral retina. Therefore, peripheral vision is thought to be preserved to a greater extent with Bevacizumab, compared with laser surgery. This medication is not yet FDA-approved, as further trials to demonstrate its long-term safety are necessary. (Mintz-Hittner H.A., K. Kennedy, A. Z. Chuang. 2011. "Efficacy of Intravitreal Bevacizumab for Stage 3+ Retinopathy of Prematurity." *New England Journal of Medicine 364*(7): 603-615.)

Chapter 4

Letting Go: Maricela Castillo

The tangled hair, stubble-covered chin, and rumpled green hospital scrubs worn by the young man who stood in front of me gave him away. "How was your night?" I asked the pediatric resident, knowing he had likely been up working for most of it.

"Oh, just spent the night tuning up Maricela Castillo," Dr. Ted Fowler replied casually. "It's cool. I'm holding her together with some shoestring reinforced with masking tape, and an extra dose of superglue. I think she will make it to her open-heart surgery tomorrow."

Leaving the county hospital's NICU behind to spend a month rotating through the NICU of the university hospital where I was an assistant professor, I was catapulted headfirst into the super-charged, high-powered world of elite academic medicine.

The old adage in medicine, "Common things occur commonly" did not apply in this NICU. While the county hospital's patients presented with bread-and-butter diagnoses, this NICU's patient population was distinctly different. Here, only a few select babies, distilled from thousands born locally, were admitted to the twenty-five beds. In addition, babies with rare diagnoses arrived from around the world, flown in on private jets. This NICU was a Mecca for infants born with complicated congenital heart lesions. Our pediatric heart surgeon, Dr. Bernard Wilain, was famous for his work with these fragile infants.

From the moment in the early 1990s that I stepped inside the heavy double doors of this singular room in the sprawling hospital, I struggled to keep my head above water. While many NICUs are populated with large numbers of premature infants and an occasional baby with a condition requiring surgery, this NICU had scarcely any premature infants and a large number of babies with complex diagnoses, many of which required surgery or other specialized procedures. I would find myself moving from emergency to emergency throughout my month in this NICU.

The NICU's one large room housed all the babies in incubators and cribs lining its perimeter. The baby's bed and all the ancillary equipment necessary to maintain life—IV poles and pumps, ventilators, and the occasional dialysis machine—stood everywhere. EEG machines offered a continuous display of brainwaves, while heart-lung bypass machines and other specialized life-support systems ticked and chattered endlessly. If a parent found a single chair nearby, they could consider themselves lucky.

On any given day, the noise in the NICU ranged from a raucous dull roar to a feverish cacophony of voices and piercing monitor alarms. It is a wonder any baby could sleep with the jack-hammering of one type of ventilator and the regular whooshing of another grinding away in the background. Sometimes the other-worldly cries of parents coming to grips with losing their baby sent everyone—staff, visitors and other parents—over the edge. The overhead lights always glared, leaving no nighttime during which babies could learn to regulate their sleep. At least the noise dropped a few decibels between midnight and 5 a.m., when the population of doctors thinned out from around a dozen to one or two overworked souls.

As the attending neonatologist in the NICU that month, I was in charge of a team of interns and residents, just as I was at the county hospital. However, here consultants abounded, eager to help figure out difficult diagnoses and to provide specialized services such as surgery or dialysis.

I went from bedside to bedside that first day, studying each baby and pondering the complex and fascinating problems they had. It took hours for my crew of interns and residents to inform me about our intriguing patients. Each baby would easily be considered interesting enough to keep the team of doctors-in-training busy all day. This NICU had such babies in abundance.

The first baby I saw on rounds had all the qualifications to be a patient in intensive care. A tube or line protruded from her every orifice and covered nearly every square inch of her torso, and connected her to a bevy of machines. Although she was a normal-sized newborn, I doubted she was the baby her parents had envisioned during the nine months they waited to meet her.

"This is Maricela," announced Dr. Fowler, the senior resident. "Maricela has a frog heart. She was flown in from a town in the Central Valley three days ago, half dead, in cardiogenic shock. We pulled her out of the soup so Dr. Wilain could do his magic." He spoke with the blasé attitude of a seasoned resident, one who had grown accustomed to facing down critically ill babies and routinely prevailing.

"*What?*" I asked. Surely the medical center was not transplanting frog hearts into babies, like the much-heralded case of Baby Fae who lived for twenty days after receiving a baboon heart in 1984.

Dr. Fowler was a head shorter and a decade younger than I, and tufts of soft hair covered his chin where stubble did not. He continued speaking in a matter-of-fact tone, never once glancing at the clipboard on which he had columns of numbers.

"A frog heart. It is what we call a heart that is unrecognizable by normal anatomic standards. It has so many things wrong that it does not fit into one of the usual diagnostic categories. In fact, it's so screwed up, her parents have been given two choices: Do nothing—in other words, *let her die*—or try for a repair. Heart transplant is not a realistic option; there just are not enough hearts for babies at this point."

I could not imagine how a parent must feel faced with such impossible choices, especially having no conception about how their lives might change, no matter which they selected.

Dr. Fowler continued. "Who would choose death? Not these parents. So, now the surgeon is trying to decide whether to do the operation in stages or go for the whole fix all at once. This is the kid I was telling you about who is scheduled for the operating room tomorrow at 7 a.m."

"Has Dr. Wilain given you any odds for the success of the repair?"

"Dr. Wilain can fix just about anything. However, frog hearts are *never* good. Trust me, it won't be pretty."

"And the parents?" I asked.

"Migrant farm workers. Left their other two kids behind with family in Mexico and came up here to earn money to send back home. Mom was picking grapes in the fields when she went into labor. Ambulance rushed her to the hospital to give birth. Baby turned blue at the referring hospital, and the rest is history." He sighed and shrugged his shoulders.

As Dr. Fowler launched into a litany of numbers describing the newborn's physiologic status in minute detail, I looked carefully at the baby. She looked perfect in every way except for an almost imperceptible rhythmic ripple about the size of a pencil eraser in the skin between the ribs overlying her heart. I also heard a loud murmur in her chest and noticed vague purple undertones to her rich brown skin.

How could she look so good when things were actually so bad? The medicine dripping through her IV kept a vital fetal blood channel open for blood to circulate through her lungs, while the ventilator forced oxygen into the lungs for the blood to absorb. She could not live her life on a continuous IV drip or tethered to a machine. The open-heart surgery designed specifically for her would be her only chance at long-term survival.

As we continued making rounds to review each baby's condition and progress over the last twenty-four hours, I examined the other patients. They included a gaunt Hispanic baby whose gigantic head harbored a brain tumor the size of a tennis ball; a petite blond who required kidney dialysis because she lacked a key metabolic enzyme; a fourteen-pound Asian newborn whose dangerously low blood sugars precipitated seizure after seizure; and a sturdy black infant who had just gotten a dose of metallic coils threaded into the arteries of his brain to treat a tangled overgrowth of abnormal blood vessels.

I had trouble imagining a routine life for any of these babies. As I reflected on the efforts the medical team was making on behalf of each baby, my thoughts drifted toward the Herculean task each of their parents would face to create a semblance of a normal life for them. Their parents' skill at navigating the complex medical systems on their children's behalf would also help determine whether the babies ultimately thrived.

I could not spare the time to contemplate the future when rounds ended several hours later. A million tasks demanded my attention: console parents, interact with consultants, interpret x-rays, field phone calls from referring doctors, review residents' orders, and write my notes. The residents had their chores: to start IVs, draw blood, track down lost lab tests, and write their own notes.

Shortly after lunch, specialists in cardiology, neurology, genetics, general surgery, nephrology, infectious disease, and neurosurgery invaded the NICU like conquering armies. The grand parades of the various physicians and their entourages continued until late in the afternoon. The noise level grew like it does in a crowded and popular restaurant as more and more people crammed into the small room, creating an undercurrent of chaos.

As the sun came obliquely through the blinds later that afternoon, I returned to Maricela's bedside. A nurse I did not recognize from morning rounds stood at her bedside; shift change had just taken place. I studied the baby's ventilator, interpreting the digital array of numbers displayed above the knobs and dials, then lifted my stethoscope from where it was draped around my neck.

"Who are you and what do you want?" barked the nurse, before I could plug the earpieces from my stethoscope into my ears.

I flinched. "I'm Dr. Hall."

"The baby's asleep. Don't touch her."

"I'm the new NICU attending. I *need* to examine her," I gently insisted.

"Oh, *you are* the new attending." The nurse, who carried herself like a veteran of all foreign wars, was surprised, but not impressed. "Well, try not to mess with her too much. I *did* just get her to sleep."

"Okay," I agreed, happy that the nurse was trying to protect the baby's quiet time.

"Hi sweet pea," I whispered, as I softly laid my hand on the baby's furry head, then listened to her heart, lungs, and belly with my stethoscope. I poked her tummy gingerly, then put the tip of my index finger on her chest and released it rapidly, watching the color return sluggishly to the imprint of my fingertip.

As I completed my exam, Maricela's parents arrived. The two of them glanced cautiously around the busy room, and then made their way over to their baby's bedside. They could not have appeared more out of place in the NICU than if they had been in a futuristic space station rotating through a different galaxy.

"Aqui está su niña," I said, using my limited Spanish. ("Your daughter is right here.")

Mother's tattered jeans and muddy sneakers were dressed up by the small, simple gold hoops that pierced both of her ears and framed her bronze face, still puffy from the effects of pregnancy. Jet-black hair tumbled down her back and matched her deep-set eyes. Warily, she reached for Maricela's hand, and the baby splayed her fingers widely when touched, then curled them around her mother's finger.

Through an interpreter, I found that mother's name was Maria and her husband was Jorge.

"Will the baby be okay, mother wants to know?" the translator asked. A suspicious frown clouded Maria's face.

"I'm very optimistic things will go well. Tell her Dr. Wilain is the best." Just then I saw the surgeon glide into the NICU. "Perfect timing. Here he comes to get consent for the operation."

Two worlds collided as Dr. Wilain stood in front of Maricela's parents in his expensive blue Egyptian cotton dress shirt and fashionable pink silk tie, covered by his starched white coat with his name written in red script above the pocket. A black Mont Blanc pen was neatly clipped in his pocket.

The translator struggled to interpret all the big words he used to describe the surgery and its possible complications, and finally the mother painstakingly printed her last name only in tilted block letters on the consent form's signature line.

As soon as she finished, Dr. Wilain turned on the heel of his Ferragamo loafers, his white coat fluttering behind him, and within seconds he disappeared.

"She'll be okay, won't she?" the translator probed again.

I did not want to tell Maricela's mother she would be okay when I was not sure she would be. And what did "okay" mean to her anyway? She might need to come up with a new definition of the word in the aftermath of Maricela's surgery.

Many of the cardiac babies needed multiple surgical repairs. Those with more complex lesions struggled the most, sometimes dying after their third or fourth surgery. It was a tough future to face, and this family had no way of knowing what it would be like. I wondered if they understood that a surgical "fix" would rarely repair the heart to a normal state, especially with a case as complicated as Maricela's.

"We do surgery on babies every day," I replied. "We'll do everything in our power to ensure she does well."

***

When I met Maricela's parents again the following afternoon, Jorge stood with his arm looped around Maria's waist, a grim expression of quiet acceptance on his face. Maricela had a four-inch wide strip of thick white tape covering her entire breastbone, and tubes filled with bright red blood snaked out of her chest on both sides. A tangle of monitor wires crisscrossed her chest and IVs stuck out of both her arms and legs. She was still under the effects of anesthesia and breathed only when the ventilator did so for her. The one thing identifying her as a baby, besides her small size, was the diaper she wore; little yellow ducks paraded across its waistband.

"How did things go in the operating room?" I asked the cardiologist, who had stood behind Dr. Wilain in the operating room for several hours trying to catch a glimpse of the surgery.

He told me how the procedure started by cooling Maricela's body until her heart shivered to a stop. The surgeon then worked feverishly to complete his reconstruction in less than sixty minutes. Leaving Maricela suspended in deep hypothermic circulatory arrest for much longer could be devastating for her future brain function. After Dr. Wilain put his last stitch in the beefy muscle of Maricela's heart, she was re-warmed until her heart resumed rhythmically pumping.

"We'll have to see how she does…it was a pretty long arrest time." The doctor adjusted his glasses over the bridge of his nose and resumed writing orders on Maricela's chart.

***

Maricela's seizures began four hours after surgery, just after I left for the day. I found out when I called the resident later that night for an update.

"She's seizing. Constantly," he exclaimed. "I've given her two different anti-convulsants, and ordered an EEG for tomorrow. I'm having neurology come by to take a look tonight."

Maricela's seizures ceased with the heavy doses of medication she received, but on the fifth post-op day Dr. Fowler called me to her bedside after rounds.

"Heart rate's 250. Should I get some ice?"

"Yeah, grab some ice. I'll run a printout of the heartbeat while you do that."

I surmised that the surgeon's scalpel must have come perilously close to her heart's natural pacemaker and interrupted its complex electrical connections. If swelling or injury prevented the pacemaker from functioning normally, the heart would trip into this frenetic rhythm, known as supraventricular tachycardia (SVT).

With her heart racing at nearly double the normal rate, Maricela would be okay for a while, but not for long. When the heart beats so fast, its ventricles—the lower pumping chambers—are unable to fill with enough blood to send out to the rest of the body. Heart failure develops over a number of hours.

One of medicine's time-honored low-tech treatments of SVT is to put ice over the patient's face. This stimulates a reaction that breaks the abnormal electrical circuit causing the runaway heart rhythm. While Dr. Fowler sprinted off to find some ice, I pushed a button on the monitor screen. From an opening at the bottom, a ribbon of paper showing the pattern of the baby's heartbeats churned out. I scrutinized it intently until Dr. Fowler returned with a plastic "zip-locked" bag filled with ice chips.

"Here goes nuthin'," he exclaimed, as he set the bag directly over the baby's forehead and eyes. We could see—although could not hear—Maricela cry, as she remained on the ventilator. We fixed our eyes on her heart monitor, and were rewarded in less than sixty seconds when her heart rate plummeted abruptly back to normal, at 120 beats per minute.

"That's so cool," said Dr. Fowler, his eyes widening.

"Wait. It's back," I said, my eyes still trained on the screen above Maricela's bedside. "Maricela, *por favor*," I warned her, "please get with the program."

"Should I try again?" asked the resident.

"Probably won't work, since she's just had heart surgery."

"Should we zap her then?"

Dr. Fowler referred to the technique known as cardioversion. I considered it a treatment of last resort. "We have time to try meds first."

The nurse drew up the drug I ordered and pushed it into Maricela's IV. Within seconds, the baby's heart rate dropped again, but just as fast it bounced right back up to 250.

When three successive doses of medication failed to bring the baby's heart rate back into the normal range for more than a minute, I instructed Dr. Fowler to notify the cardiologist on call.

Within five minutes, a guy who looked like Doogie Howser, the sixteen-year-old doctor from the 1990's TV series, showed up at Maricela's bedside. I handed him the long piece of paper showing the pattern of baby's heartbeat, and after glancing at it briefly, he confirmed the obvious. "It's SVT. Let's start some digoxin."

It took most of the afternoon for Maricela's heart rhythm to convert to normal. Dr. Fowler kept a close eye on her and updated me at regular intervals while I tended to other babies.

***

As Maricela continued to make progress through the month, we remained concerned about whether she had suffered any lasting effects from her prolonged arrest time during surgery and her subsequent seizures. A CAT scan of her brain showed an area of injury on the right side of her brain, predisposing her to left-sided weakness.

"Ella necesita fisioterapia," I told her parents, who visited only on weekends. She would require physical therapy as an outpatient to ensure optimal development.

After nearly a month in the hospital, Maricela was ready to be discharged home. The only remaining task was to instruct her parents in her care. Our social worker arranged for them to come learn how to administer her various medications. Her heart medications were dangerous enough that even a small overdose could cause her death.

Anita, a nurse who spoke Spanish fluently, inherited the job of discharge teaching. "See here?" she said in Spanish, showing Maria how to use a syringe to draw up the medication from the bottles labeled in Spanish. "It tells you how much to give, and then you measure it like this." She also had all the instructions written in Spanish on a sheet of paper.

Maria nodded her head timidly.

"Now you try." Anita handed the syringe to Maria.

Maria fumbled awkwardly with the syringe and pulled on it until it was full.

"No," corrected Anita. "Only to here." She pointed to a tiny number next to a line on the syringe, and then squirted the medicine all the way out. "Try again."

Over and over Anita tried to make her instructions clear. The more she talked, the less it seemed Maria understood. Her frustration rose; Maria seemed confused. Anita had started with the digoxin, the medicine to control baby's heart rhythm, and still needed to show Maria how to draw up four other medications, to mix the baby's formula, and to count her heart beat using a stethoscope. Changing tactics, she said, "Here, read this to me."

"No puedo leer," said Maria. ("I can't read.") Her face did not reveal shame, only honesty.

Not only was Maria unable to read, she could not write anything besides the last name she had clumsily printed on the surgical consent form. She could not add, subtract, or measure; she had never gone to school.

Jorge did not have much formal education either, although callouses on his hands were a testament to his ability to do hard work. After our social worker interviewed Maricela's parents, she told us they lived in a two-bedroom apartment with ten other people. Their living arrangements changed from time to time, as they traveled to find work when one crop in California's Central Valley was harvested and it was time to move on to the next.

"There's no way you can send this baby home with these parents," Anita argued. "They're as sweet as can be, and they love her a whole bunch, but they can't even begin to manage her medicines. Seriously, they could kill her with that digoxin."

It was true. As much as Maria and Jorge loved Maricela and wanted to take her home with them, our team decided that putting this high-tech baby back into their ultra-low-tech environment would not be safe. Her parents lacked the necessary skills to care for a medically fragile child and to negotiate the complexities of Maricela's follow-up appointments in several different clinics in the gigantic urban medical center. We recommended Maricela go to a medical foster home until her care was easier to manage. Her parents agreed, and seemed thankful for the help their daughter would continue to receive at the hands of strangers.

***

Not all parents and babies can go home together, and I was pleased that Maricela's parents were willing to sacrifice their time with her so that her complicated care could be carried out safely. Although not many children need the specialized help that a medical foster home provides, it is a valuable service to the children and families who do need it.

***

Notes:

Maricela was one of 35,000 babies born every year in the United States with a congenital heart defect; one in every 125 newborns is affected, making heart defects among the most common birth defects. (Data is from the National Heart Lung and Blood Institute, on the web at http://www.nhlbi.nih.gov/health/dci/Diseases/chd/chd_what.html.) Many factors may lead to birth of a baby with a heart defect including genetic influences, environmental issues such as certain viral infections as well as use of alcohol and possibly cocaine, several specific medications a mother might take, and some chronic maternal medical conditions, especially diabetes. To learn more about congenital heart defects, read: http://www.marchofdimes.com/birthdefects_congenitalheart.html.

Much progress has occurred in the field of pediatric heart transplantation since the first operation in 1968, when the eighteen-day-old recipient lived only five hours. Now, approximately 350-400 pediatric heart transplantations take place each year, and 70 percent of infants and children who undergo transplant live at least five years, with some surviving as long as twenty years. However, when I took care of Maricela, it was only shortly after the use of the medication cyclosporine made transplants a realistic treatment option for infants in 1985. Pediatric heart transplantation was then, and continues to be, limited by the availability of donor hearts for infants. This has made it necessary for cardiac surgeons to search for creative ways to make heart transplants available for the larger number of infants who need them. (Chinnock R.E. "Heart Transplantation." Citation online at http://emedicine.medscape.com/article/1011927-overview.)

Maricela's surgery was conducted using the technique of deep hypothermic circulatory arrest. As many as 25 percent of infants undergoing open-heart surgery with this technique may experience some type of neurologic injury, including seizures such as Maricela had. Although in most cases problems do not persist long-term, this procedure can be associated with adverse neurodevelopmental outcome when arrest time is lengthy. A "safe" duration has not been determined; it may vary with the infant's age at surgery and diagnosis, as well as many other factors. (Wypij D., J. W. Newburger, L. A. Rappaport et al. 2003. "The Effect of Duration of Deep Hypothermic Circulatory Arrest in Infant Heart Surgery on Late Neurodevelopment: The Boston Circulatory Arrest Trial." *The Journal of Thoracic and Cardiovascular Surgery 126*(5): 1397-1403.)

Dodds and Merle wrote an excellent review of what is needed to complete discharge planning for infants who have undergone heart surgery. (Dodds K. M. and C. Merle. 2005. "Discharging Neonates with Congenital Heart Disease After Cardiac Surgery: A Practical Approach." *Clinics in Perinatology 32*(4): 1031-1042.)

Medical foster care, or out-of-home care, is available for medically complex or fragile children who cannot receive safe care in their own homes. This type of care developed in response to the "boarder baby" crisis during the crack cocaine epidemic; many infants were abandoned by parents and left to languish in the hospital for lengthy periods. Medical foster care enables these and many other children—those with chronic disease, heart conditions, HIV-AIDS, cerebral palsy, respiratory problems including ventilator dependency, and developmental disabilities due to prematurity, fetal alcohol syndrome, or prenatal drug exposure—to grow and develop in a family setting instead of an institution.

A number of children enter into medical foster care because their parents have a history of abusing or neglecting them or their siblings, but some require this specialized care because their complex medical condition is more than their parents can handle, as was the case with Maricela. Most state programs for medical foster care have the goal of returning children to their families by training the families in the specifics of their child's care; however, many children in these situations are ultimately adopted by their foster parents.

Chapter 5

The Ultimate Sacrifice: Pedro Perez

Fog enshrouded the stubby mountains behind the county hospital, where I had recently returned, the afternoon I first met Ana Perez. The days of endless summer had long left Los Angeles, the gorgeous flowery floats from the Rose Bowl Parade were dismantled, and the rainy season had arrived. I knew that when I left the hospital, the bone-chilling mist falling outside would ensnarl the region's freeways; yet, I was anxious to head home. However, I still had a prenatal consultation to complete before I could leave.

"Does mom speak Spanish or English?" I asked the labor and delivery nurse taking care of the mother, Ana.

"Spanish only. She just arrived in the United States two days ago. Someone dropped her off at the hospital and she has not had any visitors since she was admitted. She seems to be quite alone."

"Will you get the hospital translator for me, please? This is going to be complicated."

Ana had been admitted at twenty-five weeks of pregnancy with bleeding. She provided a history of nausea, vomiting, and headache for the last several days, although those symptoms had subsided. I was called to talk with her about the risks and problems her baby would face if she were to deliver prematurely. I took one of the pediatric residents with me, so he could watch me do the consultation.

"See one, do one, teach one," I told the young Dr. Jimmy Kwan, reciting a time-honored motto in medicine. "Next time you can do this yourself."

Ana was a small woman who sat quietly in bed, the sheet pulled up to her waist to cover a slight bulge. If I had not been told she were pregnant, I might not have noticed. Her skin, the color of burnt orange, was set off by coarse, straight, black hair, and her dark eyes did not help me discern her emotional state.

I pulled a curtain to separate Ana's bed from the one next to her, hoping for privacy, although I knew our words could be easily overheard by the woman who lay in the next bed. With the help of the interpreter, I learned that Ana had seen a doctor once in her native El Salvador. She planned to give birth in the United States, and anticipated that her husband and son would join her soon. She had been staying with her mother's cousin.

Ana did not show much reaction when I informed her of the long list of complications her baby might face.

"Entiende?" I asked. "You understand?"

"Sí," she replied, although it was hard for me to know how much she had grasped.

"What did you think?" I asked the resident, a short, bespectacled fellow with a penchant for wearing bow ties.

"I don't think she got it," he said. "That's a huge amount of information to unload on anyone. It's got to be overwhelming."

I tacitly agreed, knowing I would have to revisit many of the topics I had covered with Ana once her baby was born.

I left the hospital when I completed my consultation with Ana. When I arrived home, the smell of jasmine flooded my senses, my own personal aromatherapy, and a perfect antidote to the maddeningly slow drive. I closed my eyes and inhaled, wanting to savor the intoxicating scent forever. At least there were benefits to this infernal rain, I thought, as I noticed how the flowers' delicate pink and white blossoms dotted the walkway into my house.

***

Back at the hospital, three days later, the NICU team was called *stat* to Ana's room. Her baby then slithered out of her, still encased in the amniotic membrane. As it lay on her bed, attached to the umbilical cord, I could see a foot stretch to touch but not penetrate the thick membrane. A nurse clamped and cut the cord, while I pulled on a pair of gloves, poked through the membranes, and cleared them from the baby's face and body. It reminded me of when I saw our cat give birth; afterward she had licked the membranes off each wet, new kitten.

The one and a half pound baby boy kicked and squirmed and mewed. After placing a breathing tube in the baby's trachea, we brought him to the NICU and initiated the usual treatments.

Ana walked to the baby's bedside unassisted several hours after that. I surmised from her appearance and her short stature—she stood barely five feet tall—that she was descended from the Mayan Indians of Central America. She came to the baby's isolette, peered in at the ruddy baby who wiggled before her, and smiled wistfully.

"Niño está bien?" she asked.

"Sí, mas o menos bien," I replied. ("More or less doing okay.")

Pedro Perez faced the usual challenges which confront premature babies. His immature lungs required the help of a ventilator. The fetal blood channel known as the ductus arteriosus remained open; a medication called indomethacin aided its closure. He was dependent on IV nutrition and tube feedings.

Something about him concerned me, however. One day, Dr. Kwan reported on rounds, "His urine output has dropped off. I'm not sure what's going on." A look of consternation clouded his thoughtful face.

The next day the baby's urine flow diminished further. "His serum creatinine is higher," the resident physician reported. "What do you think's going on?"

Serum creatinine is a blood test, which reflects the body's ability to excrete waste products it normally produces. A rising creatinine indicates the kidneys are not working as well as expected.

"Hopefully it's just a transient side-effect of one of the medications we've given him," I said.

Each morning brought worse news. "Today his blood level of potassium is high," Dr. Kwan reported. "Six point zero."

"Are you sure it's not a lab error?" I asked.

"No. It was a perfect blood draw. I did it myself," Dr. Kwan announced, proud of his newly acquired skill. It's not easy to draw blood from a one and a half pound baby.

"Ugh. *What is going on?*"

In the back of my mind, I worried. I knew that too high a potassium level could be deadly by altering the precise electrochemical environment in which the heart functions. The heart begins to quiver uncontrollably, blood is no longer pumped effectively, and the patient can die.

"We'd better bring that potassium down if we can," I instructed.

"Would an ultrasound of the kidneys help us figure out what's wrong with them?"

"Maybe," I replied, stymied. "Let's get one. Good idea."

The ultrasound revealed swollen kidneys with bright echoes, but this told us nothing about the origin of Pedro's problems.

Ana visited daily, always alone. "When is your husband coming?" Carol, our social worker, asked her in Spanish.

"Soon, I hope," came her reply, although Carol told us that Ana only understood a little Spanish, her native tongue being an indigenous dialect.

This mother was alone in a foreign country with a small, sick newborn. Even the NICU was a foreign place to her, with all its machines and noises and people in hospital scrubs. Who did she rely on for support? I wondered.

Dr. Kwan, the other residents, the nurses and I watched as Pedro continued to slip away. His body became bloated, his movements less frequent. He required more support on the ventilator, and lab tests monitoring his kidney function worsened.

"Pedro, lo siento," I whispered to him during my exam on morning rounds one day. "I'm so sorry."

My frustration at not being able to understand why Pedro's kidneys had failed was drowned by the tidal wave of resignation and defeat that swept over me. "I don't think he's going to make it," I declared to the residents and nurses making rounds with me. Dr. Kwan had just shown me the latest lab report. "I've never seen a creatinine that high...ever." I did not see how he could live much longer.

"Me neither," agreed Dr. Kwan. He paused and pursed his lips. "It's gotten to the point we're torturing him with all our blood draws. We've done so much and he's not getting any better. *At all.*"

"So it's time to talk with his parents about discontinuing life support," I said.

A nurse who'd been off for the past week asked, "Are you sure? Isn't that kind of drastic?"

"He's a hair-breadth away from death right now. As Dr. Kwan said, it's not fair to continue causing him pain...for what end?" I felt that since we did not have the means to improve his condition, our treatments had passed over into the realm of prolonging the time it would take him to die, rather than prolonging his life. It made no sense to offer false hope to his parents.

"What about dialysis?" she asked. "Kidney transplant?"

"Susan, those things aren't available for premies," I said gently. "They're technically impossible on babies this small."

"I know. I was just hoping for something…"

Ana agreed to meet with our medical team the following day at four o'clock; her husband should finally have arrived.

***

Alfonso Perez followed his wife, Ana, into the NICU at the appointed hour. He was only a shade taller than she, with skin as richly bronzed as hers. I guided them into a small room where we could talk.

As Dr. Kwan sat at my side, I explained Pedro's condition as simply as I could. "His kidneys have stopped working. He is no longer passing water. We don't know why. He can't live much longer."

"But doctor, why?" Alfonso asked.

"I'm sorry, I don't know," I answered. "Because there's nothing more we can do, I recommend we stop life support, and take him off the machine that is breathing for him. You can hold him." Neither parent had yet gotten to hold their baby; he had been too sick through the weeks of Ana's visits.

Both Ana and Alfonso looked perplexed, even stunned. As the news sunk in, Ana bit her lip but did not cry. After a long silence, Alfonso replied through an interpreter. "We are not ready to stop the machine today. We would like to hold him," he added.

When our conversation ended, I realized the medical team had made a mistake. Our group of doctors and nurses had discussed Pedro's condition for weeks now, and we were fully aware of the relentless decline in his kidney function. Yet, we had not brought the parents along on our mental journey. Even if we had thought to discuss matters in detail with them earlier, Pedro's father had not even been present and his mother barely understood Spanish. We had to give them time, I thought, but we had little.

***

Alfonso and Ana asked to talk with me when they returned the next morning. Their four-year-old son accompanied them, dressed in neat clothes, hair combed and carefully parted. He sat silently on a chair and played with his fingers while we talked.

"I wonder if this has anything to do with our baby's condition?" Alfonso asked. Then, he told me Ana's story.

Ana had given birth to her first child—the boy sitting with them—in the United States, and then returned to El Salvador with her precious cargo, a brand new U.S. citizen. She desperately wanted to have her second child in America, too, but could not get the proper visas. The couple sold half of their belongings to pay a coyote, a human smuggler, to bring her to the United States. Alfonso had handed over the cash and watched his wife disappear into the night. He had not known how she would be transported to the United States. This had to remain a secret.

After Alfonso had left, Ana was instructed to climb into the bowels of a gasoline tank truck. Having no other option, and knowing no better, she did so. Alfonso described how Ana had slid around in the darkness with several other people on the two-day trip along the bumpy highways from El Salvador, through Guatemala and Mexico. Once safely across the border in San Diego, they had been let out of the tanker, all of them sick to their stomachs, headachy and faint. They breathed fresh air for the first time, and according to Alfonso, were grateful to be in the United States and grateful to be alive.

I was stunned to hear this story. I realized that no one on our medical team had obtained information about this crucial piece of Ana's history. Since I now recognized that Ana was an undocumented immigrant, I was not surprised that she had kept this part of her backstory to herself. Our patients at the county hospital were afraid to reveal their status as "illegals," and medical staff declined to press them about it; care was provided without regard to this issue. Sometimes, however, it was difficult to render the appropriate medical care because of the lack of a complete medical and social history in this group of patients.

"It makes more sense to me now," I said to Ana and Alfonso. "Your baby's underdeveloped kidneys must have been damaged by the chemical toxins in the gasoline fumes. I have never seen anything like this, though I know gas fumes can damage adults' kidneys."

Alfonso continued speaking. "So," he said, "when the baby was born and Ana needed me to come, I sold everything we had left—all our furniture and everything—to buy airplane tickets for my son and me. I have a visa and he's a citizen here, so we were able to enter the country legally.

"Now we have nothing left," he concluded.

A few tears welled up underneath Dr. Kwan's glasses, as he sat once again by my side.

Carol put her arm around Ana and hugged and rocked the tiny woman who now cried, eyes reddened.

"I'm so sorry," I said. "I wish things were different for you both and for Pedro. I wish I could have made Pedro better."

"We understand he's not going to make it," Alfonso said. "I can tell by looking at him. He doesn't look anything like he should."

"No, he's had a rough time," I agreed.

"We're ready to let him go," he continued. Ana nodded assent.

I was grateful Pedro's parents could make the decision to stop his treatment, so that his suffering would be minimized, even as their own would continue. The plans they had so carefully crafted to start this new life in the United States, and the optimism they had brought with them from El Salvador, would have to be rechanneled.

The staff arranged some comfortable chairs for the couple, and then pulled a portable privacy screen in front of Pedro's bed. The nurses gently removed the tape from IVs, pulled them out, disconnected monitor leads, and prepared Pedro to be held. Finally, it was time to take out his breathing tube; this duty was left to me. Afterwards, we wrapped him in a clean white blanket, and Dr. Kwan placed the baby in Ana's arms. There, the tiny son of these earnest immigrants gasped twice, and then he was still.

After Pedro and his family were gone, I wondered if Pedro's parents would make the same choices if faced with them again. I thought about the allure and the promise this country holds for so many people, and marveled at the sacrifices people are willing to make to come to our "land of opportunity" in their quest for better lives.

***

Notes:

Pedro's mother was exposed to gasoline vapors, which are readily absorbed from the respiratory tract. Her symptoms included vomiting, dizziness, and drowsiness. The propensity for the inhalation of large amounts of gasoline to injure kidneys even to the extent of causing renal failure is well documented. I had to surmise that some of the toxins in his mother's system passed across the placenta to cause Pedro's renal failure. (For information on the toxicity of gasoline, please see the Medical Management Guidelines for Gasoline on the webpage for the Agency for Toxic Substances and Disease Registry at http://www.atsdr.cdc.gov/mhmi/mmg72.html.)

The NICU team was well within legal guidelines when we recommended to Pedro's parents that they discontinue his life support. The "Baby Doe" rules were first promulgated in 1984 by the Reagan administration with the intent to require life-sustaining medical care be given to all infants regardless of any disabilities. The case of an infant with Down syndrome and tracheoesophageal fistula brought this legislation into being; the infant ultimately died after her parents, on the advice of the infant's doctors, refused corrective surgery.

The Baby Doe rules have been widely debated, especially regarding whether they conflict with physicians' and parents' ability to determine what is in an infant's best interest. While the regulations were initially perceived by some to mandate full care for all infants, regardless of their condition, ongoing care was not required for situations in which: 1) The infant was chronically and irreversibly comatose; 2) The provision of treatment would merely prolong dying, and not ameliorate or correct all of the infant's life-threatening conditions; or 3) Treatment would be virtually futile in terms of the infant's survival, and the treatment itself would be inhumane.

Although Pedro was not comatose, our treatment team thought we had reached the point of prolonging his dying, and that continuing to treat him was both futile and inhumane. (1984. "Nondiscrimination on the Basis of Handicap; Procedures and Guidelines Relating to Health Care for Handicapped Infants—HHS". Final Rules. *Federal Register 49*(8): 1622 –1654. *See* also U.S. Department of Health and Human Services, 1985: 1340.15(B)2 p14887–14888. And: Kopelman L. M. 2005. "Are the 21-Year-Old Baby Doe Rules Misunderstood or Mistaken?" *Pediatrics 115*(3): 797-802.)

In recent years, a national debate has raged over provision of health care services to undocumented immigrants. While some argue that providing care to them at taxpayers' expenses takes away health care dollars away from U.S. citizens, others contend that if the states and the U.S. government do not provide routine, preventive care, such as prenatal care, these patients will end up costing the health care system far more by utilizing more expensive emergency care during times of health crises.

Others assert that illegal aliens do not impose an undue burden on our health care system. According to a study by the Rand Corporation, undocumented adults account for $6.4 billion a year in national health care expenses. The publicly funded portion of this care constituted only 1.25 percent of the $88 billion the government spent on health care services for adults (besides seniors) in 2000. ("U.S. Report: Illegal Immigrants Not a Burden to Health Care System." Online at http://www.workpermit.com/news/2006-1215/us/illegal_immigrants_not_burden_health_care.htm.)

The effect the recently enacted healthcare reform legislation (The Affordable Care Act, 2010) will have on illegal aliens' receipt of healthcare services in the United States remains to be seen. The law does prohibit undocumented workers from buying health insurance in the insurance exchanges, even if they are able to pay on their own. Whether to provide and pay for the health care needs of undocumented immigrants, and how, may be taken up in future legislation on immigration reform.

Chapter 6

A Father's Mission: Amanda Ryder

David Ryder called me at home, interrupting dinner with my two young daughters, his voice crazed. I had become well acquainted with David and his wife during the time I cared for their daughter, Amanda, in the NICU. She had been home now for several months, but earlier that day, I had admitted her to the pediatric intensive care unit (PICU) of the hospital, where another doctor was now caring for her.

"Dr. Hall, listen, the doctor here in the pediatric ICU just announced there was nothing more he could do. He told us Amanda is probably going to die in the next twenty-four hours, and if she makes it until morning we would meet the guy who's going to cover for him while he goes skiing in Colorado. Then, he left and went home to pack his bags, I guess.

"The guy is a complete jerk," he added, emphasizing each word. David and his wife had already lost Amanda's twin—suddenly and unexpectedly—in the NICU, several weeks after the twins' birth at twenty-eight weeks of pregnancy. It was clear David was not about to lose another baby without a fight of epic proportions.

David forged ahead through my silence. "Dr. Hall, come on… There's got to be something else we can do for Amanda. Can you think of anything? Anywhere else we could send her? This can't be all there is for her. I am *not* going to let it end like this."

Had the PICU doctor in the community hospital where I was now working actually told David his baby was going to die, or was that David's interpretation of their conversation? I wondered how that communication had taken place, about the words, the nuances, and the tone the doctor had used.

***

Two hours earlier, when I had arrived home, I felt dispirited by what had taken place in the emergency room earlier in the day. Amanda's mom, Jill, had called me earlier in the morning to tell me Amanda was having trouble breathing…again. Even several months after her discharge from the NICU, Amanda was still plagued by a ferocious case of bronchopulmonary dysplasia (BPD), or chronic lung disease, related to her prematurity. Her NICU course was typical for a premature infant of the mid-1990s: Her mother did not receive steroid shots before birth to help her babies' lungs mature, but Amanda did get the benefit of several doses of artificially produced surfactant to help her breathe.

When mothers at risk for preterm delivery receive a course of antenatal corticosteroids, their fetus' lung development is accelerated by the enhanced production of surfactant, the substance that enables the individual air sacs, or alveoli, to easily expand. If, after birth, babies still show signs of inadequate surfactant, this substance can be given directly into the lungs through a tube placed in the baby's trachea.

Amanda had remained on the ventilator for more than a month. However, even the oxygen she took home with her could not keep her pink when she suffered one of her terrifying bouts of wheezing.

When her breathing troubles flared up, breathing was no longer a thoughtless, casual affair. Instead, it was work. Hard work. The bronchi, or breathing tubes in her lungs, narrowed down so that Amanda needed to use considerable exertion to force each breath in and out. This caused the musical sound to her breathing, but the beauty of the sound masked its danger. A patient in the throes of an "asthma attack" experiences a distinctive feeling of suffocation, and death can result from the vise-like constriction of the airways.

When she graduated from the NICU, Amanda joined a set of preschool-aged twins at home. When one or the other contracted even a minor cold, so did Amanda, only her colds always evolved into asthma—and sometimes even pneumonia. Her multiple medications were not enough to keep the air free-flowing through her airways, and when I saw her in the emergency room shortly after her mom called me, I knew she needed to come back in the hospital at once. A private duty nurse, hired by Amanda's insurance company to help care for her at home, had accompanied Amanda and Jill to the emergency room.

Amanda knitted her brows with worry as she inhaled each shallow breath, one right after the other. Although the nasal cannula she wore piped oxygen into her lungs, her nostrils flared around the tiny tubes and her lips were purple. I instructed the nurse to increase the flow on Amanda's oxygen, and then ordered an IV, a breathing treatment, and some other medications. Next, I called Dr. Jonathan Berry, the doctor who would admit Amanda to the pediatric ICU. Although I saw Amanda weekly in our outpatient follow-up clinic, she was too old and "too big"—even though still quite tiny—to come back into the NICU.

Just after I left the emergency room, Amanda's nurse gave her a bottle of formula to drink. In a life-changing moment, Amanda choked on the milk, and formula sprayed into her trachea instead of smoothly trickling down her esophagus into her stomach. She turned the color of eggplant as violent spasms of coughing wracked her body and alternated with frantic, but ineffective, gasps. It took a few seconds for the milk to coat her main airway and ooze into its smaller, more distant branches. Soon it had filled all her tiny air sacs, obliterating any chance for the exchange of oxygen and carbon dioxide to occur. It nearly killed her on the spot.

The emergency room physician unceremoniously pushed Amanda's mom and private nurse, both in tears, out of the examining room when he was called to insert a breathing tube into Amanda's airway. After he connected her to a ventilator, the doctor whisked her upstairs to the pediatric ICU.

***

On the phone, David told me Amanda's ventilator settings had reached the upper limit, she was on 100 percent oxygen, and her IV drip medications were at their highest doses. "Freaking doctor has given up on her," he added. "And that SOB is going on some luxurious vacation tomorrow. Isn't that just dandy?" He made no attempt to mask his sarcasm.

"David, I'm so sorry this has happened," I said. I was chastising myself for not explicitly telling Amanda's nurse that her tiny charge was not to have anything by mouth. It seemed so obvious; I had wrongly assumed the nurse would know. And now Amanda would pay the price.

"I've heard the university hospital has a new kind of ventilator called a high-frequency oscillator," I told David. "Let me call over there and see if the doctors there think it might help Amanda. I'll do whatever I can to get her over there. Their PICU staff is really great. This will be her best shot." I wanted David to understand that Amanda would have an improved chance of surviving if transferred to a hospital that had better technology available to treat her, but in no way would her survival be guaranteed.

We had lost Amanda's twin at three weeks of age. Ariel was bigger at birth and was actually doing better than Amanda. She beat Amanda off the ventilator and was on a full volume of tube feedings when one day, shortly after she received a blood transfusion, she died without any warning. Seemingly a healthy premie, she simply stopped breathing and could not be brought back to life, a rare event in any NICU. As traumatic an experience as that had been for David and Jill, I guessed the loss of Amanda would be far more painful.

I hung up the phone and went back to the dinner table where I said a quick goodbye to my husband and kids. "Eat those peas, guys, or no dessert," I added.

My drive to the hospital through the light evening traffic took twenty minutes. As I cut in and out of the lanes, I talked on my cell phone to Dr. Philip Sutton, the reigning chief of the pediatric ICU at the university hospital. I told him Amanda's story and asked whether he thought he could help her.

"I'm willing to give it a try," he said. "I'll arrange for our transport team to come pick her up."

Arriving at the back entrance to the hospital, I swiped my security badge to get in the doorway, wondering how I should handle the fact that I had just hijacked Amanda's care from my hospital's PICU team. Although another doctor was technically responsible for her, I had just made my own decision about her care. I decided to call Dr. Berry once I got to the PICU to let him know what I was doing. I did not really know Dr. Berry, since he was new on staff, but I doubted he would have any objections to transferring

Amanda to a hospital where she might have a better chance of surviving.

The corridors of the hospital's second floor were already clear, and as I walked under the fluorescent lights, they emitted the faintest of buzzes; the contrast between daylight hours when the halls were always full of staff in various colors of scrubs was striking. I walked into the PICU and saw Jill bent over Amanda; David sat at her bedside.

"Dr. Hall." David stood up to greet me and shake my hand with a bone-crunching grasp. His tie looked a bit askew under the collar of his wrinkled oxford cloth shirt. His sleeves were rolled up, and his suit jacket was draped around the back of his chair. Speaking with his characteristic urgency, he said, "Thanks for coming. What did you find out?"

"Let me have a quick look at Amanda," I said. "Then, we'll talk."

"Hi, sweetie babe," I said to Amanda. I knew she wouldn't respond, since I could see she had already received medication to paralyze her so the ventilator could do the work of breathing for her. At four months of age, Amanda still weighed less than most healthy newborns; she was swallowed up in a normal-sized bed. The ventilator tubing sprouted from her mouth, another tube was threaded into her nose, monitor wires crisscrossed her chest, and lubricant gel oozed out between the lids of her eyes that were lightly taped shut with clear plastic tape. She was completely motionless except for the rise and fall of her chest with each ventilator breath.

"Dr. Sutton in the PICU at the university hospital will take Amanda," I said when I finished with my exam. "He's setting up the transport right now. She'll be in good hands. I'm going to call Dr. Berry right now and tell him."

Dr. Berry bristled a bit when I called him. "I'm doing what I can for her, given the resources at the hospital," he said curtly. "But hey, if you want to transfer her, be my guest. I won't stand in the way. I don't have any more tricks up my sleeve, that's for sure."

Before I returned to Amanda's bedside, I went to the x-ray view box to see Amanda's chest film. Amanda's lungs appeared almost completely white instead of black, indicating they were filled with fluid instead of air. I took a deep breath, exhaled slowly, and walked back over to Amanda's bedside.

Jill leaned over the railing of Amanda's bed and propped her favorite stuffed rabbit near her baby's head. I pulled up a stool and sat beside David, and we traded small talk for the several hours it took for the transport team to arrive, trying our best to keep our minds off the high-stakes game playing out in front of us. The team could not get there fast enough, I thought, as I watched Amanda's oxygen saturation slip from 80 percent down to 70 percent and occasionally even lower. I did not dare turn the ventilator up from the highest settings I had ever seen, afraid to cause one of Amanda's lungs to rupture; this would cause certain death.

At last the team rolled in, and I gave them a full report on Amanda's status, both past and present. They packed her up, and finally left the PICU at 11:30 p.m. I trailed the ambulance on the freeway for a few miles, and then turned off onto the main road leading to my home. The moon roof of my car was open to let the cool night air pour in and the strains of an Aerosmith song waft out as I sped around the curves and up the few last hills to my home. When I arrived, the house was both dark and quiet, guarded by a pumpkin with a toothy grin.

***

Amanda's medical team maintained her in a medically induced coma through Thanksgiving and on toward Christmas. I visited her several times and learned about the new ventilator being used to treat her. Each time I saw her, I marveled at the trust her parents were forced to have. Every day they saw her lying as though frozen in time; yet, they maintained hope that someday when they kissed her, she would finally awaken from her long sleep, just as Snow White did. Would she remember anything from this time, I wondered. Would she have any memory tracings deep in some part of her brain that would bubble to the surface in some unpredictable way later in life?

People sometimes dismiss the mental and emotional capabilities of babies. Research has shown, however, that fetuses as young as thirty weeks gestational age, still in the womb, form memories and act on those memories. They can remember sounds for ten minutes, and by thirty-four weeks of pregnancy, they can respond to sounds they remember for up to a month. Certainly babies several months old have memories, too. Would Amanda flinch at the sound of a jackhammer, like her ventilator, in the future? Would ringing bells, like her monitor alarms, trouble her?

Jill came to sit with Amanda nearly every day after she dropped her twins off at a babysitter's. David could only come after work. They always greeted me warmly, and together we talked about our hopes for Amanda's ultimate return home.

Once her lungs were healed to the point she could try to breathe on her own, Amanda was allowed to wake up very slowly. Although the high-frequency ventilator saved her life, the cumulative effect of having her lungs pounded with a high-pressure device for more than a month took its toll. She already had chronic lung disease going into this hospitalization, and now it was far worse. Her x-ray showed lots of scarring, the price she had to pay to regain her life. The next challenge would be to get her out of the hospital.

Amanda remained so weak after her illness, she could not even begin to take a bottle, and she had a feeding tube surgically inserted into her stomach to make feedings easier. She continued to need a high dose of oxygen and many more medications than before. This time she would have around-the-clock nursing care, minus the one nurse who inadvertently precipitated this mess. But, one task remained undone.

Amanda's discharge would take place during RSV (respiratory syncytial virus) season. RSV is a particularly formidable enemy to former premature babies with chronic lung disease. While it provokes a simple cold in older children, it induces a wheezing illness and a dangerous form of pneumonia in tiny babies. In this group, it can be lethal. If one of the twins in her family came home from daycare with a cold, Amanda could be dead within days. David, the information manager for the family, knew about this. We had spoken over the past few months about the dangers posed by RSV and how to protect Amanda against it. In his engineer's way, David wanted a definitive solution to this problem.

I told him about a new drug undergoing clinical trials in premature babies. The medication, called RespiGam, provided a super-concentrated dose of antibodies to RSV. During my training in neonatology, I worked in the lab next to the researcher who did the groundbreaking trials of this medication in rats, proving it protected them from severe RSV infection. A drug company picked up the product and was testing it in human babies.

"Can you get your hands on some of that stuff?" David implored me.

The university hospital NICU where I spent several years on staff was participating in the clinical trial, but enrollment guidelines were very strict. And Amanda was in the pediatric ICU, not the neonatal ICU. Important distinction. I called my former section chief in the NICU to inquire, but Amanda did not qualify. I was told the rules could not be bent for her without jeopardizing their participation in the national study.

"Oh come on," argued David, when he heard these details. "Surely there's got to be a way. Amanda could die without it. We can't wait until these trials are finished."

David assumed if he argued his point rationally, logic would prevail and people would do what he considered to be "the right thing." It would not be quite so easy.

"Hey, you said you know the original research guy. Right? So, call him up. Maybe he has a vial or two of the stuff left in the refrigerator in his lab."

I called my former professor in his lab back East, but came up empty-handed. "The drug company is in charge now," he reported. "I don't have anything to do with the clinical trials in babies. I just do rats. Sorry, I can't help." He did, however, give me the name of the drug company CEO, which I passed on to David.

This time David rose to the challenge, but he too hit a wall. "God-damned bureaucrats," he fumed. "The CEO says the FDA won't allow him to use RespiGam outside the trials or it will endanger his approval of the drug. My kid could die and everyone's telling me 'no dice.' God damn it again!"

"Sorry," I said. I felt like I had to apologize for the entire medical-pharmaceutical industry.

About a week later, David called me at home on Christmas Eve just as my daughters and I were just putting our presents under the tree. "Merry Christmas. You are never going to believe what I got Amanda for Christmas."

"What?" I asked, my mind devoid of any reasonable ideas.

"RespiGam," he exclaimed triumphantly.

"RespiGam? What…? How…?" I was truly amazed.

"I finally got in touch with this guy at the FDA this morning. I swear to God I kept him on the phone for a couple of hours, pleading for compassionate use of RespiGam in Amanda's case. And I'll tell you what… I think he finally gave up because he wanted to get off the phone and go home to his own kids for Christmas. He did not want to be Scrooge. Or the Grinch. I wore him down, plain and simple. He is going to ship it out to the university hospital next Monday. I got Dr. Sutton conferenced in on the call toward the end, and it is all arranged.

"How 'bout that?" he exclaimed.

I could see David grin over the phone. "Wow, awesome! Merry, merry Christmas. Congratulations. You *so* deserve it."

David had hoped—no, he had believed—he could get RespiGam for his daughter, and he had transformed his belief into action. Amanda got her RespiGam and went home in the middle of January. That winter, the baby of a close family friend of the Ryders died of RSV. Amanda did not exactly thrive that long winter, but she slowly got better.

Amanda's follow-up care stayed with the university hospital, but I checked in with David, and he with me, every so often. Once when he called, he lamented the strain Amanda's condition had placed on his marriage, and he wondered aloud if he and his wife would be able to ride it out. They did make it through the rough spots, and several years later, they moved to another state where David took a new job.

***

I received Christmas letters and pictures faithfully. Amanda at age two, sitting on David's lap on his speedboat on a lake, tethered to her oxygen tubing. Amanda at age four, splashing in the middle of their backyard pool while being held by David, tethered to her oxygen tubing. Amanda at age five, escorted by David to her first day of kindergarten, tethered to her oxygen tubing.

When Amanda was ten-years-old, I finally got to see her again. I visited her and her family when I attended a medical conference in their city. We all had dinner together at their house, during which Amanda excitedly showed me a stack of her school papers with all A's marked in red on the top. "She's a great student, a super hard worker, *and* she plays soccer," David exclaimed.

I smiled as David spoke, having no doubt in my mind that his proactive stance throughout Amanda's life had helped his daughter succeed.

After dinner David excused her from the table while her twin siblings and younger sister sat politely. "Go get your oxygen on, babe. Your lips are a bit blue."

"Awwww, Dad?" Amanda was still tiny, a wiry little girl with big glasses and a mop of unruly curly hair. I could see she liked to throw her weight around.

"Go," David directed, pointing the way.

With that, Amanda scampered out of the room. She hurried back a few minutes later, tethered to her oxygen tubing, and showed me some pictures she had drawn for a school project.

"Awesome, Amanda," I said, looking them over. "Just awesome."

Notes:

Amanda's lung disease could have potentially been minimized had her mother received a course of antenatal corticosteroids. Corticosteroid treatment of pregnant women at risk to deliver prematurely began in 1972. Steroids accelerate fetal lung development by enhancing production of surfactant, the substance that enables the individual air sacs, or alveoli, to easily expand. In 1994, an NIH Consensus Conference confirmed the value of this practice. Data clearly showed that giving a single course of corticosteroids to pregnant women at risk for preterm delivery (between twenty-four and thirty-four weeks gestation) reduces the risks of death, respiratory distress syndrome, and intraventricular hemorrhage in their preterm infants. The optimal benefit of this treatment lasts seven days. ("The Effect of Corticosteroids for Fetal Maturation on Perinatal Outcomes." 1994. NIH Consensus Statement *12*(2): 1-24. This can be found online at http://consensus.nih.gov/1994 /1994AntenatalSteroid Perinatal095html.htm.)

In the years since the Consensus Conference, usage of antenatal steroids has become the standard of care, although opportunities to give steroids are sometimes missed even now, usually in situations when delivery must be done under emergency circumstances.

Both the administration of antenatal corticosteroids to mothers at risk to deliver prematurely and the postnatal administration of surfactant for respiratory distress syndrome (surfactant deficiency) have contributed greatly to the improved survival of premature infants from the 1990s to the present. Mary Ellen Avery, a pioneering neonatologist, first discovered that the absence of surfactant, a chemical substance produced by the type-II cells of the lung, was the cause of neonatal respiratory distress syndrome. Since its commercial development, surfactant's use has been fine-tuned both in premature infants with respiratory distress syndrome and also in more mature infants with meconium aspiration syndrome, pneumonia, and other diagnoses. (Engle W. A. 2008. American Academy of Pediatrics Committee on Fetus and Newborn. "Surfactant-Replacement Therapy for Respiratory Distress in the Preterm and Term Neonate." *Pediatrics 121*(6): 419-432.)

Short-term memory has been documented in fetuses as young as thirty weeks in a study evaluating their responses to vibro-acoustic stimulation. (Dirix C. E., J. G. Jijhuis, H. W. Johngsma, and G. Hornstra. 2009. "Aspects of Fetal Learning and Memory." *Child Development 80*(4): 1251-1258.)

RSV, or respiratory syncytial virus, is a virus that is nearly ubiquitous in the winter months in North America. Nearly 100 percent of children will contract RSV by the age of three years, although in most it will cause only a mild upper respiratory tract infection with cold-like symptoms. Premature infants are at particular risk to develop more serious lower respiratory tract disease when infected with RSV, though, and in this population of infants it can be fatal.

Although Amanda received RespiGam® (RSV-IGIV) to prevent her from contracting RSV (respiratory syncytial virus) infection, a newer product—Synagis® (Palivizumab, manufactured by MedImmune)—has now replaced RespiGam. Synagis is a monoclonal antibody to the RSV virus. Monthly injections of Synagis are given to babies during RSV season if they are at high risk of severe disease with RSV. Current recommendations regarding which babies should receive Synagis can be found in the following reference: Committee on Infectious Diseases. 2009. "Modified Recommendations for Use of Palivizumab for Prevention of Respiratory Syncytial Virus Infections." *Pediatrics 124*(6): 1694-1701.

Chapter 7

Second Chances: Jésus Martinez

The first time I heard Jésus Martinez cry, his diagnosis was instantly apparent to me.

He screeched and he wailed—inconsolably—as though possessed by demons. The sound of his voice shattered the calm in the newborn nursery and I was surprised his crying did not incite a riot among the other babies, who slept quietly, oblivious to the racket. The crying was more distressing to me than the sound of fingernails scratching down a blackboard, and I wanted to put my hands over my ears. The two nurses who shuffled babies in and out of the nursery, and to and from their mother's rooms, seemed on edge, even though they had set his bassinet far over in one corner.

I followed the sound to the baby, now twelve-hours-old. A light receiving blanket hung over the top of his bassinet, an attempt by the nurses to mute the clamor of his crying. I pulled up the edge of the thin, white cotton blanket to see him writhing and flailing about in a face-down position. While all the other babies in the nursery were sleeping, all wrapped in their blankets like little burritos, he had kicked his blanket off and torn loose of it.

Jésus was a scrawny baby, not much more than skin and bones, but he seemed like a scrappy fighter. I picked him up and turned him over, trying to contain him amidst his constant motion. It felt like he might vibrate right out of my hands.

"Hey there, little guy...settle down," I said in as soft and soothing a voice as I could muster.

Jésus squinted his eyes the way babies do when crying consumes them. He barely even stopped his shrill shrieks to come up for breath. He had already rubbed the tip of his tiny nose, in the middle of his little-old-man face, until it was raw and glowing red like a hot ember. Beads of sweat covered his brow, a rarity since babies do not usually sweat until they are more than three months old. His arms trembled as his legs see-sawed up and down at the knees. They, too, were already red, the top layer of skin gone. If Jésus' thick mop of ebony hair had been standing on end, the picture of a baby who had just stuck his finger into an electrical outlet would have been complete.

That is what withdrawal from opiates—heroin, methadone, morphine, oxycodone—looked like. I had seen it before. Too many times. It did not matter what type of hospital I was practicing in—county hospital, academic medical center, or community hospital: each had their share of opiate-addicted mothers. The process of opiate withdrawal in the baby was equally ugly whether the baby's mother used heroin obtained on the street, methadone from a sanctioned treatment program, or narcotics prescribed by a doctor for pain relief.

"What's the story on this one?" I asked Annie, the nurse who was taking care of Jésus.

"Born at three this morning. Been crying since six. Hasn't slept. Wants to eat, but can't eat. Been spitting up. Diarrhea. You name it, he's got it. Withdrawal symptoms, that is."

"That bad already?" I cringed.

"Have you collected urine for a drug screen?"

Annie nodded.

"Meconium too?"

"I'm in the process of collecting that. Just waiting for him to poop again."

A newborn's urine drug screen can only detect maternal drug use if she used several days prior to delivery. Meconium, the green sticky stool passed by babies for the first day or so, can show traces of drugs in the baby's system if mother has used drugs for up to several months before delivery.

"What can you tell me about mom?" I asked.

"Well," Annie said with a harrumph, "this is her fourth baby. The first three are in foster care. Neglect due to maternal drug use." She shook her head, her frustration obvious.

"So this baby will be going into foster care, too? I mean, clearly, she's still using drugs and all..."

"Well, now, don't go jumping to conclusions. Janie from social work has already been by to check on the baby. According to her, since mom is in rehab now, she gets to keep this one," Annie countered, rolling her eyes. "Go figure."

"Oh, I get it. This is methadone withdrawal, not heroin."

Babies whose mothers try to get off heroin by getting into a methadone maintenance program suffer worse withdrawal than mothers who continue using heroin. But, at least, methadone is legal.

"Well, Annie, I'm sure you agree this baby needs to come to the NICU. This is going to be a long, drawn out process. I'll go tell mom."

"Thank you, thank you," she said, joining her hands as if to say a prayer, and bowing forward slightly. "My nerves thank you. The baby thanks you. The other babies thank you."

I knocked softly, and then pushed open the heavy door to Rosa Martinez's room. Entering from the brightly lit, busy hallway, it took my eyes a moment to adjust to the darkness and the quiet in the room. Rosa was curled up in bed with her back toward the door, a plain white sheet pulled over half her face. The aroma of fried chicken led my eyes to a tray of food sitting half-eaten on the narrow table overlying her bed. All that was left in the different partitions of a tan plastic plate were a picked-over piece of chicken, some faded green stumps representing the remains of broccoli stems, and a bit of chocolate pudding.

A man stretched out to completely fill the couch next to the bed, the toe tips of his weathered leather boots pointing toward the ceiling. The rough, scratchy movement of air in and out through his nose and mouth filled the room with a reassuring regularity. His hands, with their dark, stained fingernails, were neatly folded across his chest. A pack of cigarettes was rolled into the sleeve of his T-shirt, exposing a colorful tattoo.

"Rosa," I said quietly. No response. "Rosa, I need to talk with you." I jostled her shoulder gently as I spoke.

Her liquid brown eyes flicked open, and I sensed fear as she pulled back from my touch.

"It's about your baby. He's starting to withdraw. You were told this would happen, right? Since you've been taking methadone?"

"I was told he might have a few problems, but nothing too bad. Why? Is he in trouble?"

"He's very uncomfortable. He's crying quite a bit. He's jittery. He's not eating well. He needs to come to the NICU."

"I thought he got to come home with me. That's why I switched to the methadone. What's the NICU?" she asked, her voice tinged with suspicion.

"The NICU is where we take care of babies who need special treatment. He needs medicine to make him more comfortable."

"Can't I just give him the medicine? I want him to go home with me. I'm leaving this hell hole tomorrow. The food sucks."

"I'm sorry, but he won't be ready. When you see him again, you'll see why. He's going to be in the hospital for awhile."

"What do you mean 'awhile'?" she asked, her brows knitted above her dark eyes.

The man's snoring continued in the background.

"Withdrawal from methadone is a long process. It may take three or four weeks before the baby is ready to go home."

"Ay," she groaned, shifting her position in the bed. "Do what you have to then," she said, shaking her head back and forth.

Then she looked right at me. "But I'm telling you, I want this baby. I'm gonna take him home with me. You'll see."

I nodded in agreement, and then pulled the door to Rosa's room closed behind me, noticing as I did that she pulled the covers back up over her face, and the man on the couch twitched ever so slightly.

***

"I'm assuming you want the kid to have formula, not breast milk. Am I right?" Sandi, the NICU nurse who admitted Jésus to the NICU, held a bottle in her hand and steered it toward Jésus' mouth. She had Jésus snuggled into the crook of her arm, bound so tightly in a white blanket he looked like a mummy. The only part of his body I could see was his head, and he flung it from side to side anxiously searching for the nipple. He cried in frustration, and then latched on, grasping it for a few quick sucks. It soon slipped out of his mouth, prompting another ear-piercing wail. This time I did cover my ears.

"For now, yes, formula. But breast milk would be okay if we get negative drug screens back—showing nothing besides methadone. I'm going to go write some admit orders at the moment."

"Whatcha gonna give the baby for the pain, doctor?" Sandi asked.

"Morphine. Lots of morphine."

"Thank you. And some for the nurse as well? Or do I get combat pay instead?"

I chuckled with Sandi, as she turned her attention back to the wild child in her arms, thinking to myself how hard it must be to spend a twelve-hour shift with a baby as tightly wired as Jésus. The irony about babies with opiate withdrawal is they respond best to treatment with opiates. A number of different medications—from valium to Phenobarbital to other sorts of tranquilizers have been tried—without good success. I preferred giving morphine, but others might choose tincture of opium or even methadone.

***

When a mother uses heroin or methadone during pregnancy—and about 70,000 American women do each year—the drug gets in her bloodstream then passes across the placenta to her baby. The drug is stored in the baby's fat, its concentration building up throughout pregnancy if mom is a constant user. After the high of using, mother's and baby's blood levels gradually go down and withdrawal sets in. Withdrawal can occur repeatedly throughout pregnancy, the symptoms easing each time the mother takes more. Once the baby's cord is clamped after delivery, the baby is cut off from his supply and his blood levels drop.

To prevent babies from suffering through withdrawal "cold turkey," opiates are given in doses that are gradually lowered, minimizing their distress. Mothers who use methadone or illegal drugs during pregnancy also frequently smoke cigarettes and drink alcohol during pregnancy, which only worsens their babies' symptoms after birth.

***

I finished writing orders, and then saw that after Sandi had finished feeding Jésus, she placed him in an isolette with a dark blanket covering the top. Good. She anticipated my orders of "minimal stimulation." Babies undergoing opiate withdrawal do best if kept in dark, quiet places, and his isolette was the only dark, quiet place in the NICU right now. The sun-splashed room had a phalanx of long fluorescent lights overhead and contained twenty-five isolettes and cribs. It was bustling with the noise of nursing shift change yet again. How any of the babies could get any sleep was beyond me.

The next day when I came in, Rosa was sitting at Jésus' bedside. "Doctor, when can I hold my baby?" she asked.

"When he wakes up for a feeding," I answered.

"But my boyfriend's coming to pick me up in fifteen minutes. I have to hold the baby now. I'm gonna be leaving. He's *my* baby," she insisted, "and that nurse won't let me hold him." Rosa pointed to Javier.

Dressed in white scrub pants and top, Javier stood coolly with his arms through the porthole doors of the next baby's isolette, holding a thermometer in the baby's armpit. His dark curly hair reached the top of his scrub shirt, and his brown eyes never reflected the stress of working in the NICU. Javier did not respond to Rosa's accusation.

"What's up, Javi? What time is Jésus scheduled to eat?"

"Scheduled to eat in about forty-five minutes. That would be at 11:00."

"Do you think he could eat early this time, so mom can visit with him?"

"I just got him back to sleep about thirty minutes ago. He's been awake and crying since his last feeding. I thought he could use the rest, you know?"

I weighed the nurse's observations against the mother's wishes. I knew it best not to undercut the judgment of one of my nurses unless there was a compelling reason.

"Can't you stay a bit longer, and wait for his feeding time?" I asked mom.

"My boyfriend's working, and he's borrowing a car to come and get me in the first place. He has to be somewhere by noon. Once he takes me out of here, I'm not sure when I can come back. I'm completely dependent on him to drive me around." She had a decidedly sour look on her face. "I ain't never even got to hold my baby yet," she added.

I looked at Javier, who shrugged.

"Well, ordinarily, for babies like Jésus, rest is really important. But just this once, I'll let you wake him up early."

"Thank you, doctor. I 'preciate it."

I unhooked the side panel to the isolette, dropping the door and sliding the tray on which the baby rested toward me. As soon the baby felt the motion, he sprang to life, curving his arms out in front of his face then back to his middle in an exaggerated startle reflex. The high-pitched cry was not far behind. I caught Javier's raised eyebrows and his smirk communicating "I told you so." Just then, the smell hit me, the sour smell of baby poop.

"Looks like I need to change his diaper first," I said. I unfastened the tapes on the diaper's waistband and pulled the diaper down, discovering a slimy, yellow puddle. I nearly succeeded in getting the baby's bottom clean with the cold, wet, fresh-smelling baby wipes, when the baby squirted liquid stool from his rear end with such force it hit the end of the isolette, spraying the wall in some kind of weird modern art moment.

"Ahhhh," I protested, as Javier's smirk increased in size. He was not about to leave the baby whose diaper he was changing to come rescue me. I had to finish this myself. I got out a handful of baby wipes and tried to clean the liquid goo off the baby's bottom and legs before he could expel any more. I placed a clean diaper under him, making progress, when his penis stood straight up and squirted a stream of urine that left drops on the inner roof of the isolette. The baby continued the incessant squall he began when I woke him up.

"Javier, help! I'm a failure at this. Sorry, but can you come help me?"

Javier calmly finished diapering the baby he was with, withdrew his arms from the porthole doors and snapped them shut. "Jeez, did ya hafta leave me such a mess?" he asked, surveying the damage. "I'll have to change out the isolette after I clean the baby up."

"Look, I'm sorry, but I sure would appreciate it if you could finish this for me. I've got a ton of other kids to see." Javier nodded, taking it all in stride. "Okay, mom," I said to Rosa, "Javier will get your baby ready for you."

I continued my rounds, and after seeing two more patients I walked back by Jésus' bed. Rosa was struggling to get him to eat. He cried. He took two sucks. He spit up. He cried some more. Rosa bounced him on her knee. "Come on *papi*, take your bottle. Do it for mama. Be a good boy." He produced more shrieking, as though he were in excruciating pain.

Ay, I thought. *It's going to be a long couple of weeks.*

***

It took several days of adjusting Jésus' medication doses to finally reduce his discomfort so he could sleep for longer than two hours and take more than an ounce of formula at a time. His jitteriness and irritability lessened, but occasionally flared, especially within the few hours before his medication doses were due.

Meanwhile, Rosa arrived early in the morning for her daily visits. Her boyfriend, Roberto, took her to her methadone maintenance program to get her meds, and then dropped her off at the hospital. She spent all day at Jésus' bedside, scratching with a pencil in a paperback crossword puzzle book, and Roberto picked her up again after 5:00. Occasionally, she engaged the nurses in conversation.

"My oldest child was just like Jésus. He ate really good as a baby, and he's still a really good eater. Just last week I took him to McDonald's and he had two hamburgers. And he's still only five," she told Javier, next time he was assigned to care for Jésus. She regaled Javier with several more tales of the exploits of her children, ages five, four, three, and two.

"Hey, she's telling me this story about taking her kid to McDonald's last week," Javier told me when I came by to examine babies that day. "And the other kids too. I thought all her kids were in foster care."

"Me, too," I said, surprised. "Let's ask Janie."

Janie was a full-figured African-American woman who had a ready smile. She also had a tremendous sense of humor. She needed it. At discharge planning rounds, I asked Janie about Rosa's situation with her other children.

"They are *definitely* in foster care. She does not have any visitation with them right now. I don't know where she's getting these stories. Wishful thinking, I guess. No," the social worker insisted, "she's gotta stay in her methadone maintenance program, then show she can handle this baby before the State will even consider letting her get those other kids back."

"She's got to submit to her weekly urine drug testing to ensure she's not using anything else, and go to parenting classes. She has a whole lot ahead of her, although I will say she's off to a good start. Her urine drug screen, and the baby's urine and meconium screens, only showed the methadone. She's not using any other drugs, which is a plus. She's in a stable relationship with Roberto, whom she met in her program, even though he isn't the father of this baby. And I'm impressed with the way she's been visiting often."

"It's a start, anyway," I agreed. "Kind of unbelievable that she gets a chance with this baby, all things considered." I frowned at Janie. I knew from my experience as a social worker that mothers who abused drugs were at much higher risk to abuse or neglect their children than other mothers.

Janie must have been thinking the same thing I was. "I know. I know," she said. "I don't make the rules."

I wondered if Rosa's switch from heroin use to methadone would be matched by an improvement in her ability to care for this new baby.

Every time I saw Rosa, she wore the same thing: tight jeans over which her post-pregnancy tummy bulged at the waist, and a clingy black v-neck shirt. A flimsy gold cross hung from a thin chain around her neck. She'd plucked her eyebrows completely off and replaced them with a thin dark line of exaggerated length, and she had enlarged her red lips with an outline of pale pink lip liner.

"Doctor, can't you get Jésus off the morphine faster?" she pestered me nearly every time I saw her. "I can't wait to get him out of here."

"We can't lower his dose too fast, or the withdrawal symptoms will come back. You know how you feel if your doctor lowers your dose? Edgy, irritable, icky? That's how your baby feels, too. You remember how much he used to cry. If we drop it too fast, he'll go back to crying all the time." That was something none of us wanted to go through.

"What about him going home on morphine? What's wrong with that?"

I did not want to tell her straight out, "We're not sending your baby home on morphine because we're worried you might take it yourself," but that was the case. We never discharged a baby home on any kind of opiates, especially if the parents had a history of abusing opiates. "Our policy is to wean the baby off morphine in the hospital," I told her, "and send him home on only one medication. And that's Phenobarbital."

"I'm getting tired of this, sitting here every day. I've finished two crossword puzzle books and I don't have the money to buy me no more. I can handle him at home. Roberto will help me when he gets home from work."

"He seems fine because he's getting the medicine, and we're lowering it just a little bit every other day."

Rosa considered what I had to say, then replied, "I don't like you. I want that other doctor who was here yesterday. She understands me when I talk to her."

"Dr. Onaga?" I asked. "The short lady with the glasses?"

"Yeah, that's the one."

"She won't be back till tomorrow, but I'll let her know you'd like to talk with her when she comes in."

When I signed out my list of patients to my partner the next morning, I warned her about Rosa Martinez. "She's gonna hit you up to wean the kid's meds faster," I told her.

"We'll see," she said.

I barely made it through the NICU's double doors the following day when I was accosted by Ginger, one of our younger nurses. Her frosted hair was in disarray and she had a spot of what looked suspiciously like baby spit-up on the shoulder of her scrubs. "Dr. Hall, Baby Martinez is totally crazy today. He is *off the wall.* The night nurse told me he last slept at 10 p.m. for about twenty minutes, and he's done nothing but cry and puke his guts out ever since. I won't make it through the day with this kid unless you increase his morphine dose. Will you write his orders first?"

"What happened?" I asked. "Last time I saw him, he was doing fine."

"Oh, that mom sweet-talked Dr. Onaga into dropping the morphine dose, trying to hurry things along. Dr. "O" thought since he'd been doing okay, maybe we could push him a bit. But obviously, it backfired."

"Okay, I get it. Let's give him a 'rescue dose' now, and I'll go back up on his maintenance dose."

"And something else," she continued. "Yesterday mom brought her brother to visit. When they left, we couldn't find our diaper scale. You know, those little tiny ones we keep at the bedside? People use those to weigh their drugs. That's probably why they took it."

"Are you sure they took it?"

"I can't prove it, but it was here when they were, and missing after they left."

"That's not good…"

"No. So after you write your orders, you can come back and talk to mom about all this."

Great, I thought. *Just how I like to start my day.*

Rosa fidgeted in her chair by Jésus' bedside. She scowled as I approached. "You are back again?" she said.

"Yes, it's my day. I see Jésus doesn't feel too good today."

"He must have a virus or something. I can't believe a little change in his medication could lead to all this. Or maybe his formula doesn't agree with him. Why don't you change it?"

I found a chair and pulled it up across from Rosa's. I sat down and said, "Rosa, your baby is experiencing withdrawal. I'm sure you know what that feels like. It's not easy. We can't make him go through it any faster than we're going. It wouldn't be fair to him.

"Maybe this can be a life lesson for you," I continued. "It's time to just let go of any plans you have for when he might come home. Just go with the flow. We're not going to promise you how much longer it's going to be. Jésus will be here for as long as it takes him to get through this.

"And the nurses tell me they couldn't find one of our diaper scales after you visited yesterday. Do you know anything about that?"

"I did not take the diaper scale. No way! I'm on methadone. I don't need a scale."

"Maybe your brother does?"

"I'll ask him, but I doubt it," she snapped at me like a turtle.

"Okay, then. Please ask, because we'd like to get it back."

Rosa folded her arms tightly across her breasts, and looked down at the floor. She refused to look up, so I stood and headed off to see my next baby.

The next day the diaper scale magically reappeared. Two weeks later, Jésus was off the morphine and ready for discharge. The state social worker had cleared Rosa to take him home. I wrote his prescription for Phenobarbital and included a detailed schedule of how Rosa should adjust his dose, going down by a tiny fraction every other day. It would take her a month to taper him off the medicine. "If you lower the dose and he doesn't do well, just go back up for a couple of days," I explained. "You got it?"

"Yeah, I get it. Just lemme go already," she said.

"And one more thing," I added "No matter how bad the baby's crying gets, don't ever shake your baby. Just take a hike if you are feeling too stressed out. Call someone to help you. Okay?"

She looked at me for a second as though she heard me. "Okay," she agreed.

Roberto appeared with the baby's car seat, and within five minutes they were gone.

"Do you think she'll make it?" Ginger asked me, as the doors closed behind them.

"Not a chance in hell," said Javier, who joined us.

"Hey, whaddaya mean?" I asked. "She was here every day. She knows how to feed him. She seemed to understand the tapering schedule for the Phenobarb."

"Yeah, but…," said Javier.

"Yeah, I know," I reluctantly agreed.

***

Two weeks later, Jésus' name appeared on my schedule of appointments for follow-up clinic. I entered the room and was surprised to see Roberto, wearing the same scuffed cowboy boots with the pointed toes he had on the morning I first saw him. His Marlboros were in his hip pocket this time. "Where's Rosa?" I asked, over the din of Jésus' cries.

"Hell if I know. She split about a week ago."

"What happened? Is she coming back? How's the baby?" I could see the answer to my last question…*not very good.*

"Well, I know she tried to get him off that damn medicine, and he started to scream all the damn time. I kept telling her, 'Rosa, you can't do that.' She told me it was her baby and she'd do what she damn well pleased. That's how she is, you know."

I nodded.

"So one day, I wake up to the baby crying. I get up out of bed and she's nowhere to be found. My wallet's gone, my car keys are gone… Hell, the damn car's gone, too. That was it. Ain't never seen her back and they ain't seen her over at the place where she gets her methadone neither."

"Oh dear. I better call the social worker about this." I shook my head. After all the care we had given to both Jésus and Rosa, she'd already blown it. It seemed apparent that she had reverted to her usual way of coping with life: escaping into hard-core drug use. I doubted she would get custody of this baby or any of her other children...ever. Not after this.

"Well, ya know this ain't even my kid," Roberto interrupted my thoughts. "I mean, I love him and everything, but maybe he should be with his sisters and brother. I've gotta try and keep my job and I don't see how I can possibly take care of him."

"I understand," I said. "He needs to be with a family who can take care of him. I'm sorry it did not work out for you and Rosa."

I looked at little Jésus, just beginning his journey in life. Where would it take him, I wondered. Born addicted to methadone and now abandoned by his mother, did he even have a chance at a so-called normal life?

"Hang in there, little guy. There's still hope for you," I said, as Roberto left the room and the baby became ours.

I turned to the nurse assisting me with clinic. "Let's call Janie so she can arrange for emergency foster placement for Jésus. I'm sure that will lead to a court hearing where Rosa will lose custody—like she did with her other kids—and a more permanent placement for him. At least he'll get a chance to have a stable home life with a new family," I sighed. "And I had such high hopes for her…"

***

Notes:

Each year, up to 120,000 newborns develop neonatal abstinence syndrome due to maternal methadone exposure, as Jésus did. Methadone maintenance is the best alternative for management of opiate dependency during pregnancy, as described in the following paper. (Kandall S. R. and T. M. Doberczak. 1999. "The Methadone-Maintained Pregnancy." *Clinics in Perinatology 26*(1): 173-185.)

Although Jésus' mother did not choose to breastfeed him, the American Academy of Pediatrics considers methadone compatible with breastfeeding. (American Academy of Pediatrics, Committee on Drugs. "The Transfer of Drugs and Other Chemicals into Human Milk." 2001. *Pediatrics 108*(3): 776-789.) A methadone-maintained mother who breastfeeds her infant will not jeopardize her infant's neurobehavioral outcome, as methadone levels in breast milk are low and are not related to the mother's methadone dose. However, it is imperative that a mother in a methadone maintenance program who wishes to provide breast milk to her infant undergo urine toxicological screens to document she is not using any illicit substances. (Jansson L. M., R. Choo, M. L. Velez et al. 2008. "Methadone Maintenance and Breastfeeding in the Neonatal Period." *Pediatrics 121*(1): 106-114.)

Many substance-abusing women have been victims of childhood abuse, including sexual victimization. This, and many other social risk factors, may impair mothers' responses to their infants resulting in the perpetuation of a cycle of abuse and neglect. (Hans S. L. 1999. "Demographic and Psychosocial Characteristics of Substance-Abusing Pregnant Women." *Clinics in Perinatology 26*(1): 55-74.)

Shaken Baby Syndrome (Abusive Head Trauma) continues to be a cause of death and disability in infants and young children injured usually at the hands of their parents. The chief trigger for this type of parental abuse is infant crying. Parents who are at high risk of injuring their infants in this manner are those who are single, young, drug- and/or alcohol-dependent, those who have impulse control problems, those affected by poverty, and those who are isolated. A national campaign, "The Period of Purple Crying," is underway to educate parents about the normalcy of crying in infants and the dangers of shaking an infant. (See the website of the National Center on Shaken Baby Syndrome at www.dontshake.org or visit www.purple crying.info.)

In this story, the careful reader will note that Jésus was laid to sleep in the prone position, leading to rubbing of his nose and knees. Today, he would be more likely to be cared for in the supine position, consistent with the guidelines of the national "Back to Sleep" campaign. The American Academy of Pediatrics recommended in 1992 that infants under one year of age be placed on their backs or sides to sleep (later amended in 1996 to state that sleeping on the back is safest) to prevent Sudden Infant Death Syndrome (SIDS). The National Institute of Child Health and Human Development launched a national educational campaign to promote this practice in 1994; since that time, the incidence of SIDS has decreased by more than 50 percent. The guidelines for a safe sleep environment for babies were further refined by the American Academy of Pediatrics in

2005. (Task Force on Sudden Infant Death Syndrome. 2005. "The Changing Concept of Sudden Infant Death Syndrome: Diagnostic Coding Shifts, Controversies Regarding the Sleeping Environment, and New Variables to Consider in Reducing Risk." *Pediatrics 116*(5): 1245-1255.) To learn more about how supine-sleeping reduces the incidence of SIDS, see this resource on the internet: http://www.sidscenter.org/documents/SIDRC/BackToSleep.pdf.

Chapter 8

An Uneasy Truce: Jaxon Cranston

"Labor and delivery is setting up for an emergency C-section on a girl who was brought to the emergency room after having a seizure at school. They have no idea how many weeks pregnant she is, because she did not even know she *was* pregnant." The charge nurse rattled off the story to me in a flash of staccato words.

"That's a new one," I said. "Call me when they're ready."

Thirty minutes later, the obstetrician brought me a baby born to a fifteen-year-old girl who was out cold under general anesthesia. "The emergency room doc was working her up for seizures when they found her blood pressure was 200/120. Then, he had the bright idea to evaluate the mass he felt in her abdomen. High blood pressure, plus seizures, in a female of child-bearing age means she is pregnant until proven otherwise."

Wow, an actual case of eclampsia, I thought. Usually pregnant women who develop high blood pressure have preeclampsia; but if seizures occur, which is rare, it is called "eclampsia." The high blood pressure can also cause a cerebral hemorrhage, which may be fatal. I was glad this girl's condition had been diagnosed before things reached that point.

"Here's the abdominal mass," he said. "A bouncing, baby boy. Do you think he looks early?"

I studied the baby in front of me, whose eyes blinked repetitively as he tried to adjust to the operating room's bright lights. He had just been yanked from his dark, warm, and wet cocoon, and now he was splayed out on a hard surface in a bright, chilly, air-conditioned room. The baby probably weighed about five pounds, small for a term baby. "Maybe a couple of weeks early," I surmised. "Not too bad."

The baby certainly was not bouncing; his muscles were doughy and limp. As I wiped the cheesy white vernix off his face, I noticed his facial features were rather flat and his almond-shaped eyes slanted upwards. His lips were parted and slack, and his tongue protruded from his mouth to rest on his lower lip. I picked up the stubby fingers of his right hand and saw a telltale single crease drawn lightly across his palm, not the usual two. The wide space between his great toe and second toe—what we called "sandal toe"—completed the diagnostic picture of Down syndrome.

"How old did you say mom is?" I called over to the OB.

"Fifteen. She's a freshman in high school. At least that is what we were told."

"Well, little one," I told the baby, "you've got quite a few challenges facing you."

The NICU nurse with me in the delivery room asked, "How's that possible? A teenager having a baby with Down syndrome? I thought that only happened to older women."

"No," I explained. "The risk of Down syndrome rises exponentially after age forty, from one in a hundred, to one in thirty when mothers reach age forty-five. Although the risk is much lower in younger women, they have more babies, so they actually give birth to larger numbers of babies with Down syndrome than older women."

"Hmm," Ofelia mused, as she continued to dry the baby off. "That's kind of sad."

We took the baby to the NICU and settled him into an isolette. As I stood at the front desk writing admit orders, Charisse, our social worker, led a woman into the NICU. "This is Baby Cranston's grandma," she announced.

"Are you sure you've got this right?" the woman asked. "I'm just finding this so hard to believe..." She was quite young herself, not more than thirty-five I guessed. She was neatly dressed in a uniform, which I recognized from a local restaurant, although the uniform's crisp appearance was marred by the perspiration stains underneath her arms. Sturdy shoes, which laced up the front, gave her the appearance of a woman who spent most of the day on her feet.

"She's new to this whole Grandma thing," Charisse explained.

"Did my baby really have a baby? I've got to see this to believe it." She shook her head, a fatigued expression overtaking her. "And where is my daughter?"

So many questions. Where to start?

"The baby's over here," I said, leading her to his isolette. "This is Ofelia, his nurse." Ofelia's ebony skin contrasted starkly with the woman's alabaster complexion, and Ofelia was easily a head taller. "The baby is okay," I continued, "but I'm concerned the baby may have Down syndrome, also called Trisomy 21."

"Down syndrome?" Shock more than puzzlement registered on the woman's face.

I began the first of many explanations about how this genetic syndrome occurs. "It's an accident at the time of conception," I explained. "People with Down syndrome have forty-seven chromosomes instead of the usual forty-six, including three copies of chromosome number twenty-one instead of two."

The woman lifted her eyebrows high up onto her face and wrinkled her forehead. Her face fell flat as she exhaled.

"Your daughter's still in the operating room. She should be out soon," I reassured her.

"I still can't believe this. I just can't... I don't know...what I'm going to do..." She pursed her lips tightly then joined her fingers in a bridge to cover her nose and mouth. I worried she might faint.

Charisse stepped in and rested her hand on Lydia's shoulder. "It's okay, Lydia. We'll have plenty of time to figure everything out. I expect that Baby will be here a while, right Dr. Hall?"

"Mmm-hmm," I nodded, as I watched tears bead at the inner aspects of Lydia's eyes.

Janelle Cranston was admitted to the Adult ICU after her delivery. Her blood pressure remained dangerously high and threatened to precipitate more seizures. The heavy doses of medication required to control her hypertension made her groggy and sick to her stomach. She was not able to come to the NICU for several days. Ofelia took a Polaroid picture of Janelle's baby to her room, which the ICU staff kept dark and quiet, and the ICU nurse agreed to show it to her when the young mother felt well enough.

Meanwhile, Lydia visited the baby daily. Each time, she looked as though she were on the verge of tears.

"Do you want to hold the baby?" the nurse would ask.

"No. I'll wait and let Janelle hold him first," she replied, standing back from the baby's isolette, arms folded across her chest.

I suspected this was not how she planned to welcome a grandchild into her family. Not only that, but she had to be worried about her daughter's life-threatening health problems and perhaps even the expensive ICU bill they were creating.

"I don't have health insurance," she told us. "I've worked at this restaurant for a couple of years, but they don't give us insurance. You might as well send the bill to Uncle Sam." Her voice sounded as tired as her face looked.

"The social worker will help you apply for a medical card," I reassured her.

"Does this happen very often?" she asked. "When the person who is pregnant doesn't even know it? Janelle never told me she was pregnant, and when I asked her yesterday how long she'd known about this, she told me again, she never knew.

"Is that possible?" The woman's green eyes studied mine for an answer.

"It does seem hard to believe, doesn't it? But over the years I've heard a number of women say they did not know about their pregnancies right up until the baby was born. If you've ever been pregnant—which obviously you have—it seems impossible to believe that someone could fail to notice the changes in their body, could miss out on the thrill of recognizing the baby's kicks…"

"Yes, that's what I'm talking about," she agreed. "I just feel so stupid," Lydia continued. "I mean, my own daughter, and I did not even notice." She cringed with embarrassment. "Guess I've been too busy working to put food on the table for the both of us." Guilt marched to the forefront of our discussion and sat down between us.

"I know…" I said.

"I thought she was gaining some weight, but you can't say anything to a teenager about their weight without worrying you'll send them into anorexia or bulimia. I've seen that enough times. Those stick thin girls who look like skeletons..."

"It's a tough balance with teenagers, isn't it?"

"Yes. But I thought Janelle and I were doing okay. Janelle is a good girl. She does well in school, and she comes home afterwards and does her homework. I get home after dinner. She knows how hard I work so I can buy her all the right clothes and stuff like the other kids have.

"I still can't believe she would lie to me about being pregnant." The corners of Lydia's mouth pulled down.

"Well, Janelle may *not* have known she was pregnant," I countered. "There is an actual medical condition called 'denial of pregnancy'. Even women who have given birth before may deny their pregnancy, but most often it is seen in women who have never been pregnant. They may simply be naïve and not recognize the symptoms, they may not be very tuned into their bodies, or they may have psychological conflicts about the pregnancy. In Janelle's case, all three factors could have been at work."

Although the seizure Janelle suffered as a result of her eclampsia was a terrifying and dangerous event, at least it had brought her to medical attention. There are many reported cases of young girls and women who have suffered from denial of pregnancy, delivered their babies in isolation, and discarded them into trash bins and the like. Fortunately, Janelle's baby was spared this fate. Most women with denial of pregnancy are young, unmarried, and immature, just like Janelle. While a few are psychotic or have histories of mental illness, most have a history of normal psychological function and, in fact, are able to return to this state after giving birth.

"Hmmm," Lydia mused, as she considered what I had told her. "I don't know. I just don't know… And I don't know how we're going to care for this baby, between her school and my job..."

"When Janelle gets out of the ICU and is feeling better, let's get together with our social worker and see what the alternatives are. We'll help you two figure this out."

The baby, who remained unnamed for the first week, had the diagnosis of Down syndrome confirmed by chromosome analysis. Meanwhile, unable to finish his whole bottle in the time allotted to him, he received partial tube feedings to ensure weight gain.

When the ultrasound technician came by to scan the baby's heart to evaluate a murmur I had heard, Lydia was at his bedside, not Janelle. The technician squeezed some clear jelly onto his narrow chest, and then slid the probe back and forth across it numerous times. She snapped pictures that looked like snowstorms in the middle of a murky night: scratchy white forms on a black background.

When the technician finished, Lydia asked a nurse who'd never seen her before, "What does it show?"

"I'm sorry. I'm not authorized to tell you, since you are not the baby's mother. Federal privacy regulations prevent us from sharing private health care information with anyone but parents. Didn't someone explain that to you?"

"No. And that is ridiculous. Janelle's not going to know what to do about any of this anyway." Lydia bristled.

"Well, next time she's here, we'll have to get her to sign a release allowing us to share information with you…if that's what she wants to do."

Lydia rolled her eyes.

"I know," sympathized the nurse. "It's crazy. Of course you need to know what's going on. But we've got to follow the rules." She spoke gently but firmly.

After several days, a nurse was finally able to bring Janelle to her baby's bedside, pushing her in a wheelchair, a blanket covering her lap. The girl in front of me looked as if she had been ill for weeks, not just days. She had not been able to take a shower or wash her hair since entering the hospital, and she pushed greasy strands of dirty dishwater blonde hair out of her face. When I saw her slight figure nearly hidden under the formless hospital gown, I wondered how anyone could have missed noticing she was carrying a baby. She did not have any extra fat in which to hide a pregnancy. She wore the sober expression of one who has no idea about how she might resolve a situation, yet knows she must.

"Feeling better, Janelle?" I asked.

"Yeah, a little. My incision still hurts," she said, pointing to her pelvis, "especially when I sit up like this or try to walk."

"Well, here's your little guy. What do you think?"

She studied the baby through the plexiglass of the isolette, her face at eye level with his. He lay on his back, eyes closed, not making a sound. "I…don't…know," she said, the words coming slowly. "I know he has Down syndrome, but will he be able to go to school with other kids? Will he be able to…you know…do stuff?"

"Yes, he should be able to go to school with other kids. A lot of kids with Down syndrome are integrated into classrooms with kids who don't have disabilities. They require special attention, and he'll need extra help throughout his life. His heart checked out okay on the ultrasound we did. That's good news."

"But he'll be retarded, right?"

"He will learn things, just on his own schedule and in his own way. But to answer your question, yes, he will likely have a mild to moderate intellectual disability."

"Ugh," she sighed. She withdrew into her own thoughts.

I decided to give her a rest; adding more details could overwhelm her.

"Do you want to hold your baby?" I asked Janelle.

"No, not this time. My stomach hurts. Next time."

How hard would it be to suddenly have a baby you are not at all prepared for, I wondered. *And how do you adjust if you don't instantly fall in love with your newborn?*

Prior to Jaxon's discharge, we held a family conference to plan for his follow-up. I walked into the meeting room to find a disconnected Janelle slouched on the couch, her two-sizes-too-big plaid lumberjack shirt obscuring her tummy completely, her wrinkled jeans covering her sneakers with their laces untied. Lydia sat in an armchair across from her, erect, in her starched uniform. "I have work after this," she explained.

"So we're here to talk about Jaxon. That's what you finally decided to name the baby, right?" I asked.

"Yeah, Jaxon." Janelle nodded. Lydia quietly observed, her face not revealing any reaction.

"Well, since you are his mom," I explained, "I'm going to be addressing my comments to you. But your mom is here, too, and I trust she'll be helping you out when you get home. Have you all talked about that yet?"

"A little bit," Janelle offered.

"Yes, we have," said Lydia. "Charisse found out that the school district has a high school Janelle can transfer to, where girls who have babies can bring them to school. There's a daycare right on campus, and the girls take classes in childcare. Janelle can take care of the baby after school until I get home from work, then I can do the nighttime feedings so she can get sleep and be rested for school."

This sounded great to me. If Janelle continued going to school, perhaps she could avoid some of the known consequences of teen pregnancy: poor attainment of education beyond high school, poverty, and dependence on welfare. She was already a single parent, as most teens who give birth usually are.

"How's that sound to you, Janelle?" I asked.

Janelle simply shrugged.

"Well, Janelle, you got yourself into this fix, so now you have to grow up a bit and deal with the consequences." Lydia looked sternly at her daughter.

"I know," came her offhand reply.

"There might not be many sleepovers with your friends, and trips to the mall. We're going to have to cut back on expenses for the two of us so there's enough money to buy formula, diapers, and baby clothes."

"Mom, I *get it*, okay?" Janelle squirmed on the sofa.

"Well, I would like to know how this happened. Would you care to tell me?"

"Nope." Janelle looked blankly at her mother.

"Do you have a boyfriend? Some guy who might want to know he is a father now?" Lydia pressed.

"Nope." She shifted her weight on the couch and stared beyond her mother to the clock on the wall behind her.

Charisse broke the impasse. "Now might be a good time to talk about birth control. I assume you've never used birth control, Janelle. Am I right?"

Janelle rolled her eyes as if her whole life was on display in front of the entire universe.

"I never took her to the doctor for birth control, because frankly I never knew she needed it. All she had to do was ask," Lydia announced to the room. "At a bare minimum, she should have at least told me once she knew she was pregnant."

Was she trying to cover for her own inattentiveness to her daughter's condition? I wondered. Attempting to squeeze out a confession? Or wanting to establish a dialogue? Either way, her words did not come across well.

"Mom, I'm telling you the truth. *I did not know!* As if I could talk to you or ask you about anything anyway."

"Well, you can. I'm no prude. I had you when I was sixteen, so I know how these things happen. But honey, *we've got to talk* about it..."

Charisse spoke up. "Your six-week postpartum check-up would be a good time to discuss this with the doctor who delivered you. Janelle, would you consider taking your mom to that appointment with you?"

"Yeah," growled Janelle.

"Okay, then, why don't you two plan on that," Charisse said, giving Lydia a knowing look.

"Now, back to Jaxon," I said. "He's going to be ready to go home soon. Janelle, we'd like you to spend a night in the hospital, taking care of him and doing all of his feedings. Babies with Down syndrome can be hard to feed, so I want to make sure you have plenty of experience. Do you want to stay by yourself, or would you like your mom stay with you?"

Lydia cocked her head, looked across at Janelle, and awaited her response.

"I guess I'll have my mom stay with me," she answered with a brooding stare.

As Janelle and her mom spent the night in the hospital with Jaxon later that week, I hoped they'd made a truce and bridged their differences on behalf of their newest family member. Each would be more reliant on the other one than they could possibly know, and the sooner they learned to communicate with each other, the easier their lives as a family would be. Charisse had set up some counseling appointments to help them in this regard; Janelle would also get help dealing with the after-effects of her denial of her pregnancy and making a successful transition to parenthood.

Jaxon's special needs would keep both Janelle and Lydia quite busy as he grew. They could avail themselves of support services in the community for families whose children have Down syndrome. Children with Down syndrome are no longer shunted off to impersonal institutions or kept as family secrets as in the past. Ever since Eunice Kennedy Shriver started the Special Olympics in 1962, families have found much more acceptance integrating them into society. But even with the increased visibility of kids with Down syndrome, not every mother and every family is prepared to deal with the challenges a special-needs child will present.

I guessed that Janelle and her mom were going to need a lot of encouragement and assistance to get through the challenges facing them. I hoped, too, they could find some joy raising Jaxon.

***

Notes:

Janelle's delivery was precipitated by her condition, known as eclampsia. Preeclampsia is characterized by high blood pressure, water retention (edema), and protein in the urine (proteinuria). In severe cases, pregnant women experience headaches, blurry vision, and right upper quadrant pain. Also known as toxemia or pregnancy-induced hypertension, preeclampsia is most common in young teenage mothers like Janelle, first-time mothers (also like Janelle), mothers of multiples, and mothers older than forty years of age. When the condition progresses to seizures, it is known as eclampsia; it can be serious enough to cause stroke, liver or kidney failure, and death of mother and/or baby. Read more about preeclampsia at the Preeclampsia Foundation's website, www.preeclampsia.org.

Most women who experience the condition called "denial of pregnancy" are not mentally ill (although a minority is psychotic); they adapt favorably once their baby is born if the appropriate medical, psychological, and social support systems are put into place. (Neifert P. 2000. "Denial of Pregnancy: A Case Study and Literature Review." *Military Medicine 16*(7): 566-568.)

Some mothers with denial of pregnancy end up abandoning their infants in trash bins, alleys, warehouses, public restrooms, and parks, resulting in the babies' deaths. Babies have even been found in toilets, closets, college dorm rooms, clothes dryers, and filing cabinet drawers. More than 30,000 babies are illegally abandoned in the United States yearly, and as many as 250 are killed within hours after their birth (neonaticide), many by women who are in denial of their pregnancies.

At least forty-four states, including California, have tried to address this problem by passing "safe haven" legislation, allowing any person who has a baby to bring it to a hospital, police station, or fire department in the first few days after birth without any fear of legal reprisal. Between 2001 and 2008, more than 250 babies were surrendered in California, although not all public policy experts agree that this type of law offers the best solution to a vexing social problem. ("Left to Die in a Trash Bin." 2010. *California Catholic Daily*, March 18. Also *see* Dailard C. 2000. "The Drive to Enact 'Infant Abandonment' Laws: A Rush to Judgment?" *The Guttmacher Report on Public Policy 3*(4) at http://www.guttmacher.org/pubs/tgr/03/4/gr030401.html.) *See* also www.projectcuddle.org.

Teen pregnancy is a significant social problem in the United States. With more than 400,000 teens giving birth each year, the teen pregnancy rate in the United States is twice as high as the rate in other developed countries. The impact of teen parenthood is examined from many different angles by Hoffman and Maynard. A complex array of both personal and economic factors influences the ultimate outcome of teen parents and the children to whom they give birth. (Hoffman S.D. and R. Maynard, Editors. 1997. *Kids Having Kids: Economic Costs and Social Consequences of Teen Pregnancy*. Urban Institute Press.)

It was very unusual that Jaxon's mother, at age fifteen, would give birth to a baby with Down syndrome, also known as Trisomy 21. Most people recognize that the risk of having a baby with Down syndrome is quite high after age forty (1 in 100 at age forty, 1 in 30 at age forty-five), but many may not be aware that Down syndrome babies are born more frequently to younger mothers than to older mothers, because more young women are giving birth.

Babies with Down syndrome, one of the most common birth defects, often have multiple problems. About half will have cardiac defects, some serious enough to require heart surgery; atrioventricular canal (AV canal) and ventricular septal defect (VSD) predominate. About 12 percent will have intestinal malformations, most commonly duodenal atresia or Hirschsprung's disease. More than half will have vision or hearing problems, and a small percentage (1 percent) may be born with congenital hypothyroidism or develop leukemia at an older age. Intellectual disabilities in children with Down syndrome range from mild to moderate, and cannot be predicted at birth. Davidson has written a thorough review of health care guidelines for children with Down syndrome. (Davidson M. A. 2008. "Primary Care for Children and Adolescents with Down Syndrome." *Pediatric Clinics of North America 55*(5): 1099-1111.)

Internet resources for parents of children with Down syndrome include the National Association for Down Syndrome, at www.nads.org, the National Down Syndrome Society, at www.ndss.org, and a social networking site for parents of Down syndrome children at www.downsyndrome.com.

Chapter 9

Delivery Room Disaster: Preston Larder

"*Come now!*" the voice on the other end of the phone screamed.

I jumped into my car on that hot spring afternoon, and rolled through more than a few stop signs to get to the hospital across the San Fernando Valley as fast as I could. I knew they did not have a neonatologist on staff, or a NICU. They had to call the NICU at my hospital for help in emergencies, and today I was the one to receive their call. I tried to keep the flow of my adrenaline in reserve for when I arrived, knowing there was not much I could do about the Code Pink—the resuscitation of a baby—that was under way until I got there. Once I arrived, I sprinted from the parking lot through the unfamiliar maze of hospital corridors, stopped someone wearing a badge, and asked them to take me to labor and delivery.

After locating the operating room for labor and delivery, I donned a white-paper jump suit that zipped up the front, affectionately known as a "bunny suit," and a blue-paper hat, face mask and shoe covers. I entered the operating room and found a group of staff, some in scrubs and others in bunny suits, gathered around a baby lying motionless on a table with an overhead heat source. From what I could see, the baby's color beneath the sterile green drapes bordered on slate grey.

A doctor I had never seen before was trying to put a breathing tube in the baby's windpipe. Another doctor was attempting to thread a catheter into a blood vessel in his umbilical cord, someone was performing CPR, and a couple of nurses were frantically fumbling for supplies they thought might be needed next. A rough head count revealed approximately a dozen people in the operating room, not including the two patients, the unlucky mother and her unluckier baby.

"I'm Dr. Hall," I announced breathlessly when I arrived at the baby's bedside, trying to take in every detail of the situation all at once.

No one looked up.

"I'm the neonatologist," I said, adding a little authority to my voice.

A doctor wearing hospital-issue blue scrubs held a laryngoscope over the baby's head. He turned and handed it to me. "Here. You try. We've all tried. This baby is really hard to intubate. I have the smallest size tube now. The bigger ones did not go through the vocal cords."

I looked at the tube he offered me, which was the size intended for a one-to-two pound baby, not the proper size for a big eight-pound baby like the one lying lifeless in front of me.

"No, I'll try the bigger tube, a 3.5," I said. A murmur went through the small crowd, which consisted of an emergency room physician, a family practice doctor, the obstetrician who had delivered the baby, the pediatrician now working on the umbilical line, and the anesthesiologist who had recommended the smaller tube for the baby. Each of them had tried—and failed—to intubate the baby before my arrival.

The anesthesiologist shrugged and handed the laryngoscope to me. I leaned over and inserted its gleaming cold metal blade into the baby's mouth, lifting his tongue out of the way. Then, I reached to my side without diverting my gaze, and took the breathing tube from the respiratory therapist, and slickly slipped it between the baby's pearly white vocal cords.

"It's in," I announced, straightening my back. The other doctors stepped back, and several of them quietly left the room, seeing they were no longer needed.

For just a second I felt like I had special powers. Then, I reminded myself that this was exactly what I was paid to do for a living—resuscitate newborn babies—and none of the other doctors were. Their jobs were to take care of much bigger people. If I had not been able to get the tube in, I would not be very good at my job.

Next, I noticed the pediatrician tentatively poking around at the umbilical cord with a thin plastic catheter. I offered, "I can take over on the line." The doctor looked up. Her eyes, the only part of her face uncovered enough for me to read, showed both surprise and relief.

"What's going on?" I asked, exchanging places with her and snapping on a pair of sterile gloves.

"I just got here a few minutes before you did," she explained.

One of the nurses piped up. "Things were going fine during labor until the obstetrician broke the bag of waters. All of a sudden the mom started bleeding like crazy and the baby's heart rate dropped out, so we crashed her. He's just now eighteen minutes old."

"Crashing" a mom meant performing an emergency Cesarean section as fast as was humanly possible. It still took some time to accomplish because the operating room had to be clean and ready, an anesthesiologist had to be available to put the mom to sleep, and a scrub nurse had to be pulled in to help, as did a host of other nurses and technicians. Hospital staffs must be capable of starting a C-section within twenty minutes of a doctor's decision that emergency surgery is necessary, according to national standards. A lot can happen to the fetus in those twenty minutes.

Meanwhile, the laboring mother is undergoing trauma of her own. All of a sudden she is told she must undergo general anesthesia immediately for emergency surgery to save her baby's life. Although her doctor obtains her "informed consent," she really has no choice but to submit to surgery if she wants a chance for her baby to be born alive. I was not present to see this mom put to sleep, but I had seen it before: the tears, the wide-eyed look of terror, the protests, the fluttering eyelids as they closed with anesthesia…

I looked up and saw that the red number representing the baby's heart rate on the cardiac monitor was only sixty, half of what it should have been. A nurse continued chest compressions to make up that gap. The baby's oxygen saturation level did not even register.

Behind me I faintly heard the anesthesiologist rousing the mom. "Okay, Lori. Time to wake up. Your surgery is over. Open your eyes."

I maintained my focus on the task at hand and within a minute or two I had a lifeline in place and asked for some epinephrine to infuse. One dose resulted in the baby's heart rate climbing to above the 100 mark. I ordered CPR to be stopped.

Next, I slid a catheter in the umbilical artery, right next to the vein. The blood I pulled back from the catheter into a syringe for lab tests was thin and blue, not the bright cheery cherry red that indicated good oxygen levels. As I removed the sterile towels covering the baby, I found him to be a good-sized baby who looked normal in every single way except that his color was ashen, his feet were cold, and he was nearly dead.

Just then my transport team lumbered into the room. Megan, a NICU nurse only recently certified to do transport, pulled a guerney behind her. The transport isolette sitting on top of the guerney was so big and sturdy, it looked as though it could have safely taken the baby to the moon. Two paramedics, wearing heavy navy blue jump suits with something protruding from every pocket on every extremity—scissors, penlight, cell phone, walkie talkie—pushed from behind, their heavy boots clomping across the linoleum floor.

"Megan, wow, am I glad you are here," I said.

Megan raised her eyebrows into a big question mark as she surveyed the scene, then opened her bag and spread out all the emergency resuscitation supplies.

"Can you draw up some normal saline? Then, take the baby's temperature and get me a hat for the baby?"

I shifted my rapid-fire requests from the nurses who were already in the delivery room to my transport nurse, as she would know exactly how to find what was needed and how to do what I asked. As a NICU nurse, she had been involved in many more Code Pinks than the newborn nursery and delivery room nurses of the hospital we were visiting. She knew the drill.

"And somebody call x-ray," I said to the other nurses. "I'll need a film of both the chest and abdomen."

If an adult stops breathing, the resuscitation effort is called "Code Blue"; for babies the process is known as Code Pink. Running a Code Pink in the delivery room is like piloting a jumbo jet with engine failure. If the pilot can't fix what is wrong with the plane right away, it stalls, and then spirals out of control and crashes. As captain of the flight crew, the physician takes information in from all of the computerized display systems on the dashboard. While trying to process it all at once, he or she has to integrate it into a meaningful understanding of what the plane is actually doing. Meanwhile, the flight crew is verbally feeding the captain even more information, as well as following orders to try to return the plane to an even keel. Anticipating what the plane is going to do next and trying to keep it out of a death spiral requires all the concentration and nerve one can muster. It is draining and exhausting work.

***

Frank Sterling approached me from the other side of the room. I recognized the obstetrician and remembered when he was just a medical student and I was the attending neonatologist on his rotation in the NICU. He had recently finished his training and opened a private practice. Only the year before, his wife had given birth to a premature baby I had taken care of in our NICU. Although things turned out well for his child, he had experienced the sheer terror of having his baby whisked away unexpectedly to the NICU. I could see he was now reliving that experience vicariously through his patient.

"What do you think?" he asked. I could see from his worried look that he had an idea of how bad things were.

"Doesn't look good, Frank," I said. "But we'll have to see the blood gas. What happened anyway?"

"Things were going along fine, a little bleeding earlier in the day, then when I ruptured the membranes, she bled out. As we were wheeling her back to the operating room, the heart tones went down and then we lost them." Frank looked like he might throw up. His part in this disaster was over. Now, he had to wait and see how my part turned out.

My attention was distracted by a respiratory therapist who entered the room and made a beeline through the crowd to me. "I've got the blood gas result. You are not going to like it," he said, holding the small strip of paper in his hand.

"Tell me," I instructed.

"pH 6.98, pCO2 …"

I did not hear much after the pH of 6.98 because the number was so far away from a normal pH of 7.4 that my mind fast forwarded to the end of the story.

I turned away from Frank; I had work to do.

"Call the blood bank and get me some O-negative uncrossmatched blood. *Stat!*" I expected someone would grab my order in mid-air to make sure it got carried out. Megan was busy working with the baby, and one of the delivery room nurses would have to do it.

The baby needed blood, and he needed it now. I surmised he might have lost anywhere from half, to nearly all of his blood volume before birth. His heart was not only struggling to pump around the inadequate amount of blood that was left, but to continue pumping in the inhospitable environment of extreme acidosis. I thought it was ominous that his heart was beating so slowly, when beating faster than usual would be a normal first response to anemia.

The baby's heart was like the engine of a car and right now it was running on gasoline fumes, the tank being virtually empty. The car was sputtering as it limped off to the side of the road, and I could see it was about ready to conk out completely at any moment. The baby needed a fill-up of his gas tank, in the form of a blood transfusion.

One of the nurses scuttled over to the phone to call the blood bank while Megan set about carrying out my orders.

"Megan, let's give some more normal saline." The saline would improve his blood volume, even if it did not have precious oxygen-carrying red cells in it.

Megan was taking the baby's temperature. She stopped and looked up at me, her eyes pleading for clarity about which task she should actually complete. She plainly could not do the long list of things I had given her to do, not all at once anyway. If we were in our NICU, at least five experienced NICU nurses would be crowding around to share the burden of carrying out all the orders. So many things needed to be done simultaneously, and one NICU nurse could not do it all…alone.

"The blood bank wants to know the hematocrit, and they want a specimen for type and crossmatch before they'll release the blood." The nurse on the phone with blood bank held the receiver out to her side as she yelled to me across the din of the room.

"Tell them again I want *uncrossmatched* blood and I need it right now. We don't have time for a crossmatch."

A crossmatch is a critically important test to make sure blood being transfused into a person is compatible with his or her blood type, so there will not be an adverse reaction. When a patient's life is hanging in the balance, though, a physician can order blood that has not been tested for compatibility against the patient's own blood type. It was a risk I was willing to take.

The nurse turned back to the phone but I could not hear what she said. Then she half-shouted, "They're going to send up some papers for you to sign before they'll release the blood. This is outside their standard of practice so they need your signature."

I strode over to the phone and took it from the nurse's hand. "This is Dr. Hall. I'm taking care of this baby. The baby has practically *bled to death* and I need some blood for him *right now*. I don't have time to deal with paperwork. *I need the blood now. Do you get it?*"

My voice was not loud, but I spat out the words so the blood bank technician would understand clearly there was no time to spare. The person on the other end of the phone finally relented. She agreed to send up the blood and the paperwork together. I could fill the forms out when I had time. I hung up the phone, still boiling inside.

"The heart rate is back down to sixty," one of the delivery room nurses snapped at me.

"Start CPR and draw up more epinephrine. And Megan, is that saline in yet?"

"Nope," Megan replied in her normally small voice that was always a surprise considering she was nearly six-feet tall.

"Get it in. Push it as fast as you can."

Megan's shoulders were all hunched up, her mouth was pinched and she had seemingly shrunk several inches. The paramedics were leaning against the wall taking it all in like it was an episode of the TV show *ER*.

Just then, an x-ray technician entered the room driving a machine that looked and sounded like an armored tank. She maneuvered it to the baby's bedside and snapped his picture. I followed her out of the room to look for the radiology view box so I could see the film as soon as she trotted down two floors to develop the film in the radiology department, then sprinted back to my location with it in hand. Within a few minutes, she returned; I breathed a small sigh of relief as I saw that all the tubes and lines I had placed were in good position on the film.

I strode back to the operating room through a hallway filled with nurses standing around like horrified bystanders at the scene of a gory car crash. Entering the mess that was the operating room, with paper wrappings and empty syringes and towels littering the floor, I picked out a man who looked as if he must be Dad. He was the only one not dressed in scrubs and he had a dazed look on his face, as though he had just awakened in the middle of a dream…a bad dream. He was standing next to his wife, who was still flat on her back in a daze in the center of the operating room. I introduced myself to him.

"Everything's gonna be okay, isn't it?" he asked before I could even start to tell him that it might not be.

"Your baby is in very critical and unstable condition. Does he have a name yet?"

"We're going to call him Preston. Preston Larder. I'm Ethan Larder and this is my wife Lori." He tilted his head in his wife's direction. She was too groggy to notice.

"Nice to meet you Ethan," I replied. "Your baby has probably lost a lot of blood, his heart's having a hard time, and he has a lot of acid in his blood. We have a lot of work to do to turn things around."

"But you'll be able to, won't you?" Ethan Larder spoke as though he was having an out-of-body experience. His wife's eyes opened and tried to focus, then closed again.

"I'm going to try my best. It'll be tough. I'm going to be honest with you. His heart rate and blood pressure have been so low for so long now that he could suffer permanent brain damage."

"Brain damage?" A look of sheer disbelief overtook him. "How will you know? *And what happened?*"

"We won't know for some time how the baby will do. That's why we'll just keep doing what we're doing and hope for the best. Now, I had better get back to him." The man, who seemed stunned, nodded as I returned to his baby.

"Megan, let's switch the baby to the transport ventilator." I spewed out a string of numbers that represented the ventilator settings and Megan grimaced as she dialed the knobs on the machine. Once the baby was hooked up, his oxygen saturation began to improve.

I reached into my bunny suit to pull my cell phone out of the top pocket of my blouse, and called the charge nurse who was awaiting our return to the NICU. The operating room was no place for a cell phone, but at least the surgery was over. "Get a high frequency ventilator set up. And call the blood bank and tell them we're going to need some blood right away."

What would happen to this baby? I knew the statistics cold: At least 50 percent of babies in his condition would die within the next couple of days and at least 50 percent of those who survived would have significant long-term disabilities. If Preston landed in the group who did not do well, his meaningful participation in life, if he was granted one, would be minimal. That left just a 25 percent chance that he could have some semblance of a normal life.

My gut told me he was headed toward the bottom 50 percent, but I had to keep moving forward as though he had the potential to reach the top 25 percent. These were the times when I wished for a crystal ball. I wondered if I saw death as the outcome in the crystal ball, whether it would make the process of getting there any easier.

I reminded myself of the progress I had made since my arrival. The baby had a secure airway, and his heart rate and oxygen saturation were both improved. Blood for a transfusion should arrive in the operating room any minute. Things were looking up. I could afford to generate a little guarded optimism for the baby, even if it were based on shaky pretenses.

When I returned to Preston's bedside, Megan informed me his blood pressure had not even registered when she tried to measure it, although his heart rate was now in the normal range. I rattled off a medication to treat his hypotension and a dose for her to infuse. It was up to Megan to do the mathematical calculations to determine how to mix the drip and how fast to run the IV.

Megan stood, befuddled and probably in shock herself, tapping numbers into a calculator. Soon, she was on her cell phone calling back to the pharmacist in our hospital to ask for help. It is one thing to sit in a CPR recertification class and have twenty minutes to figure out the composition of an IV drip, and then run the numbers three different ways to check if you completed the assignment correctly. It is another thing entirely to remember the mathematical formula, when preparing the medicine is only one of twenty-five things you should have finished five minutes ago to save a baby's life.

As I paced while waiting for the blood to arrive from the blood bank, Dr. Frank Sterling stood in the background exchanging words in hushed tones with his scrub nurse. Shortly, he approached me again, still covered in the blue-paper garb of a surgeon. He'd pulled his face mask down around his neck revealing bloodshot eyes and a red nose. Beads of perspiration covered his brow.

"Was this your patient or did you just happen to be the only obstetrician in the hospital?" I asked, guessing it was his patient.

"Yup, she's one of the very first patients I've taken care of through the whole pregnancy. Really sweet lady. Super nice husband. Good people."

Bad things really did happen to good people with alarming regularity, I mused. They happened so often, in fact, that I recommended the book *When Bad Things Happen to Good People* written by Rabbi Harold S. Kushner to families so that they could benefit from the author's reassuring words.

Frank continued. "I did the C-section as fast as I could. I wish anesthesia hadn't taken so long. I'm thinkin' now this must have been vasa previa, but I've never seen it before and I had no idea. How could I have missed it? What should I have done differently?"

In vasa previa, the blood vessels that are normally safely encased in the umbilical cord and cushioned by its gooey Wharton's jelly are instead woven into the fetal membranes, the bag of waters in which the fetus resides. The unprotected blood vessels tear when the bag of waters is broken, and the fetus can bleed to death within minutes. The risk of death in this situation is high.

Frank was wracked with regret, and I could see the process of second-guessing himself had set in. Recognizing something instantaneously that you have only ever read about in books is a difficult challenge. You can still berate yourself for not meeting the challenge, and we doctors often find fault with ourselves before anyone else has a chance to.

"Look, I'm sure you did everything the way you normally would," I replied. "You just got burned by some really bad luck. And so did mom. If this were vasa previa and you did not know beforehand, I'm not sure anything could have been done differently. Don't beat yourself up about it." Vasa previa can be diagnosed by specialized ultrasound techniques before delivery, but this is only done if mother has known risk factors.

"Let me know how things go, okay?" Frank asked, ready to leave the operating room.

"Sure, no problem," I replied softly, and headed back to the baby.

Just then a lab technician burst through the operating room door holding aloft a plastic bag filled with a thick dark purple substance, packed red blood cells.

"Hooray!" I cheered. "Liquid gold. Get it hooked up, Megan, then let's pack the baby up and get back to home base."

Just as we were leaving the operating room, with the blood transfusion snaking through the catheter in the baby's umbilical vein, someone handed me a lab slip. I glanced down and saw the numbers, the lowest I had ever seen for this lab test: Hemoglobin 2 mg/dL, Hematocrit 6 percent.

The baby had indeed bled to death…almost. I shivered at the thought.

***

Megan ferried Preston back to our NICU via ambulance with sirens blazing, while I followed in my car, driving past palm trees swaying in the light afternoon breeze. When we arrived, everything was ready. Things went smoothly as I ordered another blood transfusion, two more IV drips for his blood pressure, medication to prevent seizures, ventilator changes, more x-rays, and more lab tests. A cadre of nurses scurried to complete all the necessary tasks I gave them like worker ants doing the bidding of the queen.

In the midst of the controlled chaos, Dr. Kimberly Stratton, one of the hospital pediatricians, walked through the NICU. She briefly posed with her eyes closed, arms extended and fingers curled into a meditation position, middle finger touching her thumb. I could almost hear her say "Ommmm" across the room. I knew by the message she was sending me that she sensed my deep involvement with this critically ill baby. I felt some of the tension ease out of my shoulders, and I smiled as I dug back into the set of orders I was working on.

After about an hour, Dr. Sterling wandered into the NICU looking like he was the distraught parent of the baby.

"What are you doing here?" I greeted him.

"I couldn't focus at the office. I left a bit early to come over and see how the baby is doing. How is he?" he asked, leaning heavily on my desk.

"Touch and go," I said. "His blood count is improving, so I'm going to stay upbeat. I figure if I get to normal by morning I'll be doing well. Maybe then I'll be able to dial down some of the blood pressure meds."

Frank closed his eyes briefly and I could see a wave of nausea take hold of him.

"Look," I said when he opened them again, "I'm gonna keep working and see how far I get. Why don't you go home and get some rest? Sticking around here isn't going to do much for your mental health."

He nodded. Then, he went over to the baby's bedside and said his goodbyes to Preston's father. "Good luck," he said. "Doctor Hall is going to do her best for Preston and we'll just keep all our fingers crossed."

The night nurse and I were in constant contact about Preston. It seemed like he was the only baby in the NICU that night. Although his blood pH improved with treatment, it took a long time to get his blood pressure close to the normal range, he never once urinated, and he still barely responded when he was touched.

Exhausted and drained, I had no choice but to maintain my vigil at the hospital all through the night. I gave him numerous transfusions of different blood products, dialed all three of his blood pressure medications up to the max, adjusted his ventilator, and spoke many times with his father. I never even made it into the NICU's on-call room, although I laid my head down on the desk outside of Preston's room for a brief nap.

"His color is better," his Dad said halfway through the night, hoping against hope.

"Yes, a tiny bit better…" I covered my mouth as I yawned, barely able to keep my eyes open. I wanted to hope, too.

***

Neonatology is a team effort. Morning brought reinforcements as always, a new starting line-up and a fresh doctor to act as quarterback to move the ball down the field in Preston's case. Neonatologists work in groups, taking turns covering twenty-four-hour shifts during which one is responsible for all the patients in the NICU. A good system to communicate what has happened during one's shift is essential, so the doctor—and nurses and nurse practitioners—taking over have a complete understanding of what is going on with each individual baby's care.

The hand-off went smoothly as I signed out Preston's care plan in excruciating detail. At the end of my report, all that my favorite partner, Dr. Katherine Warren, could say was, "And I am supposed to keep this going? You don't have a DNR (do not resuscitate) order yet?"

"Katherine, he has a chance. His hematocrit is coming up, and his pH has been almost normal since midnight."

Dr. Warren, always blunt to a fault, merely said, "A snowball's chance in hell." She laughed heartily, which only made me feel worse. "Brain's probably gone," she added cryptically.

I felt like I was a balloon she had just pricked, suddenly deflated. After hours of slaving over Preston, in an instant I realized that all my work since arriving in the delivery room many hours ago may have been for nothing. Even though I had known the odds were heavily stacked against this baby, I had spent every ounce of my strength trying to force his survival by providing meticulous care. Had I been fooling myself? The quality of my care might have nothing to do with his survival. And was continuing Preston's care a reasonable thing to do…or not?

"Hey, you can bring up DNR with the family if you want. Maybe get an EEG first, though. You could be right. What we're doing probably *is* futile," I said, reluctantly. At that moment, I did not have enough strength left to consider the point very thoughtfully, much less argue it.

I returned to the call room to pick up my things, and then headed home. A Beethoven symphony played on the car radio, and I let my mind follow the violin line, the flowing flutes, and the tinkling run of piano notes. Trying to keep them all separate in my head, while at the same time listening to the orchestra play as one, left no room for extraneous thoughts of Preston Larder, let alone room to focus on driving while so tired.

Once home, I changed into my nightgown and pulled the shades to block out the bright morning sun, then crawled into bed, glad my kids were in school that day. I tossed fitfully for two hours, unable to get images of Preston and his father out of my head. Something kept pushing the rewind button in my head. I revisited the sequence of decisions I made the previous night, wondering if I made them fast enough and in the proper order. I found myself going through exactly the same self-questioning process I had calmly warned Frank Sterling against doing in the delivery room.

I awoke, still exhausted, when my cat walked over my back, her paws sinking through the blankets. When I realized where I was, my first thought was Preston. Was he still alive? I got out of bed, but refused to let myself call Katherine in the NICU to find out. I spent the rest of the day pushing memories of my night on call out of my head.

I returned to the NICU at 8 a.m. the next day, having no idea whether Preston would be there or not. Now it was Katherine's turn to look spent, and indeed she did.

"Tag, you're it," she said, rather unenthusiastically, a half-drunk cup of coffee on the desk near her stack of charts.

"Is the Larder baby still here? Do you have a DNR order yet?" I asked, afraid to hear the answer.

"Yes and no. I mean, yes he's still here and no way is he DNR." She perked up considerably. "I've got him all tuned up. He's peeing, his blood pressure is finally normal, and his hematocrit is a perfect 45 percent. I do very good work."

"Indeed you do," I exclaimed. "Indeed you do…"

"Oh, and an EEG showed good baseline reactivity. I think his brain will be fine."

I closed my eyes and said a small prayer of thanks.

***

It was many days before Preston was ready to "graduate" from the NICU, but the time did come. An MRI of his brain carried out before discharge had a few minor spots of possible injury, but even our dour neurologist could not find it in himself to give Preston a bad prognosis. He, too, remained positive.

I called Frank Sterling to let him know Preston was going home soon, and told him about the optimistic outlook we all had for his future development.

"Wow, amazing," he said. "Great work!"

"Thanks," I said. "We're lucky he pulled through."

One afternoon later that week I dropped by Preston's bedside to thank his parents for the big basket of homemade chocolate chip cookies they brought in for the NICU staff. "Thanks for the cookies. They're awesome. I'm gonna put a couple away for my next night on call."

"Oh, no," said Ethan, his wife at his side, holding a snoozing Preston contentedly in her arms. "It's *we* who have to thank *you*.

"I don't know if you know this," he continued," "but Lori and I lost a child in an auto accident about three years ago. It was a huge deal for us to get over." His voice wavered for a moment. He inhaled deeply and looked down at Preston. "But, we finally decided to get pregnant again. We were so scared, and then when this happened, we thought maybe we weren't meant to be parents."

Shocked by his words, I wondered how I could not have known this information. Perhaps Ethan and Lori had been holding their breaths through Preston's hospitalization, afraid to truly believe he would survive and do well.

A shiver went up my spine as I realized how close we'd come to losing Preston.

I was reminded that parents' unspoken histories can greatly influence their current coping styles, and that the medical team needs to engage parents as fully as possible to learn how past events may color their views of their present situation.

As I left the hospital that afternoon and joined the millions crowding Southern California's freeways, I was happy I never had to recommend Rabbi Kushner's book to this couple. They already knew from their experience with their first child that bad things could happen to good people. But now, all seemed right with the world, as good things were finally happening to them.

***

Notes:

The condition which affected Preston's placenta, vasa previa, is a difficult diagnosis to make. It can be identified by transvaginal color flow Doppler ultrasound, which is performed if the mother has one of the following risk factors: bilobed or low-lying placenta, multiple pregnancies, pregnancy resulting from *in vitro* fertilization, marginal or velamentous insertion of the umbilical cord (the cord inserts on the edge of the placental disk instead of in the center), or blood vessel felt when the doctor performs a vaginal exam.

If vasa previa is identified antenatally, the baby's outcome is improved if Cesarean delivery is scheduled for thirty-five weeks and delivery is done under controlled circumstances. (Lijoi A. F. and J. Brady. 2003. "Vasa Previa Diagnosis and Management." *Journal of American Board of Family Medicine 16*(6): 543-548.)

Megan, the nurse who helped me at Preston's delivery, understandably had some trouble calculating the composition and drip rate of Preston's IV while under pressure. Computerized programs are now available to perform calculations for medications, especially those delivered by intravenous drips. Many such programs are available as applications for hand-held devices such as smart phones and personal digital assistants, and these have been shown to improve medication safety by reducing errors. At the time, neither Megan nor I had access to an electronic program to assist us in solving this problem. (Bates D. W., M. Cohen, L. L. Leap et al. 2001. "Reducing the Frequency of Errors in Medicine Using Information Technology." *Journal of the American Medical Informatics Association 8*(4): 299-308.)

My physician partner asked me about Do Not Resuscitate (DNR) orders for Preston. DNR orders involve withholding life-sustaining care, such as attempting CPR in the case of a cardiac arrest, and sometimes withdrawing life-sustaining care that is already in place, such as discontinuing mechanical ventilation in a moribund infant. Much less common would be a situation in which mechanical ventilation would be discontinued in an infant whose cardiorespiratory status is stable but who has severe neurologic injury.

The basis for any DNR orders is the notion that the care being provided is futile. Decisions to stop providing full intensive care or to withdraw care already being provided should never be made in a unilateral fashion by either doctor or parent. These decisions are best made in close consultation between the medical staff and the patient's family; sometimes hospitals' ethics committees are involved as well. (Singh J., J. Y. Lantos, W. Meadow. 2004. "End-of-Life After Birth: Death and Dying in a Neonatal Intensive Care Unit." *Pediatrics 114*(6): 1620-1626.)

I was worried that Preston would suffer the ill effects of hypoxic-ischemic encephalopathy (HIE). HIE is a form of brain injury resulting from low blood-oxygen levels and/or low blood pressure, usually occurring around the time of birth in newborns. Although at the time Preston was born, there was no treatment that was proven to improve survival or long-term neurodevelopmental outcome, in recent years new treatments have been introduced.

Both total body hypothermia and selective head cooling have been shown to improve long-term neurological outcome in survivors of HIE. These therapies involve cooling the baby's whole body or just the baby's head, in an attempt to slow the baby's brain metabolism and limit secondary cell death after an episode of hypoxia and/or ischemic has already occurred. (Shah P. S. 2010. "Hypothermia: A Systematic Review and Meta-Analysis of Clinical Trials." *Seminars in Fetal and Neonatal Medicine 15*(5): 238-246.)

"Hand-off" communications between health care professionals are vitally important and are increasingly recognized to be at the root of many medical errors. Improving hand-off communications is a patient safety goal put forth by The Joint Commission. The directive states that hand-offs between staff members should "include up-to-date information regarding the patient's care, treatment and services, condition and any recent or anticipated changes." (www.jointcommission.org)

Rabbi Kushner's book has brought solace to many people. (Kushner H. S. 2002. *When Bad Things Happen to Good People.* Harpswell, Maine: Anchor Publishing.)

Part Two

A New NICU in the Midwest

Chapter 10

Transitions

In 2007, after spending eighteen years in Southern California, I moved back to the Midwest, where I had grown up, to take a position as Medical Director of a Neonatal Intensive Care Unit with nearly twice as many beds as the NICUs in which I had previously worked. I loved a challenge.

If Los Angeles was famous for freeways with seven lanes of Mercedes and BMWs going an average speed of nineteen miles per hour in both directions, travel in the Midwest could be characterized by solitary Ford pick-up trucks zooming down lonely roads, flanked on both sides by eight-foot tall rows of corn. While Los Angeles was endless summer, punctuated only every few years by a rainy season, the Midwest had four distinct seasons with color changes in the landscape that brought each new one to life. Snow, sleet, drizzle, ice storms, thunder, lightning—even tornados—imparted a sense of drama and struggle to my new life, and replaced the perpetual sunshine, as well as the laid-back, devil-may-care attitudes it engendered. The glitz and glamour of Los Angeles faded into the past, as the serious Midwesterners with whom I now worked forged ahead with a great sense of purpose, their eyes on completion of the tasks in front of them.

The many California NICUs in which I worked had nothing on the newly constructed NICU I found in the Midwest. Quiet and serenity replaced noise, chaos, and calamity as babies and their families were accorded private rooms. Constant artificial daytime gave way to darkness and growth-inducing sleep for the babies. A top-quality, reliable stethoscope at every baby's bedside rendered time-wasting hunts for stethoscopes obsolete. Having an electronic radiology viewing station across from the doctors' desk made analyzing x-rays a simple pleasure instead of an exercise in frustration, wondering how soon the film would be brought back to the NICU in an emergency. Gone were the worries about the financial viability of the State of California, and its health care system in particular, as resources abounded in support of my new NICU. One thing remained the same: I found a constant supply of newborns and their families in crisis.

***

Notes:

Evidence has been mounting over the years that a private room model for NICUs may be preferable to large, open-room NICUs because of the developmental advantages conferred to the infants. Exposure to light and sound can be better controlled in private rooms, which may enhance the infant's healing environment. (Carlson B., K. Schwarzkopf, S. Ecklund. 2006. "Challenges in Design and Transition to a Private Room Model in the Neonatal Intensive Care Unit." *Advances in Neonatal Care 6*(5): 271-280.) Several other advantages to private room NICUs are improved infection control and more privacy for families.

Another study found even more advantages to single family rooms in the NICU. Infants' medical progress in the quieter, more controlled environment afforded by single rooms was improved in many ways. Infants not only had fewer instances of hospital-acquired infection, they also had improved survival. Mothers and babies had greater breastfeeding success, with a greater proportion breastfeeding at discharge than those in multi-patient wards. (Domanico R., D. K. Davis, F. Coleman, B.O. Davis. 2011. "Documenting the NICU Design Dilemma: Comparative Patient Progress in Open-Ward and Single Family Room Units." *Journal of Perinatology 31*(4): 281-288.)

Chapter 11

Broken Hearts: Jadyn Danziger

This is a strange case of heart failure, I thought, as I listened to Dr. Kelly Donahue rattle off details about the baby he had admitted to the NICU several days earlier. He reduced his report on Baby Danziger to a series of numbers and measurements: blood pressure, heart rate, respiratory rate, oxygen saturation, lab values, medication doses, and on and on. The story perplexed me; I could not quite put it all together.

Jadyn's mother, Kourtney, had arrived at the high-risk OB clinic at our hospital on referral from her obstetrician in the rural community where she lived, several hours away. He had detected something amiss on an ultrasound two-thirds of the way through her pregnancy. She was only thirty-two weeks pregnant; yet, her uterus measured the size of a thirty-six week pregnancy. An ultrasound showed she had an excessive amount of amniotic fluid, called polyhydramnios, its cause unknown.

"How many pregnancies does this make for you?" Dr. Richard Snyder, our high-risk specialist, had asked Kourtney. He had called me down to his clinic to hear her story firsthand.

"This is my second. I've felt fine. No problems." Confidence permeated the woman's voice. Perhaps the doctor who had sent her here was wrong.

As the obstetrician maneuvered the ultrasound machine's transducer through puddles of warm jelly he'd squirted onto her belly, he squinted at the images of her fetus it produced.

"Hmmm…heart's definitely bigger than normal… pumping faster than usual but not very effectively, I'm sorry to say." A kindly, grandfatherly type with bushy white hair, he knew how to deliver bad news with the gentlest of touches, always apologetically.

"What's that mean? Is the baby okay?" The woman remained flat on her back, her belly her most prominent feature. Her smile flattened.

"Give me another couple of minutes. I'm measuring the blood flow across the placenta."

Whoosh, whoosh, whoosh. Every beat of the fetus' heart pulsed loudly, filling the small exam room, while spikes traced across the screen. Switching to another view, Dr. Snyder watched as blotches of red and blue crashed into each other on the screen, indicating the mixing of venous and arterial blood in the heart. The regular tempo of the noise generated by the baby's heartbeat provided a reassuring backdrop to the exam, but the doctor's words did not reassure.

"Things do not look good. The circulation from the placenta, across the umbilical cord to the baby, isn't normal. A huge amount of blood—much greater than normal—is flowing into her heart, and she's struggling to pump it out. I am afraid you might lose her if we don't deliver her very soon.

"You did know it's a girl, right?" He tacked on the question at the last minute, a twinge of guilt lacing his voice for having possibly revealed what might have been a surprise.

"Yes, we're calling her Jadyn. But I'm only thirty-two weeks along. Isn't that too early for her to be born? Can we wait?" Kourtney's cheery mien began to dissolve; tears loomed on the horizon.

"It's definitely early," said Dr. Snyder,"but I think this is the only chance the baby has for survival. In most cases, the best place for the fetus at this stage of pregnancy is in the womb, but in Jadyn's case I can't say that's true.

"You see, I've just found an irregularity in the placenta, called a chorioangioma. It's a benign tumor."

"A tumor? Like cancer?" Tears dripped over the edge of both her eyelids.

"No, it's not malignant. It's a tangled overgrowth of abnormal blood vessels. Her heart's got to pump extra blood around to supply this thing, and it's creating undue stress on her. We've got to deliver her and hope she does better on the outside."

Kourtney looked at Dr. Snyder expectantly. "Deliver her?" she asked warily.

***

Jadyn was born not long after Kourtney's clinic appointment, and soon it was my turn to look at the baby and ponder her condition. An ultrasound after birth had shown her bigger-than-normal heart was still pumping fast and furiously, but only very small volumes of blood were being ejected into her aorta. A cardiologist recommended medications to improve the heart's contractility and to support her blood pressure.

I approached Jadyn's isolette and greeted her parents. "Does this young lady belong to you?" I asked.

"Yup. We've got a little girl already and she's our second," her mother answered. "I'm Kourtney and this is Dan." For a woman who'd given birth only several days before, Kourtney looked remarkably well. Her luminous blue eyes reflected the thrill of seeing her newborn; yet, I perceived wariness in them, too.

A blanket decorated with all the animals of Noah's Ark hung over the newborn's isolette to block the light that shone evenly over the large room. I pulled it back to get a better look at her, and the baby scrunched her eyelids together and crinkled her forehead in response to the brightness. "She certainly looks nice and rosy pink," I said. "Small, but pink."

"That's good, isn't it?" asked Kourtney.

"Yes, pink is always good." I poked my hands through the porthole doors of the isolette and reveled in the warmth inside; it felt as warm as a sunny day at the beach. "Hey, Jadyn," I said, "did you know mommy and daddy are here?"

I started my exam, pulling aside the monitor wires to place my stethoscope on Jadyn's chest, and worked my way around the other tubes and lines coursing into her body. I heard the harsh murmur Dr. Donahue had told me about. I could also feel the baby's miniature heart, probably the size of a walnut, heave under my hand when I placed the stethoscope over her chest. Probing her belly, I felt her liver's edge midway down her abdomen, a bit lower than usual, likely the result of heart failure, I guessed. The ventilator sighed regularly, and her IV pumps ticked and groaned as they propelled yellow nutritional fluids and invisible medications into the lines, which disappeared into the stump of her umbilical cord.

"From what I know about her," I said, as I finished my exam, "I guess she needs 'Tincture of Time.' Just some time for her heart to adjust and recover from the extra load it had to pump while she was inside you." "Tincture of Time" was one of my favorite prescriptions; it meant that with watching and waiting, conditions should gradually improve on their own.

Tincture of Time was apparently the wrong prescription, though. I returned to the NICU two days after I first met Jadyn to find she had not improved at all. She was stuck on all the same medications and had not been weaned at all from the ventilator.

"She should be getting better by now if the placental lesion was the sole cause of her failure," the cardiologist maintained when he called to check on Jadyn's progress.

"I know," I agreed. "It is disturbing."

"I can't figure out what's going on with her," he said, and I could tell it bothered him, too. Making a diagnosis could seem like playing chess. Moving pieces around the board—obtaining different tests—the goal was to figure out a checkmate and clinch the diagnosis. Usually, heart failure could be attributed to a structural anomaly of the heart, an atypical heart rhythm, some type of infection, or a metabolic imbalance. But, so far, no test we had completed could explain Jadyn's ongoing heart failure. "I'm going to come by this afternoon and have another look," the cardiologist added.

Always a good idea, I thought, *to return to the patient and get back to old-fashioned bedside medicine.* In the physical exam, was there anything we had missed? I examined Jadyn once again and scrutinized every inch of her three-pound body. I could see her cry but could not hear her protests since the breathing tube in her throat prevented her from making any noise. Her heart exam remained unchanged, and her lungs sounded clear. Then, I noticed a tiny red dot on her arm…then one on her leg…and another one on the tip of her inch-long index finger. The closer I looked, the more I found: ten in all, but none was larger than the head of a pin.

"Hey, did you notice these little red spots?" I asked her nurse.

"Yeah," she replied, looking up at me through glasses, which magnified her eyes out of proportion to the rest of her face. "I first saw those yesterday. They are so small I wasn't sure they were really there, especially because they disappear if you press on them. But today, they are more noticeable. What are they? They don't look like a rash; they're too far apart."

"They're hemangiomas," I said, referring to the lesions, which were made up of clusters of abnormally growing blood vessels. "They're just showing up. They'll get bigger. And when there are this many on the skin, it sometimes means there are internal hemangiomas." *Check*, I thought. I just needed one more move to announce checkmate.

I surmised there must be a large hemangioma residing in Jadyn's liver, altering her circulation and straining her heart. I picked up the stethoscope and laid it on the skin of Jadyn's abdomen over her swollen liver. *Whoosh, whoosh, whoosh.* The hum of blood flowing at high velocity was unmistakable. More evidence. Her enlarged liver must be a *cause* of her heart failure, not necessarily a result.

"Let's get an ultrasound of her liver," I told the nurse. "Today."

The ultrasound discovered multiple cavernous blood vessels distorting the normal architecture of the baby's liver, a malformation similar to the lesion in her placenta. *Checkmate.* This was not a good game to win, though, because winning meant the baby might lose.

I retreated to my office and sampled the thick medical texts on the shelf, reading all about this diagnosis I had studied in medical school but had never before encountered.

When the cardiologist appeared later that afternoon, I announced, "Got it figured out. There is a vascular lesion in the baby's liver, and she has multiple cutaneous hemangiomas. She probably has them everywhere inside her body, too, not just in the liver. Disseminated neonatal hemangiomatosis."

He winced. "Ouch. Not a good diagnosis. And you beat me to it. Darn it!"

Together we told Kourtney and Dan how Jadyn's heart could not keep up with the demands to feed the hungry beast residing in her liver *and* supply well-oxygenated blood to the rest of her body. There could be more lesions lurking inside, we explained.

Kourtney held a crumpled tissue to her face. "I thought we delivered her early so we could do something to make her better. What happens next?" She looked as though she wished the baby were back safely inside her, before she had been told of all these problems, and before she had agreed to delivery. *Oh, to yearn to turn back the hands of time*, I thought. *That's a dangerous mental path to tread.*

"The treatment choices are difficult," I said. "Sometimes chemotherapy can shrink the lesion, but since she only weighs three pounds, she is far too small and premature to tolerate chemo. Radiation sometimes works to lessen the tumor's size, but again, it is not an option for her. Steroids have too many side effects. Coils can be threaded into the abnormal blood vessels, to block the flow; that would be a dicey thing to do with Jadyn. And then, there is surgery, either to take out the abnormal part of the liver or give her a new one with a transplant. I doubt if such surgery has ever been done on a baby her size."

Dan was not very tall, but he was as compact as a pro wrestler and seemed just as tough. In an unwavering voice, he asked, "Doctor, which treatment do you recommend?" He wanted to grapple with this thing inside his baby and bring it down firmly to the ground under his domination.

"We don't do any of those treatments here in our community hospital," I explained. "She will need to go to the children's hospital; the specialists there can advise you. She needs to be seen by hematologists, dermatologists, gastroenterologists, surgeons, and interventional radiologists. It is where I would want my child to be if she had a problem like this. Trust me, they provide excellent and expert care."

Kourtney's tears were instinctive; I would have worried if she did not cry.

"I'm sorry about this," I said, "but at least now we know exactly what we are fighting, so we can figure out which treatment may help her. I'll go arrange her transfer."

Kourtney nodded wordlessly, and Dan inhaled sharply.

I left the baby's bedside and Dan followed close on my heels. "Doc, can I have a word with you in private?"

"Sure. Let's go in here where it's quieter." I led him to a small room reserved for parent conferences.

"Give it to me straight," he said. "What are her chances? My wife doesn't really want to know, but I do. Just give me the statistics, please."

I was not used to being pinned down so directly. I answered based on what I had read about the condition. "I would say her overall survival chances are about 30 percent. We have to hope that her heart will function sufficiently well, while she grows big enough to be able to tolerate one of these treatments. It will be a race against time."

"I know they will do everything they possibly can for her at the children's hospital. I hope things will turn out well for you all." That was all I could do at this point…cross my fingers and pray, along with Jadyn's parents. Although her chances for survival were small, there was no sense in closing off any options prematurely. In going to the children's hospital, Jadyn would undergo further exploration as the doctors there gathered yet more information about her condition. Over time, things should become clearer to her doctors and to her parents.

As Dan nodded, he clenched his teeth and the muscle across his jaw contracted tightly.

"Can we bring our four-year-old daughter in to see her? She's out in the waiting room with her grandparents."

"Sounds like an excellent plan," I said gently.

I was back by Jadyn's side when Kourtney bravely carried her daughter into the NICU. The little girl with the blond pageboy hair cut, set off by a pink ribbon, clutched Peter Cottontail to her chest.

"Eden brought Jadyn her favorite character from the Peter Rabbit books," she announced.

As Eden pointed to her baby sister, Kourtney softly told her how sick her baby sister was and how she and Daddy hoped they would all be together someday soon. "We will say our prayers for her tonight, okay sweetie?"

Shortly, Kourtney handed Eden to Dan, who carried her out of the NICU to her waiting grandparents. As Kourtney stood with tears dripping down her face, I gave her a hug and wished her safe travels, and within a few hours the family began the next part of their journey.

***

I kept up with Jadyn's progress by phoning her new doctors for regular updates. The parade of consultants visited her; yet, none could suggest a viable treatment option for this baby who remained nearly six weeks shy of her due date. The risk of death from the proposed treatments outweighed the slim benefits each one might offer. Meanwhile, even more medications were added to treat her heart failure, without any positive effect, and her liver function deteriorated as the hemangioma enlarged.

Several weeks later, Kourtney surprised me with a phone call. "Doctor Hall, we're having a conference with Jadyn's team at the children's hospital tomorrow, and I wanted to invite you to come. We're going to talk about the possibility of discontinuing her life support. I thought you might have something to contribute." Kourtney sounded remarkably even-keeled, like she was managing a continuing medical education course on end-of-life care. I imagined that her close involvement and proactive style in making this decision gave her some measure of control in what otherwise was a situation that was completely out of her control. Jadyn's parents had given her every opportunity to live, but now their hopes for her were colliding head-on with the reality of her condition. They did not seem to be harboring false hope.

"Oh gosh," I said. "I'm so sorry to hear it has come to this. How are you doing?"

"Dan and I are okay. We know there's probably not much more they can offer Jadyn. Even if she was bigger and more mature, she would have a tough go of it. We have read a lot on this diagnosis and have known from the beginning what she has been up against."

"It's true about this being a tough go," I said. "Listen, I'm very sorry, but I'm on call here tomorrow and I will not be able to leave the hospital. My thoughts and prayers will be with you. Thank you for thinking of me and letting me know about Jadyn."

"Thank you for everything you did for her."

"I just wish we could have done more." Our conversation felt like a good-bye. As I hung up the phone, I thought Kourtney was handling the situation as well as could be expected.

At their meeting the next day, Kourtney and Dan agreed with Jadyn's medical team to discontinue their daughter's life support. Sadness engulfed me when I heard about her passing from the neonatologist taking care of her. How are new parents able to let go of their dreams when they are forced to do so, I wondered.

***

Three days later, in the middle of morning rounds, the NICU secretary motioned for me to come to the phone. "Dr. Snyder asked me to pull you out of rounds," she said. "He says it's urgent."

I picked up the phone. "Hi, Richard. What's up?"

"You are not going to believe this. Kourtney Danziger collapsed this morning and was taken to the emergency room coding. The baby's funeral is tomorrow, and now Kourtney's in the ICU on life support."

"What?" I asked. "She's so young, and seemed so healthy… What happened?" Words poured out as my mind raced forward. I could see Kourtney's luminous eyes in my mind. "Is she in our ICU?"

"No, she's at the hospital nearest to where she and her husband live. It wasn't a heart attack. The cardiologists say it's a classic case of 'broken heart syndrome.' I've never heard of it before, but apparently massive emotional stress causes the release of epinephrine and other hormones that stun the heart muscle. The old pump just fails.

"Just thought you would want to know."

"Wow, unbelievable." Suddenly I felt leaden and numb. "Thanks for letting me know."

I returned to my NICU team and told them what had happened. The news about Kourtney rippled out first to all the nurses, like concentric rings produced on the surface of a pond when a stone is thrown into it, and then to the other therapists and social workers who came in and out of the NICU all day long. A subdued pall hung over the NICU for the rest of the day, and I slipped out over lunch to buy a "Get Well" card to send to Kourtney.

The following day, things were back to normal with the crush of patients and parents, doctors and nurses, coming and going from the NICU. But Kourtney Danziger remained at the forefront of my thoughts. Word filtered back to us over the next several weeks that Kourtney had actually experienced a blockage in one of her coronary arteries, leading to a massive heart attack. She remained in intensive care and had been placed on a heart-transplant list.

Without a new heart herself, Kourtney was in grave danger of dying. She must now look exactly like her tiny daughter had looked: covered with tubes and lines and monitor patches, and anxiously awaiting a treatment that was her only chance. I could not imagine how Dan must be feeling, having to transfer any hope he may have had for his infant daughter's survival to his wife.

About two months later, even as Kourtney remained hospital-bound, awaiting transplant, I received a letter from Dan. He thanked me for the "world class care" my team and I had provided to Jadyn.

"We all wish that things would have worked out differently, but they are what they are," he wrote. "Thank you and all of your staff for everything they did for Kourtney, Jadyn and me."

I wondered how Jadyn's father had the resilience to marshal his inner resources and cope with the challenges facing him, and still have the energy and presence of mind to express gratitude to those he encountered on his journey. The pressures he faced might have left another person immobilized with grief.

I set his letter, stained with my wet tears, down on my desk and marveled at how some people can face such tremendous adversity in their lives with grit, grace, and utter generosity of spirit.

***

Notes:

To read more about the very rare condition from which Jadyn suffered, diffuse neonatal hemangiomatosis, see the following references: Golitz L.E., M. D. Rudikoff, O. P. O'Meara. 1986. "Diffuse Neonatal Hemangiomatosis." *Pediatric Dermatology 3*(2): 145-152 and Bakaris S., H. Karabiber, M. Yuksel et al. 2004. "Case of Large Placental Chorioangioma Associated with Diffuse Neonatal Hemangiomatosis." *Pediatric and Developmental Pathology 7*(3): 258-261.

Kourtney's doctors first thought she had experienced the broken heart syndrome, an entity that has only recently been described. Researchers studied patients who had symptoms similar to heart attacks but did not have the typical coronary artery disease responsible for heart attacks. They concluded that emotional stress can overstimulate the sympathetic nervous system to cause severe dysfunction of the left ventricle, the main pumping chamber of the heart. (Wittstein I. S., D. R. Thiemann, J. A. Lima et al. 2005. "Neurohumoral Features of Myocardial Stunning Due to Sudden Emotional Stress." *The New England Journal of Medicine 352*(6): 539-548.) A nonmedical interpretation of Dr. Wittstein's study can be found on the internet. (Stein R. 2005. "Study Suggests You Can Die of a Broken Heart." www.washingtonpost.com, February 10.)

It was then found that Kourtney had instead suffered a myocardial infarction (MI), or "heart attack," something that rarely occurs in women of childbearing age. Pregnancy is known to increase the risk of MI three-to-fourfold. General factors that place a woman at risk of having an MI during pregnancy include an age greater than thirty-five years, black race, hypertension, diabetes mellitus, and smoking. Risk factors specific to pregnancy include preeclampsia (a form of pregnancy-associated hypertension), postpartum hemorrhage, transfusion, and postpartum infection. (James A. H., M. G. Jamison, M. S. Biswas et al. 2006. "Acute Myocardial Infarction in Pregnancy: A United States Population-Based Study." *Circulation 113*(12): 1564-1571.)

Chapter 12

A Fierce Devotion: Grace Blakelely

"Storm's acomin'," the helicopter pilot said. "We've gotta get outta here."

"Give us a second, will you? The baby was just born," I replied. "We'll pack her up as fast as we can." We had arrived to ferry Baby Girl Blakeley from the community hospital where she had been born weighing just four pounds back to our NICU, where she would be able to grow to a size that would enable her to go home safely.

At best, my exam of the baby was cursory. She was obviously small, as we had been told before her birth she would be. We had stretched clear plastic oxygen tubing from ear to ear over the middle of her china doll face. In the rush of activity to get her loaded into our transport isolette, I did not think about how still she lay.

My skin felt sticky under my weighty flight suit as we wheeled the baby out to the waiting craft. Unrealized rain hung like a threat in the sky as we lifted up into the inky night.

During our earlier flight out to the small town to pick up this tiny baby, the helicopter had swayed gently in the late afternoon sun, tousled by the breeze. I felt as if I were riding in the aerial tram across Disneyland, although the wide-open spaces reminded me I was definitely no longer in California. I had looked down to see monopoly houses, Tonka trucks®, and Hot Wheels® cars below. When we left the city limits, we flew low enough to see cows nibble at bright bits of grass, which only recently emerged from the otherwise barren land, land now recovering from a harsh winter. I thought nothing of it when the shadows from converging clouds created a patchwork effect over the ground, but now they were completely closed in, creating a murky grey ceiling overhead.

A silver streak sprang forth from the clouds to our left and shattered the peaceful darkness. The streak snaked to the ground in a split second, spawning eerie tendrils from its core. The steely beam was as well defined as a filament in an incandescent light bulb, and it generated a similar glow as its central core burned out. The horizon rumbled angrily, and further ahead of us on the other side, a flash of light blazed like a bomb explosion. With the excellent visibility, I saw a soft blurring of the horizon where rain fell miles ahead. Our transport team had front row seats for an IMAX movie entitled "Spring Storms."

I looked over at Suzie, the flight nurse who accompanied me. She bent down to peer into the baby's isolette. If the baby cried, we would not have heard it, given the deafening drone of the chopper's blades above us. Although I could not see the baby from where I sat, the colorful cadences dancing across her monitor screen reassured me her heart rate and breathing pattern were normal. Even though she appeared to be in stable condition, I was happy that the time to return the baby to our NICU would be cut in half since we were going by helicopter instead of ambulance...that is, unless our flight were interrupted by the ever-more threatening weather.

Moments later, our pilot Philip called the Dispatch Center. As our helmets were all hooked into the radio system, I overheard his conversation. "What is our best route back to the hospital?" he asked.

The woman running dispatch told him the location of the storm cells and the wind speed along our route. Although the main storm system was moving in from the west, and our flight path was due north, some rogue cells with bad weather lurked to our east. Philip and the woman wrestled with the question of whether we would make it to our destination ahead of the westerly storm, and whether we would run into a storm cell if we jagged east to fly around the far side of the storms.

"I think you can fly up right between the cells," suggested the woman.

Oh my God, please, no, I thought. Squeezed into the seat behind Philip, who always preached safety first, my knees touched the back of his seat.

I hoped Philip, a decorated hero in Vietnam, did not feel like he had to be a hero now. Would he attempt to outrun the storm and deliver us to the hospital come hell or high water? My definition of "hero" in this situation would be someone who could just say *to hell with the transport* and land the helicopter.

But where?

As the light show continued all around us like a gargantuan fireworks display, I waited until Philip's conversation finished, then angled my microphone in close to my mouth to speak.

"Philip, let's go down. This…does not…look good." I did not want our patient to be added to the list of those who have died nationally as a result of accidents in medical transport helicopters. The importance of safety during transport has to trump the importance of speed in getting the patient to their destination in every case.

"We'll be okay, Dr. Hall. I'll figure it out. Let me talk with dispatch a bit more." Philip's tone was reassuring, and I had to trust that he took as much pride in doing his job as a consummate professional as I did mine.

I made a conscious effort to relax but could not. I leaned forward to scan the horizon while I strained to hear every word of Philip's transmissions to and from dispatch. As we chugged forward in the thick air, I heard, "They are reporting rain at the hospital," and a few seconds later, "Thunder in the vicinity of the hospital." I groaned to myself and wondered what our options were, as the lights of the city began to sprout ahead of us.

"Order us an ambulance," Philip directed the lady on dispatch.

Shortly, we drifted downward, and Philip announced, "Make sure things are secure for landing. Small local airport in front of us." The chopper banked to the side and fluttered like a leaf, passing a line of blue lights. We skittered to a landing in front of a hangar that appeared from nowhere. I noticed the windsock on the roof of the hangar fell limply. Within a minute of our landing, it swirled around erratically, buffeted by wind that pelted the helicopter with fat new raindrops.

Suzie and I waited with our tiny patient while Philip disappeared into the hangar. A few minutes later sirens pierced through the crash of the rain, and an ambulance pulled up behind us. We unloaded our precious cargo, cocooned inside the heavy transport apparatus, and wheeled her over to the ambulance. The emergency medical technicians strained to hoist the isolette into the back of the ambulance, and then Suzie and I piled in next, as wet as Labradors after a summer swim.

"Do you want sirens going back to the hospital?" the driver asked.

"No. I think we're fine without them." Now that we were safely out of the sky, the last thing we needed was to skid through an intersection on the city's slick streets. Driving at something less than the emergency medical technicians' usual breakneck speed would be just fine.

We finally arrived at the hospital and took the baby inside the NICU. The rest of the night slipped by quietly; burrowed deep within the hospital, I could neither see nor hear the ongoing storm.

***

The morning after I admitted Baby Blakeley to the NICU, one of the nurses called me to her bedside. "Dr. Hall…don't you think this baby looks just a bit…different?" Monica asked.

"Hmm," I said, glancing through the plastic walls of the isolette. "What are you concerned about?"

"She just doesn't look right. Her eyes are kind of small, her nasal bridge seems flat, her ears might be low set. Her fingers are funny and she keeps her fists balled up most of the time. See the slackness in her skin? I don't know. I think she might have a syndrome."

"Oh dear." That seemed to be my favorite expression for times like these. "You could be right," I said, on closer examination. "I guess I did not look that carefully last night."

"What is going on with you, sweetheart?" I asked the baby.

The findings Monica pointed out were subtle, but I decided to convene the group of doctors and nurse practitioners making rounds that day at the baby's bedside.

"What do you all think?" I asked, as one by one they evaluated the baby's appearance.

"Get chromosomes," said my physician partner, Dr. Sonya Sondheim. "Definitely. Something's not right."

When the baby's parents arrived from their small town the following day, I spoke with them. "The baby's doing pretty well, but she has a heart murmur, and she's still requiring oxygen. We are a little concerned about how she looks, so we're getting chromosomes."

"Why? What don't you like about how she looks?" Tracy, the baby's mother, said.

I described our concerns about the baby's facial features. Mom quickly replied, "She looks just like our first baby. She looks fine to me."

"Well, she is a cute baby. We'll let you know when we get the results. In the meantime, we're going to get a cardiac echo, an ultrasound of her heart, to evaluate the murmur.

"What's her name, by the way?"

"It's Grace," said Joey, Tracy's husband whom I had met briefly while on transport. His face crumpled with concern as he stared at the baby.

That afternoon, an echocardiogram showed a large hole in Grace's heart: a VSD, or ventricular septal defect.

"Is that bad?" asked Tracy.

"This one is large enough to cause her problems. She may have trouble breathing, and she might need surgery."

"Why didn't the ultrasounds I had during my pregnancy show this problem with her heart?"

"Sometimes ultrasounds are just done to determine the baby's due date, and the baby isn't really carefully examined," I explained. Most of the new mothers I had seen recently only wanted a 3-D snapshot of baby from their prenatal ultrasound—for the baby book—and did not think much about the ultrasound's importance beyond that. Ultrasounds are now used fairly routinely to help establish a baby's due date and to check whether the fetus is growing well; not every ultrasound is performed with the purpose to detect physical abnormalities. These more careful exams are only carried out if there are certain clues during pregnancy that the fetus could have a problem.

"If something was wrong, the doctors should have seen it," said Joey. "I never really trusted that doctor you were going to," he added.

"Now wait a minute, honey. He's a good doctor. But you are right, it's not good that he missed something this big," countered Tracy. "Gracie's gonna be just fine, though. Aren't you, sweet thing, mama's little girl?" Tracy cooed at the baby, who appeared oblivious to the sound of her voice.

We tried to get Grace to take a bottle, although she had no reaction when the nurse placed a nipple in her mouth. Bad sign. We don't ask babies to do much, so if they can't do one of the main things necessary to stay alive—eat—we are very concerned. Although she was small for her gestational age, Grace was thirty-seven weeks old and should have been able to suck and swallow.

"She'll learn. I'm not worried," insisted Tracy. "I want to take her home."

"You can't take her home until she can eat," I explained.

"You know, she's our baby, and we'll take her home whenever we damn well please." Joey surprised me with the force of his statement.

Tracy turned to look at him and smiled. "It's okay, honey; we'll take her home soon. Let's give her a little longer, though."

The week dragged on as we awaited the chromosome results.

"Grace has Trisomy 18," I told Tracy and Joey, once the results came back. "Normally we have twenty-three pairs of chromosomes, for a total of forty-six. She has an extra chromosome on number eighteen, for a total of forty-seven. This is the result of an accident that occurred at the time of conception. There was nothing you did that caused this."

"I don't understand," said Joey, the anger in his voice rising. "How could they have not detected this on those ultrasounds Tracy had. How many did they do, three?" His questioning glance found Tracy.

"Yes, three. I'm really confused. What does this mean?"

"Trisomy 18 is a genetic defect. That extra chromosome has gummed up the works of the baby's DNA. DNA provides the instructions for how the body is to develop—like a blueprint for a house—and if the DNA message isn't right, the baby does not form normally."

"So what does that mean for her?" Tracy asked.

"It explains why she has the heart defect, and she probably has some other abnormalities of her internal organs. We should at least do an ultrasound of her kidneys."

"She'll be all right, won't she? I mean, like, normal, you know?" I sensed that Tracy was almost afraid to hear my answer.

"Unfortunately, babies with Trisomy 18 are not normal. They do not develop beyond the level of a two-month-old...They will never walk or talk... I'm so sorry," I added. I paused, giving some time for this news to sink in, and I wanted to give Grace's parents plenty of time to express their thoughts and reactions.

When I started my training many years earlier, Trisomy 18 was universally accepted to be a "lethal anomaly," meaning all babies born with it were expected to die, about half within the first six months, and the other half by one-year of age. Either they simply stopped breathing, or they passed away from their heart defects. Because their prognosis for what the medical community considered to be a "meaningful life" was nil, congenital anomalies such as heart defects were not repaired.

What doctors and nurses consider to be a meaningful life is often quite different than what parents think, though.

"This can't be right," insisted Tracy. "She looks exactly like Johnny, her brother. He looked this way, too, when he was born, and he was slow to eat. He's seven now and he's a complete terror. You would never know he was slow at birth."

"Well, these are the results. We can talk about them more over the next couple of days. Why don't you two take some time to digest this information and we can meet again tomorrow to discuss it, or whenever you are ready."

I shook my head after leaving Grace's room. This was such a tough diagnosis to deliver. I would not want to believe it about my child, either.

***

When I saw them next, Tracy held Grace, nestled on her chest and covered snugly with a blanket for privacy and warmth. They swayed back and forth contentedly in a rocking chair, looking like they had all the time in the world together.

"I see you are doing 'kangaroo care' with Grace," I said. "Terrific! Did you know kangaroo care began in Third World countries as a way to keep babies warm without incubators? The skin-to-skin contact is very therapeutic for babies and moms."

"Yeah, it's great to finally hold her," said Tracy. A woman who was older than Tracy, but younger than I was, accompanied Joey and her. She had the type of smile people have when they do not know what to say. "This is my mom," Tracy added.

"Hey, I looked up Trisomy 18 on the internet," she continued. "I think Grace has the mosaic form."

A mosaic form would mean that some of Grace's cells had an extra eighteenth chromosome, and some did not.

Children with mosaic forms of chromosomal abnormalities are usually less affected than those who have extra, broken, or rearranged chromosomes in every one of their cells.

"She doesn't have a cleft lip or palate, and she doesn't have any of those esophagus or stomach problems I read about." Tracy outlined as strong a case against Trisomy 18 as she could muster.

"We did find out yesterday that she has a horseshoe-shaped kidney," I mentioned.

"No one told us that," said Joey.

"I was just coming in to tell you," I said. "The shape of her kidney may not affect its function, but it is an abnormality seen in Trisomy 18."

"I still think she's mosaic." Tracy was adamant. She quickened the pace of her rocking.

"The chromosome report doesn't show that she's a mosaic. All her cells are affected. Here," I offered. "You can read the report yourselves."

Tracy took the paper I held out to her, and Joey looked over her shoulder. Grandma watched them both. The parents looked up after a minute. The expressions on their faces suggested they did not yet want to believe what they had read.

"I'm sorry," I said. "This must be hard for you."

Tracy tried hard to hold back tears, but they came anyway, although just for a fleeting second. She clutched her baby to her chest more tightly. Her mom stepped forward and put her hand on Tracy's shoulder.

"Doctor, what does Trisomy 18 mean?" the grandmother asked. The woman's rigid smile was replaced by a weary expression that told me she had experienced life's trials and tribulations.

I explained once again how babies with Trisomy 18 are created, and gently reviewed their prognosis. I studied

Tracy's and Joey's faces as I did. They winced when I mentioned death again, and a sorrowful expression replaced the look of concern on Grandma's face.

"You kids can get through this," Grandma said. "We did it with your brother, Tracy.

"He had Down syndrome," she explained to me. Ah, Trisomy 21, I noted.

"I don't want it this way, mom. I want my baby to be normal." There was no stopping Tracy's tears now. Her mother's eyes misted as she watched Tracy hug Grace as though she would never let her go.

"We can all love Gracie just the same, no matter how many chromosomes she has," grandmother said softly.

Tracy accepted the tissue box I offered her. Joey rested his chin on the palm of his hand, and supported his elbow with his other hand. His stance reminded me of Rodin's Thinker statue.

As I left Grace's room after our conversation, I was happy to see that Big Al was Grace's nurse that day. Big Al looked as though he had missed his calling as a pro football player, but his mellow man-to-man chats with so many fathers of our NICU babies helped them recover from that helpless, almost incapacitating, feeling of not being able to make things right for their wives and children. I was hopeful he would continue to help Joey and the rest of Grace's family work through their feelings about her condition.

Several days later, Tracy told me she had been searching the internet again.

"Did you come across the SOFT website yet?" I asked. "It's a supportive community for parents of babies with trisomies, and it has good, reliable information about Trisomy 18."

"No, I did not come across that. But I did find pictures of survivors of Trisomy 18 who lived to be twenty-one-years-old. Grace is going to grow up, and go to school, and we're going to go to her wedding."

I knew rare survivors of Trisomy 18 existed, but they were invariably severely mentally retarded and physically incapacitated. Best not to argue with Tracy, though, I thought. Not wanting to take hope away from her, I had to let her decide what she wanted to hope for. Without hope, how could she possibly go forward? I wondered, though, whether Tracy's view of her daughter's future meant she was in denial, unable to let go of the vision of having a normal daughter she must have carried during her pregnancy, or whether it was an act of defiance that enabled her to cope with her daughter's condition on her own terms.

"Hey, let's get the show on the road," urged Joey. "Our family is the most important thing to us. I've taken a leave from my job so I can be home to help. Right now we're staying at the Ronald McDonald House so we can visit every day. But we're anxious to take Grace home, unless she can get the hole in her heart fixed first."

"I'm so glad you found the Ronald McDonald House," I said. "Great place.

"Grace's heart is doing okay, just now. She's off the oxygen. You can see how things go for a while, and decide later if you want her to have heart surgery."

"Why wouldn't we, if her heart needs repair?" he asked.

"We don't want her to suffer," Tracy added. "But we're not going to give up on her."

I reminded them that statistics predicted half the babies born with Grace's problems would not survive beyond six-months of age. I did not, however, want to describe the surgery as futile.

"We've already talked about it. We want her to have surgery. We're going to give her everything she needs," Joey stated with finality.

"Okay, then. We've already arranged for her to follow-up with the cardiologist."

***

The family's desires mirrored those of many families whose babies have chromosomal syndromes previously considered to be lethal. Although the life expectancy of babies with Trisomy 18 is almost always severely shortened, this is no longer seen as a justification for withholding medical treatment. Most doctors now agree that babies with trisomies should be offered the same treatment options for their birth defects as babies without a trisomy.

However, decisions are left up to the parents, and quality-of-life considerations are factored in. Not every family will choose to pursue each available treatment option for their baby, given that these things may not substantially prolong or improve the baby's life. The psychological cost of living with a disabled child must also be considered. The stress of caring for such a child leads to higher rates of divorce, separation, or parental abandonment than average.

***

"Now," I said, "we have to figure out what we're going to do about her eating…or rather, her lack of eating."

"Just give me some more time with the bottle," begged Tracy. "I think she's improving. Really." Grace lay in her crib wearing a white one-piece outfit with pink script writing. "If mommy says no, ask grandma," it read. She still moved only rarely and her doughy muscles remained slack.

"Fair enough," I agreed. "We'll give her another week or two, but if she hasn't improved by then, we should discuss surgical placement of a feeding tube into her stomach. We call it a G-tube, for gastrostomy tube. It will make her care much simpler. You won't have to spend hours trying to get her to take a bottle."

"I don't want her to have a tube." Tracy frowned.

"I know you don't," I said. "But there might not be any other choice."

Grace's room became an oasis in the NICU. Every time I entered, the lights were low and the strains of a different lullaby floated out of the CD player her parents had brought, creating a soothing atmosphere. *All Through the Night*, *Brahm's Lullaby*, *Beautiful Dreamer*...I loved them all, and remembered fondly the nights when I sang them to my own babies. Scrapbook pages featuring pictures of Grace as "Our Little Angel" hung on the wall. A mobile with brightly colored turtles and fish swam above her crib, and two lacy, frilly dresses with satin bows, the size a six-month-old baby would wear, hung on the door of the cabinet.

The nurses rarely left Grace alone. If her parents were not around, a nurse or a volunteer usually held her, gravitating as they did to the more fragile babies who were always so easy to cuddle. "She's so sweet," they would all say, and I would agree.

"Dr. Hall, we are so ready to take Grace home," Tracy said to me one day. "The Ronald McDonald House is great, but we need to get back home."

"Let's just go for the G-tube," Joey added. "We need to be a family again. It's too hard having Grace here and Johnny at home with Grandma. And Johnny doesn't do too well here."

Johnny buzzed around the room as we spoke. He clambered up on the metal railings of the crib to peer in, then jumped down to the floor, toppled to the ground, and rolled around like he had just escaped from a burning plane.

Grace's surgery for placement of the G-tube was uneventful. The following week her parents spent the night with her in our family room, demonstrating their proficiency with her tube and administering the medications she would need at home.

It was a bittersweet day as the Blakeley family left the NICU. The nurses crowded around to bid farewell to their favorite little charge. Some of them stayed to help Tracy, Joey, and Tracy's mother pack away all her belongings, including a guest book in which each had inscribed little notes to Grace. "You are such a darling girl," one wrote. "You are so lucky your parents love you so much," wrote another one.

Before they left, Tracy gave me a single long-stemmed rose. "To remember us by," she said.

"Don't worry," I said. "I won't forget you. Come back to visit."

To Joey and Tracy, as well as to Tracy's mother, family meant everything. No member was less than any other, and all were wanted and loved. Despite Tracy's fervent desire for Grace to be normal, I knew that ultimately her syndrome would make little difference to her mother. To be a family and have that time together —however short it might be— was all that mattered.

***

Notes:

Grace was transported in by helicopter, which is not a risk-free endeavor for either the patient or the medical transport staff. During a six-month period in late 2009-early 2010, four medical transport helicopters crashed in the United States, killing twelve people but fortunately no patients. Bad weather and thunderstorms were implicated in two of the crashes. ("Brownsville Medical Helicopter Crash is Nation's Fourth in Six Months." 2010. *The Commercial Appeal*, March 26.)

The condition with which Grace was diagnosed, Trisomy 18, is a genetic syndrome in which there are three copies, instead of the usual two, of the eighteenth chromosome. About 95 percent of fetuses with Trisomy 18 will die before birth due to multiple organ involvement. The incidence of this disorder among live-born infants is one in 6,500.

Although Trisomy 18 was previously thought to be "lethal," it has since been determined that it and other syndromes like it are not necessarily lethal, although only 5-10 percent of affected children live past their first birthdays. An article by Koogler et al. provides an historical overview of this transition in thinking, as well as a thorough discussion of the ethical arguments about how decision-making for infants with potentially lethal birth defects should be approached. Even the title of this article, "Lethal Language, Lethal Decisions," suggests that what doctors say to parents about these anomalies has the strong potential to influence decisions parents may make. The authors' conclusion is that decisions to withhold or treat infants with serious, life-threatening anomalies should be the province of the parents. (Koogler T. K., B. S. Wilson, L. F. Ross. 2003. "Lethal Language, Lethal Decisions." *Hastings Center Report 33*(4): 37-41.)

A study demonstrating that providing neonatal intensive care for babies with Trisomy 18 improves their survival (although survival at one year was only 25 percent) was conducted by Kosho et al. (Kosho T., T. Nakamura, H. Kawame et al. 2006. "Neonatal Management of Trisomy 18: Clinical Details of Twenty-four Patients Receiving Intensive

Treatment." *American Journal of Medical Genetics 140A*(9): 937-944.)

Another study showed that medical providers' opinions regarding whether Trisomy 18 is a lethal anomaly are shifting. Increasingly, providers are allowing parental autonomy to dictate resuscitation decisions regarding babies with Trisomy 18, whereas previously resuscitation in the delivery room was not offered to these infants. (McGraw M. P. and J. M. Perlman. 2008. "Attitudes of Neonatologists Toward Delivery Room Management of Confirmed Trisomy 18: Potential Factors Influencing a Changing Dynamic." *Pediatrics 121*(6): 1106-1110.)

Reliable internet resources for people seeking more information about Trisomy 18 include: Support Organization for Trisomy 18, 13 and Related Disorders (SOFT), at www.trisomy.org, and Trisomy 18 Foundation, at www.trisomy18.org.

When talking with Grace's parents about her diagnosis and prognosis, my challenge was to present a realistic picture of what lay ahead while not decimating all their hopes for her future. Jerome Groopman quotes Oliver Wendell Holmes' admonition to "beware how you take away hope from another human being" in his book *The Anatomy of Hope* (2004. New York: Pocket Books). Groopman also discusses how having hope under extreme circumstances may be an act of defiance that allows a person to be in control of his or her situation, including holding out for a miracle even when it seems most unlikely to occur.

My focus in talking with parents who have a baby who will likely be severely disabled or who may die is to focus on making their time with their baby "quality time." I encourage parents to love and bond with their baby as much as possible, and in all cases I address the guilt parents (especially mothers) might feel for having given birth to a baby who is less than perfect by usual standards. I encourage both parents to understand that the mother has done nothing "wrong" to cause her baby's condition.

Kangaroo care, or skin-to-skin contact between parent and baby, has been widely adopted in most NICUs in the United States. This low-tech therapy was first implemented in Third World countries (including Bogota, Columbia) to improve survival in the absence of high-tech medical equipment, with the thought that skin-to-skin contact would help maintain the baby's temperature and facilitate breastfeeding. Kangaroo care was found to decrease infant death from 70 to 30 percent, and it has since been used around the world to improve mother-infant bonding as well as to improve the health of babies. (Charpak N., J. Ruiz, J. Zupan et al. 2005. "Kangaroo Mother Care: 25 Years After." *Acta Paediatrica 94*(5): 514-522. *See* also Browne J. 2004. "Early Relationship Environments: Physiology of Skin-to-Skin Contact for Parents and Their Preterm Infants." *Clinics in Perinatology 31*(2): 287-298.)

Joey's distress reminded me that fathers, in particular, feel a lack of control when their infants are ill in the NICU, and suggestions for activities to help fathers regain their sense of control can be found in a paper by Arockiasamy. (Arockiasamy V., L. Holsti, S. Albersheim. 2008. "Fathers' Experiences in the Neonatal Intensive Care Unit: A Search for Control." *Pediatrics 121*(2): e215-222.)

The importance of male nurses in the NICU, such as the one depicted in this story, is often overlooked. The very vital role of male nurses in the NICU is explored in a paper by Peterson. His contention is that male nurses are singularly able to help NICU fathers cope with their situation in ways that are healthy and successful. (Peterson S. W. 2008. "Father Surrogate: Historical Perceptions and Perspectives of Men in Nursing and Their Relationship with Fathers in the NICU." *Neonatal Network 27*(4): 239-243.)

The Ronald McDonald House is a home-away-from home for parents coping with the hospitalization of their sick child. From its inception in 1974 in Philadelphia, the Ronald McDonald House Charities have established 300 houses in cities around the country. This invaluable resource provides a place for parents to stay close to the hospital, and a supportive group environment for families at little-or-no cost to them. Their presence on the web is located at www.rmhc.org.

Chapter 13

Rendezvous in the Emergency Room: Devon Winston

I reached for the telephone as it jangled in the darkness, drank in the message in a state of minimal consciousness, and replaced the receiver in its cradle, all without turning on the call room light. My deliciously deep sleep was over for the night. I had just learned that a baby who had been born at home thirty minutes earlier at twenty-four weeks gestation was being rushed to the hospital by ambulance. After years of taking calls from home, I was actually happy I was now doing "in-house" call so I could respond immediately to give the baby his or her best chance for survival.

I got to the emergency room five minutes later, a split second before an emergency medical technician charged in with a bundled up extra-large man's grey sweatshirt. He placed it in a small heap in front of me, and then backed out of the room. I unwrapped the sweatshirt to find a little baby, one that could fit in the palm of my hand. He was lifeless but not yet purple or cold. Soon, a nurse was delicately performing chest compressions, using two fingers to apply pressure to his robin-sized chest to a depth of half an inch twice every second.

I had at most twenty minutes to bring this baby back to life. That was a generous estimate considering how many minutes had already passed since his mother involuntarily expelled him while vomiting on the floor of her bathroom.

My charge nurse, Cathy, and a respiratory therapist came with me from the NICU to the emergency room. The trauma room where we met our miniscule patient was already full of emergency room staff, none of whom I had ever seen before. Each shouted frantically to the next to get a different piece of equipment. In spite of the din surrounding us, I started quietly issuing commands to Cathy and then to the other nurses in the room. "Let's take the baby's temperature and warm him up. I need a laryngoscope and the smallest size of endotracheal tube. Someone draw up some epinephrine."

As Cathy rifled through the drawers of the emergency room crash cart looking for the supplies I demanded, the emergency room nurses shrank into the background of the room, more than happy to cede their roles to the NICU team. Two-hundred-fifty pound adults with heart attacks were their daily fare, but a micro-premie, a baby with a palm of a hand as big as a dime, was nothing they knew anything about.

While I prepared to intubate the baby, an emergency room nurse asked me, "Doctor, what's your name?" She was the self-appointed scribe for the Code Pink, and she would record every detail for later scrutiny in the monthly Morbidity and Mortality meetings of both the emergency room and the NICU. If I made any mistakes, they would be documented, analyzed against national performance standards, and brought to my attention for correction in the future.

"Hall," I replied, never taking my eyes off the baby, whose heart rate was dangerously low at fifty beats per minute. "H-A-L-L."

Out of the corner of my eye I noticed several teary-eyed people huddled together, looking through the glass door of the trauma room. I reached over and yanked the curtain closed.

The baby's head was no bigger than a lemon, and his tiny mouth barely admitted my laryngoscope. The light on the end of the instrument illuminated his white vocal cords and thankfully I was able to slip the breathing tube into his windpipe on the first try. The respiratory therapist inflated his lungs and immediately his chest began to rise. His heart rate did not respond, however. "Let me have some epi," I said, guessing the dose based on his estimated weight of just over a pound.

Cathy handed me the syringe and I squirted the medicine down the tube going into his lungs. I quickly announced that the epi was in, so it could be duly recorded with a time stamp. Meanwhile, I scooped the baby off the sweatshirt brought from home, and Cathy took his temperature. When she announced it was 94.5 degrees, I scrunched a pink and blue striped cotton hat on his hairless head to warm him up, noticing as I did tiny eyelids as tightly sealed as those of a newborn kitten. The minutes ticked away as we worked on him, and soon five of them had passed; it was time for another dose of epi.

I repeated the dose, but the baby still did not move. His little popsicle-stick legs lay limply in front of him. A nurse I did not know continued CPR, but I could not have picked her face out of a police lineup if my life depended on it.

I opened my procedure tray and Cathy struggled to keep up with my demands for instruments while I fought to stay one step ahead of her. I dabbed a bit of antiseptic solution around the base of the baby's umbilical cord, tied it tightly, and sliced the cord off with a scalpel. I bent over the baby with two tiny sets of forceps, one in each hand, identifying the vessels in the cord marked by pinpoints of dark blood. My luck held. Within a minute, I successfully snaked tiny catheters into both the umbilical vein and artery, and asked for another dose of epinephrine.

This time I infused the drug through the IV line and seconds later, the baby's heart rate was more than 100. I ordered CPR to stop. Next, we poured a dose of surfactant down his breathing tube, and the white milky liquid slithered into his lungs allowing for better inflation of his air sacs, the alveoli. A few minutes later, the baby started to breathe on his own. This was a major milestone. We brought the baby back to life within twenty minutes of his arrival in the emergency room, but his NICU journey was just beginning.

I exhaled deeply, and wiped the sweat from under my bangs. Cathy and I secured all the IV lines, hooked the baby up to all the monitors, and bundled him into our transport isolette to make the trip upstairs to the NICU. Over the next hour, I checked his x-rays and blood tests, wrote orders for IV fluids and medications, and wrote my note admitting him to the NICU in the electronic medical record.

As I trudged up the stairwell to the postpartum floor to inform the baby's mother of her newborn's status, I reflected on the fact that at the beginning of my career, I would never even have been called to resuscitate a baby born so early. Yet now, I could not remember the last time when a parent had not desired and even demanded that her extremely preterm baby—no matter how small—be given every possible chance to survive. I wondered what this baby's mother would be like. Chances were she was a teenager who had not yet told anyone she was pregnant, or a drug addict who lived on the streets. Such stereotypes often seemed to fit women whose babies enter the world so precariously and without warning.

The woman I found lying in bed did not match the pictures I had conjured up at all. She was nearly forty-years-old, and her beautifully manicured fingernails gave the impression that she was elegantly dressed even though she wore a standard-issue hospital gown. Immediately my sentiments changed, from wanting to judge the mother for not taking care of herself and her pregnancy to wanting to judge the doctor who perhaps missed the signs of her impending premature labor.

My tiny patient's brand new mother sat expressionless in her bed, eyes focused on the wall straight ahead of her. She answered my questions in a monotone, her words quiet and measured. I couldn't read her face: Was she furious? Embarrassed? Humiliated? Profoundly sad? Scared? Or just in shock over the evening's events?

Her extra-large husband sat on the couch next to her bed wearing a T-shirt, sweatpants, and high-topped sneakers. He bantered with me, obviously enjoying his celebratory mood over having a son, Devon Winston, Junior. His wife Diana summoned him when she felt herself extrude the baby, and he proudly recounted the story of how he caught the baby, and how it cried and wriggled around as he held it.

I reassured them both that their baby was alive, and that I was doing everything I could to take good care of him. I then told them about Devon's chances for survival—about 40-50 percent at best—followed by an abbreviated list of the possible complications he could encounter. The biggest threat facing any extremely premature baby is intraventricular hemorrhaging, or bleeding into the spaces of the brain that produce cerebrospinal fluid. The after-effects of such bleeding can be life-changing. I mentioned this in my list of complications but figured we would have enough time to delve into this unpleasant topic in the future if we had to.

I doubted whether much of what I said was getting through the wall the mom already had constructed around herself, and Dad seemed too giddy to take much in. I knew I would need to repeat my words in the coming days to make them fully aware of what life might be like in both the short-term and the long-term with their extremely premature baby. The one sentiment I tried to make perfectly clear to both parents was that my team and I would share the journey with them, no matter where it led.

After talking with the parents, I arrived back at my call room door, exhausted. I fell into bed and slept fitfully from 5:00 a.m. until my 6:30 alarm went off, and then forced myself out of bed once again so I could make rounds before my partners arrived at 8:00. We finished sign-out rounds quickly enough given the amount of new information I had to hand off to the oncoming crew, and when we were done, I headed straight home. Now that I had made certain that Devon got a second chance at life, I wondered what was next for him?

***

Three days after Devon entered the world and the NICU, he suffered an intraventricular hemorrhage—a very large one. An ultrasound of his brain showed blood filling both of his ventricles, stretching them beyond their normal size. This was certainly bad news. Devon might be afflicted with cerebral palsy as he grew. He might never be able to walk or talk or see or hear. Then again, he might be one of the ones who did well. There was absolutely no way to know. Would he bring sorrow or joy into his parents' lives?

In spite of the bleeding in his brain, Devon was stable in every other way. He did have many more days—even months—ahead of him in the NICU just to get big enough to be able to go home. And he was still at risk for any one of a number of life-threatening complications. Since Devon's chances for "intact survival" (in other words, survival without some disability) were now very slim, I felt I should present Devon's parents with the option of discontinuing life support.

I broached the subject with them gently and tentatively. Mom still appeared stoic and guarded, sitting by Devon's isolette with her hand through the open porthole door. She cupped one hand over his head and gently rested the other over his belly as I spoke.

"We got the results of Devon's head ultrasound. Unfortunately, he has some bleeding in his brain." There was no way to downplay the news, and I did not think it would be fair to try to minimize what had happened to Devon.

I continued on, telling Diana that Devon had a 50-50 chance of getting better or developing hydrocephalus. If his ventricles continued enlarging, his normal brain tissue would be compressed and damaged by the pressure.

I paused to let the parents take in this information. Diana tilted her head to the side and pursed her lips as she studied her baby's tiny frame in the dark isolette. A brightly patterned baby blanket draped over the top of the isolette blocked out light from the room, and Devon's eyes were further covered to minimize the light reaching them. Tucked into a little nest, a soft mini-bed with a two-inch bumper all around it, his frame was confined as though he were still in the womb. Just then Devon stretched one leg out, dangling his inch-long foot just over the bottom edge of his nest. Neither parent said anything. Diana avoided eye contact with me, and Devon, Sr. had a blank stare.

"You know, we are not obligated to continue life support for Devon. If we think…or you think…that his outcome is going to be really bad…if that's not something you want…we can always reevaluate…"

Diana did not look up but she did answer in clearly measured tones. "No, we'll take whatever we get. What happens, happens. It's okay. We'll deal with it."

"Umm-hmm," added Dad quietly. "Umm-hmm."

***

Over the next several months, Devon grew nicely, got off the ventilator and off IV fluids, and required very few medications.

Diana evolved into quite a doting mother. Devon was her first child. She was one of those mothers who called every three hours throughout the night—each and every night—when she got up to pump breast milk. She was at Devon's bedside nearly all day, every day. I frequently popped my head through the door or went in and sat down to chat with her. With time, she warmed up and began smiling more frequently.

Devon's room started to look very lived-in. Crayon drawings from his five-year-old cousin adorned the wall. Cards with congratulatory wishes filled his bedside table. Pictures of his Mom and Dad hung on his bulletin board, and the outside door to his room was elaborately decorated so that it was easily recognizable as his and his alone, a virtual shrine to this new life. It was clear to all that Devon was very much a treasured little boy.

We continued to repeat ultrasounds of Devon's brain regularly and to measure his head circumference weekly. One day I stopped in to tell Diana the results of Devon's most recent ultrasound. I had been worried about what it might show, because the soft spot on his head, the anterior fontanelle, could now be easily felt raising up a bit over the contour of his skull; his head circumference was also growing at a faster pace than expected. These findings suggested he had developed hydrocephalus that finally needed treatment, and this was indeed true.

Diana had just given Devon a bath, and the room still smelled like baby lotion, a smell which evoked fond memories of when I was a young mother and my own two girls were babies. Devon was smartly dressed in a little blue sleeper with a puppy dog pattern, and his hair was neatly smoothed down. His big eyes shone grey-blue, and as Diana held him in her arms, I thought about how he was starting to look like a real baby, a baby who had most definitely come to life. I had been feeling better and better about his chances for normal development.

"What a gorgeous young man you have there!" I told Diana. Then, directing my comments to the baby, "You are getting so big, aren't you Devon?"

The baby gurgled contentedly.

"It's hard to believe how much he's grown, isn't it?" I asked.

"Sure is," Diana replied proudly.

"Well, the time has come for him to get a shunt in his brain, to drain the extra fluid that's been building up; this is the recommended treatment for his hydrocephalus. It's a surgical procedure…"

Diana did not skip a beat. "Okay," she said, pinching her baby's cheek lightly. "We'll just do what the doctor says, won't we?"

"He's on the schedule for Thursday," I told her. "The neurosurgeon will meet with you to go over all the risks associated with surgery. Once the surgery is out of the way, Devon will be ready to go home soon. Enjoy your visit."

Devon's surgery came and went without a hitch. He made rapid progress toward discharge, surprising everyone when he took to the bottle then the breast eagerly; he gained weight day after day. And finally, on the 106th day of his life, he got to go home.

First came the hospital baby pictures, for which Diana dressed Devon in a blue baseball uniform complete with little baseball cap. Next was the parade around the NICU, with Diana carrying Devon around to say goodbye to all the nurses and doctors who cared for him over the past three and a half months. As Diana bundled him into his car seat that afternoon, with her husband at her side, she radiated happiness.

It was afternoons like this that made working in the NICU such a rewarding experience. Although Devon might ultimately experience developmental delays or be diagnosed with cerebral palsy, he could also develop normally; only time would tell. I smiled as Devon and his parents left through the NICU's double doors, Dad pushing Mom in a wheelchair with Devon in his car seat on her lap. Devon had started out his journey in life at home with both parents, and now he was returning there with them, just as they had hoped he would be able to.

About a month later, Diana and Devon, Sr. brought Devon, Jr. back to the NICU just to show him off. They had an appointment in the area, and stopped in to say hi. "We miss you guys," Diana said. "You became our family."

Several nurses came with me out of the NICU to see our little graduate. We took turns fawning over him, passing him around and exclaiming about how great he looked, how much weight he had gained, and how happy he and both parents seemed.

"Yes, we are really, really happy," said Diana. "Everything's going great."

A little over a month later, word spread quickly around the NICU that Devon had died suddenly and unexpectedly. Diana found him in his bed, not breathing—most likely from Sudden Infant Death Syndrome—and an ambulance brought him into the emergency room. Only this time, he could not be resuscitated. Thankfully, I was not the doctor on call when he was brought in. It was a lot easier to resuscitate the anonymous baby I had never met before, on his first trip to the emergency room, than to consider resuscitating this baby I had grown quite fond of over the past number of months.

Some people always cry at weddings. I always cry at funerals. Devon's memorial service was the first service I ever attended of any of my patients who passed away. I suppose what kept me from attending patients' funerals in the past was that I was afraid—as "the doctor"—to cry in front of a lot of people. Even after twenty years as a neonatologist, I still shed tears with nearly every death of a baby in my care, but only in front of the parents and the few nurses who were involved. I am sure my feelings about showing emotion in public when I am identified as a physician (instead of as a family member or friend) goes back to an incident that happened while I was a medical student.

***

I had entered medical school fresh from my previous position as a social worker. My social work training encouraged me to demonstrate empathy, and this was my natural tendency anyway. One day as a medical student on rounds with the surgical team, a teenage girl had to have the dressing in a surgical wound changed by her doctor.

When her incision could not be sewn shut in the operating room, the surgeon packed gauze in the space between the two edges of skin. The soiled gauze had to be pulled out daily, and fresh, clean gauze placed back on the raw tissues. The wound was supposed to gradually close from the bottom up toward the skin. I knew the dressing change would be painful, and because this young girl looked scared without any of her family around, I instinctively sat down on the bed and reached for her hand to hold.

In front of the whole rounding group of nurses, doctors and other students, the chief surgeon called out to me, "You. Get up. That is not your role anymore. You are to be *professional* about this."

When I complied with his demands, he stepped in front of me and completed the procedure on the girl as tears streamed down her face. Although the attending surgeon's charge to me was clear—I was to transform myself immediately from bleeding heart social worker to starched white coat physician—when I walked out of that patient's room, I did not think I wanted to be that type of doctor. But neither have I ever forgotten the surgeon's admonition to have a professional mien. The tug between these two opposites has been with me throughout my career.

***

I wondered how I would handle my emotions the day of Devon's funeral. Would I wear my heart on my sleeve or keep it safely hidden behind my best professional façade?

I drove up to the funeral home nervously. As soon as I entered the building and saw Diana in the foyer greeting people, I started crying—almost sobbing—and could not stop. We hugged each other as I whispered to her, "It's just not fair."

"It's okay. It's gonna be okay," she whispered back, squeezing me tight.

"You were such a fantastic mother," I said through my tears.

"Thank you, Dr. Hall," she said softly. Her agony was palpable. "Now go up and look at Devon." She beckoned toward the front of the room where the wake was being held.

I let go of her and approached the front of the room, passing friends of the family and relatives, and a few of the NICU nurses who were sitting in pews on either side. I came to his miniature coffin. Devon was once again decked out, this time in a tiny suit with a white shirt and black tie. His cheeks were surprisingly pink, and his little hands were folded across his chest. A rosary had been slipped in between them. His coffin was lined with white satin, and a stuffed puppy dog sat near his chest. A big spray of yellow roses bloomed tentatively off to one side. The whole scene was beautiful and peaceful.

I turned around to leave and hugged Diana again, both of us still crying. I stepped outside and the cold wind stung my face and froze my tears. They were tears for Devon and his parents, and for all the babies I lost during my years of practice. Seeing families suffer the loss of a child never gets any easier.

***

Notes:

I doubt Devon would have survived at birth if I, or another neonatologist, had not been immediately available to take care of him upon his arrival in the emergency room. Over the years, neonatologists—especially those in large, busy NICUs—have increasingly moved toward taking "in-house" call instead of being on beeper call from home, to provide the best care in a timely fashion to our tiny patients. Interestingly, studies have documented that most very low birth weight infants are born during evening and night hours; as many as 60 percent of NICU admissions take place at night. It has also been shown that sick infants face an increased risk of dying if admitted to the NICU at night, particularly if experienced in-house physicians are not available. In-house attending physicians contributed to improved survival of infants in the NICU between 1989 and 1995. (Gould J. B., C. Qin, G. Chavez. 2005. "Time of Birth and the Risk of Neonatal Death." *Obstetrics and Gynecology 106*(2): 352-358. *See* also Lee S. K., D. S. Lee, W. L. Andrews et al. 2003. "Higher Mortality Rates among Inborn Infants Admitted to Neonatal Intensive Care Units at Night." *Journal of Pediatrics 143*(5): 592-597. *See* also Stephansson O., P. W. Dickman, A. L. Johansson et al. 2003. "Time of Birth and Risk of Intrapartum and Early Neonatal Death." *Epidemiology 14*(2): 218-222. *See* also Richardson D. Y., J. E. Gray, S. L. Gortmaker et al. 1998. "Declining Severity Adjusted Mortality: Evidence of Improving Neonatal Intensive Care." *Pediatrics 102*(4 Pt 1): 893-899.)

When Devon experienced a significant intraventricular hemorrhage, I felt it was imperative to collaborate with his parents on making a decision regarding continuation of his treatment. Previously, doctors often acted in a "paternalistic" mode and unilaterally made life-and-death decisions that should rightfully be shared with the patient or, as in this case, the patient's family. The differences between parents' and physicians' opinions about quality of life are explored in an article by medical ethicist Norman Fost. (Fost N. 1999. "Decisions Regarding Treatment of Seriously Ill Newborns." *Journal of the American Medical Association 281*(21): 2041-2043.) A study of attitudinal differences toward disabilities in former preterm infants showed that parents of preterm infants were more likely to want to save their infants in spite of the risk the infant might be disabled than health care workers were. Implications for counseling parents who have given birth to at-risk preterm infants are highlighted. (Lam

H. S., S. P. S. Wong, F. Y. B. Liu et al. 2009. "Attitudes Toward Neonatal Intensive Care Treatment of Preterm Infants With a High Risk of Developing Long-Term Disabilities." *Pediatrics 123*(6): 1501-1515.)

While both severe intraventricular hemorrhage and post-hemorrhagic hydrocephalus are risk factors for long-term developmental problems, as many as 15-35 percent of affected infants may develop normally or have only a mild developmental delay. Outcome tends to be worse, however, if an infant requires placement of a ventriculoperitoneal shunt. (Resch B., A. Gerdermann et al. 1996. "Neurodevelopmental Outcome of Hydrocephalus Following Intra-/Periventricular Hemorrhage in Preterm Infants: Short- and Long-Term Results." *Child's Nervous System 12*(1): 27-33.)

This Lovely Life, by Vicki Forman (2009. New York: Mariner Books), is a beautiful and touching memoir lovingly written by a parent of twenty-three-week gestation twins who were cared for in a Neonatal Intensive Care Unit. The author writes of the disagreement she had with her twins' medical team, and how doctors' independent decisions left her and her husband feeling they had no say in what happened with their babies. Forman describes the agony but also the joy she faced with the birth, subsequent care, and ultimately the death of her extremely premature babies.

A moving account of a family's experience raising a premature infant who suffered a massive intraventricular hemorrhage is Marianne Leone's book (*Knowing Jesse: A Mother's Story of Grief, Grace, and Everyday Bliss.* 2010. New York: Simon and Schuster). Although Jesse ultimately developed disabling cerebral palsy and was never verbal, he was highly intelligent and had a vibrant, engaging personality. Each of these mothers' memoirs illustrates the fortitude of the human spirit, as both sets of parents not only coped with unimaginable stress and grief but found unrivaled happiness and love in the experience of parenting their children who were born premature.

Sudden Infant Death Syndrome, or SIDS, is the sudden death of an infant less than one year-old that remains unexplained after an autopsy, death-scene investigation, and case history review. It is the leading cause of death in infants from one month to one year of age. SIDS occurs more commonly in boys than in girls, and the peak incidence is at five months of age. Prematurity and low birth weight are two of the most important risk factors for SIDS, and the risk of SIDS may continue longer in premature than in term infants. (Halloran D. R. and G. R. Alexander. 2006. "Preterm Delivery and Age of SIDS Death." *Annals of Epidemiology 16*(8): 600-606.)

Prematurity is likely a risk factor for SIDS because the breathing control center is immature in premature infants. There are many steps which can be taken to reduce the risk of SIDS. Mothers should not smoke during or after pregnancy. A baby should be placed on his or her back instead of stomach to sleep. Care should be taken to not overheat a baby during sleep or breastfeeding. Parents should ensure their baby's sleep environment is safe by eliminating pillows and soft bedding in which the infant could suffocate. (*See* the American SIDS Institute at www.sids.org) and the SIDS Network at http://sids-network.org.)

Chapter 14

A "Normal" Premie: Elizabeth Markham

Kate Markham got the shock of her life when her doctor told her she was five centimeters dilated. After a week of feeling miserable, she had finally gotten in to see her doctor at twenty-eight weeks of pregnancy. Within an hour, she found herself loaded into a helicopter to be flown from the college town where she was a graduate student to our hospital. Upon arrival, her baby, who was breech (bottom down), was delivered by C-section. It was Labor Day weekend, and Kate's due date was Thanksgiving.

Doug Markham was at his wife's side during her delivery, and he accompanied me as I brought his two-pound seven-ounce daughter from the delivery room into the NICU. Anxious to see her and learn that everything was okay, he looked crestfallen when I asked him to step out of Elizabeth's room so I could place a catheter into her umbilical artery. This was a sterile procedure, I explained, in which only gowned medical personnel could participate.

An hour later, I found him in the waiting room and invited him back to his baby's bedside. Taller than myself, with neatly trimmed blonde hair and a ready smile, Doug stood up and accompanied me into his baby's room. His calm blue eyes quickly gravitated to his brand new baby in her isolette, but they also scanned each piece of equipment in the room as the bedside nurse carefully explained the purpose of every item.

Several hours later, Kate was wheeled into Elizabeth's room, her broad, ungainly hospital bed just barely squeezing through the doors. Brushing a wisp of her short hair out of her face, she leaned forward so she could get a better view of her little one. "Oh, look at her Doug…she's so tiny." Tears bubbled up in Kate's eyes, and I recognized in her face the guilt many mothers of premature infants instantly feel. What did I do wrong to cause this, women in her situation invariably wonder. In Kate's case, as is often true, there would be no answer to that question.

Kate continued examining her baby with her hand extended through the isolette's door, her fingers just touching the palm of the baby's hand. "Her eyes are both still sealed shut, and those bruises all over her head and face…poor dear! I've never seen skin so paper thin and sticky. Is that normal? And look Doug, her ears are so thin they're plastered to her head."

"She's a little more bruised than usual from delivery," I said, "but other than that she looks just like she should for her gestational age. This is what a premie looks like. Different than what you expected, huh?"

"I've heard about premature babies," Kate replied, "but I've never seen one up close. She looks so fragile." Kate looked a bit fragile herself, and shaken by her experience.

Kate only had time to receive one shot of steroids to help her baby's lungs mature before her baby was born, and Elizabeth needed the help of a ventilator for the first few days. However, soon we were able to take her off the ventilator and place her on nasal cannula oxygen. Her parents celebrated this small victory; now they could hear Elizabeth's weak cry for the first time, but only when they put their ears up close to the isolette's doors.

Another first took place when Elizabeth was three-days-old: her parents held her for a total of six minutes. That was not nearly enough. Because the baby had to remain in her isolette to stay warm, Kate could not scoop Elizabeth up in her arms whenever she wanted to.

"I get so frustrated when I hear her little cries and I can't pick her up," Kate remarked to me several days later.

As Elizabeth became more stable, her parents were soon able to take their baby out of her temperature-controlled environment to spend longer periods of time with her nestled skin-to-skin in kangaroo care. Kate, in particular, reveled in these sessions, as they were the only times she really felt as though she had control over what happened to her baby. Although she was intimately involved in Elizabeth's care on a daily basis, taking her temperature, and changing her diaper, when possible, Kate still had to defer to the nurses when Elizabeth had an episode of apnea (a pause in her breathing), or bradycardia (a drop in her heart rate). Sometimes the spells lasted long enough that Elizabeth's face turned blue, and her monitor alarmed for a desat (desaturation, a low oxygen level). Concern clouded Kate's face at these times, and sometimes she cried. Kate's sentiments mirrored those of nearly all NICU mothers; she could not wait for the day when her baby's "spells" ceased and she would no longer have to worry about them.

The university where Kate and Doug were both students was an hour's drive from the hospital, and so they chose to move in to the Ronald McDonald house near the hospital and make it their home for the duration of their daughter's hospital stay. They made arrangements with their professors to cyber-commute. Dressed casually in jeans—the uniform of students everywhere—the young parents began toting their laptop computers into Elizabeth's private room. While the baby slept, which was nearly all the time, they did homework. Each of them appeared to have the task orientation and work ethic necessary to be a successful graduate student. But now they had a baby in the NICU to consider.

Both parents spent considerable time detailing Elizabeth's progress on the blog they wrote for friends and family. Kate wrote: "Elizabeth gained 10 grams today. That's not bad." "Little Elizabeth tolerated her feedings over the night: no spitting up, no residuals, and regular stools." "Things are looking up for our daughter. She only had 15 desats over the night and no bradys. Praise God." "Elizabeth's blood transfusion is complete. For the rest of her life, she'll have to answer yes on all of those medical and insurance forms that ask if she's ever had a blood transfusion." Since Doug was an engineering student, his blogs featured "tech spotlights," detailing his fascination with all the equipment being used in Elizabeth's care; he liked to speculate on the design and inner workings of the machines.

I had seen Kate and Doug leaving Elizabeth's room late at night, and once again I had seen them first thing in the morning as I made my rounds through the NICU after my night on call. It was clear they did not want to let too many hours elapse when at least one of them was not present at Elizabeth's bedside. Kate seemed more tired with each passing day, until finally one of our seasoned nurses sat down and had a talk with her.

"Are you taking care of yourself?" she asked.

With that, Kate burst into tears. "I'm having trouble getting my life back into a routine," she said. "Just trying to balance school, family, pumping breast milk for the baby, and getting sleep is so hard…"

"You know when you go on a plane flight, and they tell you that in case of an emergency you need to put on the oxygen mask first, so you can take care of your child? That's what being in the NICU is like. You have to take care of yourself, so that you'll be better able to take care of your baby. You look like you need more rest. You don't have to be here so many hours of the day," the nurse continued. "That's what we're here for. We'll take care of your precious baby."

When the nurse recounted this exchange to me, I was glad she had offered her advice to Kate. It matched my belief that as a health care team, we had to be as concerned with how the parents were adapting to life in the NICU as we were with how their babies were progressing.

Kate and Doug tried to take the nurse's advice and expand their life beyond their schoolwork, parenthood, and the NICU, by going on a date one night. However, they came back and reported to the nurse that they had spent the whole evening talking over dinner about their baby.

They did become part of the community of parents at the Ronald McDonald House whose babies were in the NICU, and as the days stretched out into weeks and months, they traded stories, triumphs, and setbacks with the other parents they befriended.

One day, Carol, who was the nurse practitioner taking care of Elizabeth, and I walked into Elizabeth's room, after foaming our hands with alcohol, to complete our daily exams.

"Hey, pretty girl," I said to the baby, as I put her through the paces of her exam. "How are you today?" She was wearing a sleeper outfit for the first time. A gold crown, with "Princess" written in pink script beneath it, expressed Elizabeth's position in their family perfectly.

"She's graduated to real clothes finally!" Kate's excitement was palpable and her eyes sparkled. "And she's outgrown the extra small premie diapers and is now wearing the regular premie diapers."

"Terrific. She's gaining weight well. She must like your milk," said Carol.

"At least that's one thing I can do for her," Kate replied, smiling.

"How are things going otherwise?" I asked Kate.

"Well," she replied, her tone becoming more serious, "I've been feeling a bit down lately, wondering why this had to happen to us, why our life had to take this detour. You know, we're the kind of people who have a plan, and we carry out the plan. This premie thing wasn't a part of our plan; it must have been part of God's plan for us. I think he's trying to teach us patience and gratitude.

"A couple of nights ago," she continued, "I talked to Shauna, who has the twenty-three-weeker in the NICU right now. Boy, after talking to her I feel really grateful that I made it all the way to twenty-eight weeks with Elizabeth. When Elizabeth's had a good day, I feel guilty telling Shauna about it, in case her baby's had a bad day."

"Yes, twenty-three-weekers are a handful," I said. "Problem after problem. Lucky for Shauna her baby is doing well right now. But it's been tough for all of them: the baby, Shauna and her husband."

"Yeah, she told me. After talking to her, I was able to put our situation in perspective a bit more. I'm just happy Elizabeth is doing well. For a while there, I was going back and forth between hope and despair nearly every day."

I suspected Kate had been going through the "baby blues." I thought back over Elizabeth's stay to that point in the NICU. Nothing unusual or untoward had happened; she had not encountered any major complications. As I wondered what the source of Kate's despair might be, I reminded myself that what seems like a "normal" course for a premature baby to the medical team is anything but that to the baby's parents; it is all "abnormal" to them. No matter how good a baby looks to the doctors at the time of admission, the first question in the parents' mind, and frequently on their lips, is invariably: "Will she be okay? Will she survive?"

The NICU mother's experience begins with fear, when she suffers the trauma of getting the news that her baby must be delivered early—usually urgently—because of some problem. Her feelings progress to guilt, as she considers that she somehow failed as a woman (why couldn't I give birth at the usual time, like everyone else? she wonders) and also failed her baby. From there, she grieves the loss of her dream of giving birth to the quintessential happy, healthy Gerber Baby. Her emotional journey only becomes more difficult as she struggles with the separation created between her and her child by virtue of the baby needing intensive medical observation, and the lack of control that it imposes on her. In addition to all this, new mothers have to contend with changes in their hormone levels that normally occur after giving birth.

Fathers go through their own adaptations to NICU parenthood, and many feel challenged to show they are somehow maintaining control of the family's new situation. The struggle can get to them, too.

Late one afternoon, I dropped into Elizabeth's room to find Kate and Doug giggling.

"What's so funny, guys?" I asked. "Let me in on the joke!"

Kate said, "Doug's been sitting in the comfortable chair over there, trying to take a nap for the past hour. But stuff kept happening. First Elizabeth's monitor alarm went off. Then, the nurse came in to take her vitals. Next, Elizabeth cried because her diaper was wet and we had to get up and change it. Then, it was time for her feeding. Finally Doug said, 'It just doesn't look like it's working out for me to take a nap.' In the sweetest voice I could muster, I told him, 'Welcome to parenthood!'"

Doug grinned sheepishly, and then opened his eyes widely so he did not appear so sleepy. I guessed that taking shifts at Elizabeth's bedside while working hard to complete all his assignments toward his degree was taking its toll on him, too.

"Yup, this is Parenthood 101," I said. "Soon you'll be ready for Parenthood 202. That starts when you take your baby home with you. Are you ready?"

"Yes, we're going back home for a baby shower this weekend, and we'll make sure everything's in place at our apartment. We can't wait!" Kate's enthusiasm was infectious.

When Kate and Doug returned from their baby shower, Carol and I held a discharge planning conference with them. We reviewed Elizabeth's NICU course to make sure they understood the results of all the tests she had undergone, and then turned our discussions toward her future. We gave them our usual warning not to take their baby out into crowds for the first several months after discharge, particularly since we were now entering the winter cold virus season. Premature babies' underdeveloped immune systems leave them vulnerable to infections.

"Wow, we're really social people so staying inside with the baby and not taking her out to visit our friends, to church…that will be hard for us," said Elizabeth. "I've been looking forward to the time when I can show her off." The corners of her mouth drew into a frown.

"It's for her safety," Carol said gently. "We also recommend she get Synagis, the vaccination to prevent RSV infection."

"Okay. I know all about Synagis from the parenting class we took. So, when does she get to go home?" Kate asked. "Our little wiggle worm *did* earn the triple crown over the last twenty-four hours. She's kept her temperature up outside of her isolette, she's taken all of her feedings, and even nursed once really well, and her breathing has been good…no apnea or brady episodes."

Doug smiled broadly at his daughter's accomplishments.

"Super!" Carol said. "We'll get your training arranged for her home monitor. The monitor will be just another pair of eyes and ears for you at home, since it seems like Elizabeth hasn't completely outgrown her apnea. It will alert you if she has any spells, and you'll be able to intervene and help her if she does. She probably won't have to use it for too long, maybe a month or two at the most."

"That sounds great. I know we'll sleep better at night having the security of the monitor. Otherwise, I probably would be obsessing over every breath she takes." Kate looked at Doug, who nodded his head in agreement.

"Well, maybe you won't sleep better," I teased, "if she has lots of alarms."

We concluded our conference, and the next day the woman who came to do the monitor training told Kate and Doug that their baby would probably get to go home in the next day or two, since monitor training was usually the last thing to take place before discharge. This sent them into "freakout mode," as Kate later described it to Carol, as they scurried to ready themselves for the next stage of their lives together, heads spinning.

Disappointment set in, though, when Elizabeth's discharge was delayed several more days because of her sluggish feeding. I saw that Kate was feeling let down when I stopped in to speak with her.

"Sorry Elizabeth has to stay a few more days," I explained, "but we don't want to discharge her until she's a reasonably vigorous feeder. Right now she's still inconsistent. We don't want you to get her home and have to worry about whether she'll finish her feeding."

"I know." Kate let out a sigh of exasperation. "Patience, that's my mantra. One day at a time. It's just that we'd gotten our hopes up so high…"

Finally, seventy-one days after Elizabeth's birth, and two weeks before her due date, Kate and Doug hugged Carol first, and then me, and then took Elizabeth, their "normal" premie, home.

***

Three months later, Kate and Doug brought Elizabeth to her follow-up clinic appointment on a day when several inches of crusty snow covered the roads and sidewalks. At six-months-old, Elizabeth was smiling, pushing up well when placed on her tummy, making some cooing sounds: everything a three-month-old baby should be doing, which was appropriate, since she had been born three months early. And she was adorable, with her wisps of blonde hair and gorgeous blue eyes, although her weight was at the lower end of the growth chart.

"So how has Parenthood 202 been for you?" I asked.

"It's been surprisingly rough," Kate replied honestly. "The first night at home was a disaster. I set my alarm for her 2 a.m. feeding, and at 3 a.m. I woke up, realizing I had missed her feeding time. Our alarm hadn't gone off. When I figured out what happened, I got so upset that I started crying, and then both Doug and the baby woke up. Doug had his hands full trying to take care of the two crying girls in his life. It was a big mess, trust me. But, things are better now." Sweet smiles drew across their faces, as Kate and Doug remembered that night.

"Well, Elizabeth looks fantastic, guys. Slender, but developing normally. How's she been eating?"

"Want to see my spreadsheet?" Kate asked, ever the good student.

"A spreadsheet?" I was incredulous.

"Yes. When we got Elizabeth home, we found it was really hard to keep her on the same schedule she had in the NICU. We tried, but it did not work. We had to go into experimental mode, just trying to figure out what would work. She's never been a great eater, if you'll remember, and I've been really nervous about whether she's getting enough. So I record everything: how much she eats each day, how many wet diapers, how many poops, and any special notes."

Surveying the piece of paper she handed me, I remarked, "This is a very complete record. Good job."

"So what would you say is a magic number of how much she has to eat each day?" Kate pressed.

"You know what? Don't focus on a specific number. Let your pediatrician check her weight often, and if she needs more, he'll tell you. Don't you worry; she's gaining well enough."

"Well, you'll be happy to know we still haven't taken Elizabeth out of the house yet, except to doctors' visits. And because I've been so worried she'd get an infection and have to come back to the hospital, I'm being very strict with my family and anyone who comes to see her about using the hand sanitizer. I don't want anyone with germs anywhere near her!"

"Yeah," added Doug, "I think we have like five bottles of it in the apartment, or maybe it's five in one room. I don't know the exact count, but I do know we have plenty of it."

Kate blushed. "I'm just trying to protect my baby," she said.

"I'm glad she hasn't gotten sick," I told them. "That's great. But you don't have to go overboard with the hand sanitizer, especially since her contact with outsiders is so limited."

"We're just being extra careful," said Kate.

We set up Elizabeth's next appointment for May, and after carefully bundling Elizabeth in her white snowsuit, the young family departed into the biting, crystalline air of mid-winter.

***

Spring was in full bloom when the Markhams arrived for Elizabeth's next clinic visit. Supple, new leaves had sprouted on all the trees, bright red tulips lined the walkway into the hospital, and the breeze was soft and warm.

"So tell me how things are going with your little princess," I said.

"She's doing fine, but mommy has not been," Kate answered solemnly. Her face was a bit thinner than before, and drawn.

"What's been going on?" I asked.

"I think I'm finally getting through it, but Dr. Hall, I've been so depressed. It's gotten so bad I even went to see a counselor. He told me I have postpartum depression."

"Wow. I had no idea," I said, although I remembered she had had what I thought were the "baby blues." Kate had usually seemed so upbeat about everything, so quick to smile—and, I remembered, so quick with her tears also. I knew that postpartum depression usually shows up in the first few months after delivery, so in Kate's case it was a little delayed. Dealing with the sadness and guilt that often come after giving birth to a premature baby, or one with a birth defect, can make a woman more susceptible to postpartum depression. I felt certain that the additional stresses in Kate's life—completing her educational degree, changing her routines radically to meet the needs of her still-fragile daughter, and planning to move to a new city after graduation—further increased her risks for depression.

"Tell me more," I urged Kate.

"I think part of my problem is that when we brought Elizabeth home, I felt like I had to recreate the NICU environment with its schedule, and strictly adhere to it. And you know from our last clinic visit, I became a complete psycho germ-o-phobe. Since we were taught to be so cautious with the alcohol hand gel in the hospital, I continued being that way at home. When my mom came to visit, I made her clean her hands about 500 times during the week. And I've had this kid in total lockdown! I only took her to church for the first time a couple of weeks ago. I was pretty much sick to my stomach the whole time we were there. I couldn't listen to the preacher. All I could hear were the million coughs and sneezes that were in the sanctuary. It made me mad that people would come to church when they were clearly sick."

Doug nodded his head as Kate spoke, giving his encouragement as she continued.

"Finally, one of the therapists who comes to our house to work with Elizabeth sat me down and said, 'Kate, you are obsessing over this. You've got to find a balance between living your life and worrying about germs.' That did it. I pretty much broke down crying. I had been trying so hard to do everything right, and..."

Kate had to stop and catch her breath and hold back tears as she told me her story.

"I realized I've deprived Elizabeth of experiences with other people because of my anxiety. We've all missed out on a lot, and I've been grieving that, and grieving over how Elizabeth's birth happened…"

I reached out and put my arms around Kate, hugging her tightly. "I'm glad you are getting some help for yourself. I'm sorry it's been so tough for you all, but at least now you are on the road to recovery, right?"

"Yes, and I've decided to become a volunteer at the Ronald McDonald House. My counselor says that would be the best therapy, to walk right back into it."

"They'll be lucky to have you. That sounds fantastic.

"And school…are you done with it yet?" I asked.

"We graduate next weekend, and then we're moving. Doug got a great job, and I'm going to be a stay-at-home mom, at least for a couple of years. We're excited; but boy, it's been a lot of work preparing for the move."

"Congratulations on your degrees, the new job and the move. Wow, nothing but stress in your lives, huh?"

"We're on top of it now," Doug said.

"Well, good. Now, let me have a look at Miss Elizabeth."

"Isn't she just precious?" Kate asked, addressing herself to Elizabeth with her face down at the baby's eye level, smiling broadly.

Elizabeth's exam was again reassuring. At nine-months-old, she could now sit and roll over, as well as babble a bit. It was easy to tell Kate and Doug, "She's right on target. She looks absolutely fantastic."

As Kate pulled Elizabeth's pastel yellow sundress over the baby's head and slipped her miniature white sandals onto her chubby pink feet, I was glad that Kate had recognized her need for help in dealing with her postpartum depression. Although her baby looked to be developing normally, I knew that when mothers with depression do not get help, the bond between mother and child can be disrupted and their babies may suffer behavioral and developmental problems.

"You are lucky you have such a good guy there with you," I told her, nodding my head in Doug's direction. Having observed through Elizabeth's NICU stay how close her parents' bond seemed to be, I added, "I'm sure he's helped you get through this."

"Oh, definitely. Doug, my family, my counselor, and of course, my faith."

As I waved goodbye to Kate and Doug, I felt certain that together they would get through the ups and downs of parenting their NICU graduate.

***

Notes:

Although as many as 80 percent of women have the "baby blues" shortly after delivery, Kate Markham was one of the 10-20 percent of women who suffer postpartum depression in the first few months after giving birth. Depression around the time of birth (perinatal depression) has been called "the most underdiagnosed obstetric complication in America," with more than 400,000 infants being born each year to mothers who suffer from depression.

Maternal depression can lead to multiple problems between mother and child. The mother may discontinue breastfeeding early on, depriving the infant of both the health and social benefits of nursing; infant attachment and bonding can be interrupted, adversely affecting the infant's early brain development; and in extreme cases, the mother may either abuse or neglect her child. The American Academy of Pediatrics advises primary care practitioners, including pediatricians, to screen for maternal depression during routine well-child care visits. (Earls M. F. 2010. "Incorporating Recognition and Management of Perinatal and Postpartum Depression into Pediatric Practice." *Pediatrics 126*(5): 1032-1038.)

Postpartum depression is more likely to occur in women who have previously experienced depression, those who have significant stress in their lives, or those who lack adequate social supports. It can be a disabling condition in mothers, with symptoms including exhaustion, inability to sleep, sadness, poor appetite, rapid mood swings, thoughts of harming oneself or one's baby, and loss of pleasure in normal activities. An excellent patient education publication on the topic is on the website of American Congress of Obstetricians and Gynecologists at www.acog.org. More information about postpartum depression is available on the websites for Postpartum Education for Parents (www.sbpep.org) and Postpartum Support International (www.postpartum.net).

The actress Brooke Shields has written about her personal experience with postpartum depression in her memoir, *Down Came the Rain: My Journey Through Postpartum Depression* (2005. New York: Hyperion).

A neonatal nurse practitioner greatly assisted in Elizabeth's care while in the NICU, as they do with so many NICU patients. In California I had never worked with nurse practitioners, but in my new NICU I easily became accustomed to their role as "physician extenders" and embraced all they could do on behalf of babies and families. Around the world, advanced neonatal nurse practitioners are increasingly supplementing the work force in NICUs, as shortages of neonatologists and reduced work hours for resident physicians combine to create staffing shortages. (Juretschke L. J. 2003. "New Standards for Resident Duty Hours and the Potential Impact on the Neonatal Nurse Practitioner Role." *Advances in Neonatal Care 3*(4): 159-161. Also *see* Smith S. L. and M. A. Hall. 2003. "Developing a

Neonatal Workforce: Role Evolution and Retention of Advanced Neonatal Nurse Practitioners." *Archives of Disease in Childhood: Fetal and Neonatal Edition 88*(5): F426-429.)

Chapter 15

Loving Samantha: Samantha Driscoll

One evening, I was asked to talk with Joanna, who was admitted to the hospital on referral from her doctor who practiced in a town more than an hour away. She was thirty-seven weeks pregnant with an anencephalic fetus and was in very early labor. I went to see her with Abigail, my charge nurse in the NICU that night, hoping to determine how she wanted to manage the delivery of her baby with this fatal birth defect, and more importantly, what she wanted her experience to be like with her baby after its birth.

Abigail and I entered Joanna's room to find a woman reclining about half way back in the large hospital bed, propped up with pillows. Her wavy brown hair fell down and touched the shoulders of her hospital-issue gown, which was white with a nondescript tiny blue check pattern. The small gold cross she wore just brushed the upper border of the gown. Her husband, Dave, was dressed in a Rolling Stones T-shirt and skinny black jeans; he sat quietly hunched forward in a chair beside her bed.

"I'm Dr. Hall," I said upon meeting the two of them, "and this is Abigail. We're here to talk about your baby's birth. What do you know about anencephaly?"

"My doctor told me not to look up anything about the baby on the internet," Joanna answered. "And he told me that if I delivered in the hospital in our small town, they would take the baby away from me after birth and I wouldn't be able to see it. That's why I wanted to come here."

"So did you look it up?" I asked.

"No," she said. "But my brother is an emergency medical technician, and he sees all kinds of stuff. He did research on anencephaly and said the pictures were so awful, he couldn't even look at them." She grimaced. "It seems so unfair," she continued. "I've always taken my one-a-day vitamins, even before I became pregnant."

Joanna was referring to the important role folic acid plays in preventing anencephaly and related defects. The March of Dimes in 1998 began promoting awareness of the significance of getting adequate folic acid during pregnancy, with a goal of reducing the incidence of this birth defect.

"Folic acid can definitely minimize your risk, but it can't completely eliminate the possibility of having a baby with this problem," I explained.

Joanna's belly bumped up from beneath the sheets of her bed, and her fingers periodically went to a spot on her abdomen as she cringed with pain. Her husband did not appear to be alert or engaged with our discussion; yet, I had the distinct feeling he was listening. He tapped his foot while he stared at the floor.

"Anencephaly occurs at about twenty-six to twenty-eight days of gestation," I began, "before you probably even knew you were pregnant. It's a failure of the neural tube to close." I pulled apart my hands to draw a neural tube in the air. It is one of the earliest fetal structures. "If the neural tube doesn't close at the bottom end, it creates spina bifida. If it doesn't close at the top end, anencephaly is the result. In anencephaly, the brain doesn't form normally and the skull doesn't form around the brain.

"Unfortunately, there's really nothing we can do about anencephaly; there's no way to fix it. Babies who have it live for a short time only."

Joanna sighed as though she had heard this part before, the part about not being able to fix it.

"So, what we usually do," I continued, "is try to figure out how to make your time with this baby 'quality time.'"

Joanna's drawn face made her underlying sadness appear more pronounced, and she looked older than her thirty-two years. She nodded as I spoke.

"It's already so hard to say goodbye to this baby and it's just going to get harder," she said.

"We'll help with that," I reassured her.

"I know that you had a previous pregnancy loss at twenty-eight weeks," I continued on. "What was that experience like for you?"

Joanna began her story. "My pregnancy was going along just fine. I felt great. I loved being pregnant. Then one day it occurred to me that I hadn't felt the baby move for a while. He had always kicked and turned, and then he seemed to stop, but I really wasn't sure. I called my doctor and went right in. On the ultrasound, the baby's heart wasn't beating. He was already gone."

A few tears began to leak from the corners of Joanna's eyes, barely visible under the heavy rim of her glasses. Her husband still tapped his foot on the floor, steadily, without a break.

"I had to go through labor and deliver him normally, but when he was born I cried so hard my OB took him away. He said I had already been through enough, I shouldn't have to see him. He gave me a sedative to knock me out, so I never did get to see the baby. I think that's why I've had trouble getting over it."

"Oh dear," I sighed, caressing Joanna's arm. "You probably thought that you had your one bad thing happen to you, your turn was over, and nothing like that should ever happen to you again." Her head bobbed up and down in a nod.

"And now here you are," I said.

Several early tears now grew into small rivers cascading down her full cheeks. Joanna sobbed, then immediately caught her breath. "I'm sorry," she whispered, tightly holding on to the air in her lungs. Just then she squirmed uncomfortably, as another contraction constricted her belly.

"No, no…you don't have to be sorry. This is really tough for you," I said, as my own voice wavered a bit. I gave her a few minutes to catch her breath while I steadied myself. Her husband, who never looked up, kept his hands clasped in between his knees, his foot still moving.

"We can make this experience so much better for you," I promised. "We have a palliative care program for babies with birth defects who aren't expected to survive long after birth. We also call it a comfort care program," I explained. "Instead of providing intensive care for your baby, our goal with comfort care is simply to make the baby—and you—as comfortable as possible. We want to help *you* decide how *you* want things to go."

"So, let's talk about what kind of delivery you want, what will make you comfortable, who do you want to have in the room with you, and so on. First, let me ask, is it a girl or a boy?"

"It's a girl. Her name is Samantha. Samantha Hope."

"Oh, what a pretty name. Samantha Hope. I like that. So, back to your delivery…"

"I would like to be awake. I know that."

"Awake is good," I agreed. "Any pain meds during labor? How are you doing with those contractions?" I noticed she'd winced a few more times during our conversation, but she could still talk without stopping during the pains. "You can have an epidural or IV pain meds, your choice."

"I've heard good things about epidurals. I'll go for that."

"Okay. And what about friends and family? Do you have others you want with you during labor and delivery, in addition to your husband?"

"Yes. Actually, my parents are driving up from home with our seven-year-old son Ryan. I had him before I lost the other baby. It seems like he was born so long ago. I can hardly remember what a normal delivery is like."

"Okay, so your parents and your son…"

"Yes, and Dave's parents are coming too, and my brother, his wife and their daughter, my niece. She's twelve. Do you have rules that limit the number of people that can be in the room when I deliver?"

"Your brother? The one who couldn't look at the pictures?" I asked.

"Yeah, Bob." Joanna smiled wanly. "He wants to be there for me. We've always been close. He's an old softie, underneath it all."

"Okay. To answer your question, in cases like yours, we don't limit the number of people in the room when you deliver. You are in the driver's seat. It's completely up to you and what you feel comfortable with." My goal was to give Joanna control of her situation, so that she would find it more emotionally satisfying than her previous birth experience.

I felt happy Joanna wanted to include her son and her niece. My thoughts about children's experience of death were formed during my days as a social worker, after the very young single mother of a four-year-old boy in the day care center for which I worked was killed one Saturday night in a gruesome freeway car crash.

I visited the grandparents who were then caring for the boy. "What are you going to tell him about his mother?" I asked. "Do you need help in talking with him about this?"

"No, I do not need help," the grandmother sternly insisted. "He doesn't need to know the details, except that she's not coming home."

I had wanted to persuade the boy's grandmother to discuss her daughter's death with the child in a way he could understand. At least then he'd have a better chance of dealing with it in a healthy way. When talk of death in a family is squelched, children often imagine, in their magical way of thinking, they must have done something bad to cause the death. Yet, this woman remained firm in her convictions that the matter would not be discussed. I never learned whether her viewpoint was borne out of ignorance, her inability to deal with her own grief at losing her daughter, or perhaps with her anger at being saddled with the responsibility of a young child at her advancing age.

The boy's confusion and sadness stayed with him a very long time.

Since then, I've always made a special effort to attend to the emotional needs of children who lose siblings, even if those siblings are brand new babies they scarcely have gotten a chance to meet.

"Now, what about someone from your church?" I continued with Joanna. "Do you have a priest or minister you wish to have with you? We can always call someone affiliated with the hospital if you'd like…"

"Hmm, Dave, what do you think?" Joanna turned to look at her husband.

Dave lifted his head for the first time since our conversation began. "I think I would like someone to be there. There's probably not enough time for our priest to get here, so if we could use the person the hospital usually calls, that'd be great." Dave stopped tapping his toe while he spoke.

A young labor and delivery nurse dressed in hot pink scrubs and white Reebok tennis shoes came silently into the room and checked Joanna's IV. Next, she checked the stretchy belt encircling Joanna's abdomen that was hooked into the electronic fetal-monitoring machine. It picked up impulses from the baby's heart and amplified them into a steady thump, thump, thump, a reassuring noise providing the background for our conversation.

"Hey," I said, as the sound registered. "You know, you don't have to have this fetal monitor machine on you, if you don't want. The only reason we monitor is so we can do a C-section if we find your baby's in distress. But in your case, doing a C-section is not going to help your baby. Do you want to take this thing off?"

"Can I? It's so tight. Yeah, I would love to be done with it."

I looked at the nurse and motioned for her to take it off.

"Whew," said Joanna, rubbing her belly after the belt was unfastened. "That feels better."

"All right," I said, "once the baby is born, do you want to have her in the room with you? Do you want to hold her? Give her a bath perhaps?"

"Will you have a hat she can wear?" Joanna asked timidly. I knew she was thinking about her baby's deformed head, and how hard that might be for her to see. *Her imagination must be running wild*, I thought.

"Absolutely. We have hats for all the babies. And clothes we can dress her in. She'll be beautiful."

"Yes, I definitely want to hold her. And if she looks okay—you know…" Joanna paused, as she swallowed hard.

"She'll look okay. You'll see," I reassured her.

"Then, I want my family to see her, my son, everyone..."

"No problem. No problem at all. And I can be there to check her out and make sure she's comfortable, not in any pain. I'll be in the hospital all night tonight."

"Oh, good. I was worried about whether she'd feel pain," Joanna said. It was Dave's turn to wince.

"I want to tell you about something else we have that is so wonderful," I said. "It's a volunteer photography service called *Now I Lay Me Down to Sleep*. It was started by a woman who had to make the decision to take her child off life support due to a fatal illness, and a photographer who took pictures of her family with the baby. Together, these women have a mission to memorialize babies who die, whether they pass before or after birth. They've created a nationwide network of people who donate their time and their hearts to this cause.

"We've used them before and they create amazingly beautiful, really touching portraits of families with their babies. And the best thing about the photographers is, they come when they're needed, whether it's in the middle of the night or on a weekend. Are you interested?"

Joanna held her hand up like a stop sign while she breathed through a short contraction. When it passed, she said, "It sounds lovely. Yes, I'm absolutely interested."

"We'll call them now and give them a heads-up. And we'll see you when Samantha's ready to come out." I looked over at Abigail, who indicated her agreement, then squeezed Joanna's hand. She eked out a small smile and thanked me for coming.

I followed Abigail out of the room and into the hallway. After I pulled the heavy door closed behind us, she said, "That was really hard. I don't know why, but I always tear up in these situations. I have to watch myself or I'll start crying."

"Me too," I said.

***

That evening, I attended a C-section for a baby whose mother had diabetes, admitted a baby with respiratory distress from the newborn nursery, and made rounds in the NICU, chatting with the night nurses about the babies assigned to each of them. At each baby's bedside, they posed questions to me.

"Can Jazmin have more to eat?" "Can I turn Lucas' oxygen concentration down?" "Should Jonah's medication be increased?" After answering them and making a final sweep of the NICU at about midnight, I climbed into the bed in my call room.

At 5 a.m., Abigail called me. "They're ready for us in Room 251. It's Joanna. She's ready to deliver."

I got out of bed, ran my fingers through my hair to fluff it up, pulled the drawstring at the waist of my scrubs tight, and slipped into my clogs. I met Abigail in the hall and we walked together to the labor and delivery floor.

"I called the photographer from *Now I Lay Me Down to Sleep*," she told me. "He'll be here any minute. The priest is on his way, and I've got some clothes and a Memory Box." We had planned to assemble some items from the baby's hospital stay, including copies of her footprints and a lock of her hair, in a specially decorated box for the baby's parents to take home to remember her by.

Leave it to Abigail to always have everything perfectly prepared, I thought. "Great," I said.

We arrived at Joanna's room and parted a crowd of people to get through the door. We entered to find Dave holding one of Joanna's hands, and a woman who looked just like Joanna, only thirty years older, holding her other hand. Joanna's chin was touching her chest and she was pushing with all her might. As her baby slowly emerged, the obstetrician said, "Joanna, look. Right now. Your baby's coming *right now*!"

Samantha popped out and everyone's attention was immediately riveted on her, as the obstetrician held her in his arms and clamped the umbilical cord. Handing the scissors to Dave, he prodded, "Here, you do the honors."

Dave stepped up and cut the cord between the two clamps, and then the obstetrician brought the baby over to Abigail and me at our warming table. Abigail used the blue bulb syringe to suction secretions out of the baby's mouth while I quickly toweled her off. Through the gaping defect on the back of her skull, I could see her lumpy soft purple brain, encased only in a glistening translucent membrane. I gently pulled a pink hat knit from fluffy yarn over her head, while Abigail put a diaper on her. Then, I wrapped her in a white blanket. She was taking slow, shallow breaths.

"Come on, Samantha, let's go meet your parents. Here's your baby," I said, handing the bundle to Joanna. "See how great she looks?"

"Is she breathing?" Joanna asked anxiously.

"Yes, she is," I reassured her.

"How long will she breathe?"

"I don't know. We'll just watch her. She'll let us know."

Joanna studied Samantha's face, and then lightly touched the back of her head through her pink hat. After satisfying herself with her exam, she said, "Dave, get everyone else." By this time, the obstetrician had finished his work.

The door opened wide and the family rushed in: another grandma, two grandpas, an aunt and uncle, her brother, and a cousin. A bearded gentleman whose long black robe dusted the tops of his scuffed black shoes trailed in behind them.

"Is the baby finally here?" asked the grandma who wasn't in the room during the birth.

"Yeah. Here she is," said Dave, gesturing for his mother to come closer.

The grandma pulled out her digital camera and began taking pictures like crazy.

A boy with red hair and sleep in his eyes stood at the back of the crowd.

"Ryan, come here," Joanna called. "Come meet your sister."

Dave went over to Ryan and put his arm around the boy's shoulder, and guided him up to his mother's bedside. The boy's eyes opened wider the closer he got. Being still quite short, Ryan couldn't see the baby his mother was holding very well. Dave helped him climb up on the bed next to Joanna.

"Look, here she is," Joanna cooed.

"Mom, why do her eyes look so funny?" Ryan asked. The baby's eyes were bulbous and protuberant, but otherwise her facial features were perfect.

"That's just what she looks like. Isn't she beautiful?" Joanna stroked the baby's cheek with her fingertip. She was beaming.

The clergyman stepped forward from the fringes of the room and introduced himself as Father O'Hearne. "Can I baptize the baby?"

"Yes, we'd love it if you would," said Joanna.

"Gather round then everyone, and hold hands," he commanded. Father O'Hearne stepped forward into the group of family encircling Joanna's bed, brought a small jar of water out of his satchel, and also pulled out a prayer book.

He opened the book to a page marked by a purple velvet bookmark.

"Joanna, Dave and friends," he intoned, "we are gathered here today to baptize Samantha, and to bring her into the Holy Family, to receive the love of the Holy Spirit."

He read a prayer from the book, formed the sign of the cross over Samantha, and touched her head lightly, sprinkling a few drops of holy water on her. Joanna gazed lovingly at Samantha during the brief ceremony, and held Dave's hands tightly as the priest completed his ritual, murmured his goodbyes and well wishes, then left the room.

A knock on the door signaled the entrance of the photographer. He introduced himself and explained he would simply take pictures while the family went about their business of becoming acquainted with Samantha. "Just do whatever you would normally do, and don't mind me. I'm going to produce a beautiful photo album for you, so you can just enjoy your baby and not have to worry about taking pictures yourselves."

"Thank you so much," said Joanna.

Joanna cradled the baby in both arms and held her up close to her face, murmuring to her, "We've waited so long to meet you, and now you are here. I'm sorry this happened to you, baby. We're going to miss you so, my sweet little girl."

Joanna finally let Dave have a turn holding the baby, and when he had his fill, the family members passed her around, taking their turns. Everyone seemed to delight in that wonderful feeling of holding a tiny new life in their arms, remarking on how perfect Samantha's ten little fingers were as they curled over the top edge of the blanket, how cute her tiny nose was, how beautiful her miniature rosebud mouth appeared. Samantha remained quiet and peaceful, and fairly pink.

When she was returned to Joanna, I suggested, "Let's unwrap her so you can see her little body and count each of her ten itty-bitty toes."

As we did so, Ryan asked, "Mom, how come she doesn't cry?"

"I think she's just so happy to be a member of our family, she doesn't need to cry, Ry."

The boy considered this for a minute, then broke into a big smile and said, "Oh," as in "Oh, I get it."

The baby looked absolutely perfect in every single way.

"Jo, she's a cutie," said Bob. "She looks great." As their eyes met, a look of relief passed between them.

The photographer snapped lots of great shots: Joanna's index finger lying across the palm of Samantha's hand, Dave cradling the bottoms of Samantha's wrinkled feet in his big, sturdy hands, Samantha's face held side by side with Ryan's. After the baby was again wrapped in her blanket, Ryan had his picture taken while holding her on his lap in the rocking chair; Uncle Bob posed while cuddling her up to his shoulder; and Cousin Sandra wanted her picture to include the teddy bear she brought Samantha as a present.

As the photographer stayed busy, I remembered the words to my favorite childhood prayer.

Now I lay me down to sleep
I pray the Lord my soul to keep.
If I should die before I wake
I pray the Lord my soul to take.
If I should live for other days
I pray the Lord to guide my ways.

I loved the prayer's simple words; even as an adult they brought me a feeling of comfort and solace.

Abigail went back to the NICU, but I stayed with the family. I felt like a movie director who set up a scene, started filming, and let the actors improvise. So far they were doing a superb job.

"Is her heart still beating?" Joanna asked me after about an hour.

"Let me listen," I said, coming forward from the back of the room where I had been leaning against the wall. I pulled my stethoscope off from around my neck and opened Samantha's blanket. I rubbed the bell in my hands to warm it, then placed it on her chest. I closed my eyes and concentrated very hard, listening for any beats. I knew if there were any, they would be few and far between, and only barely perceptible. After nearly a minute, I opened my eyes and lifted my head up. "She's gone," I simply said.

Joanna took off her glasses to wipe her eyes and Dave came over to tenderly kiss the top of her head. "It's okay, babe. It's okay," he said, pulling his fingers through her hair and digging them into the back of her neck for a brief massage.

"Who would like to give the baby a bath?" I asked the family. "We can wash her off, then dress her in some clothes?"

"I would love to," said Joanna's mother warmly. "Ryan, will you help me?"

"I'll help," offered Sandra, stepping forward.

"No, I'll help," insisted Ryan. "She asked me first." He was fully awake by now.

"You can both help," said the grandma.

I put the pink plastic tub in the sink and filled it with warm water and two squirts of Johnson's Baby Shampoo, then got out of the way. As the fragrant smell of baby shampoo permeated the room, it felt even cozier than before. Grandma and Ryan undressed Samantha, leaving her hat in place, and then carefully lowered her into the tub. Sandra squeezed in next to them, and used the washcloth to wipe the baby's soft, smooth skin. Ryan enjoyed cupping his hand and lightly splashing water onto her chest. Dave sat on top of the covers of Joanna's bed and snuggled with her.

Just as the first beams of daylight came through the window of Joanna's room, Grandma put one hand under Samantha's shoulders and one under her bottom, and lifted her onto the clean towel I had waiting. She dried her off a bit, then took her back to Joanna. The photographer was in every corner of the room. Snap. Snap. Flash. Snap.

I brought two dresses over for Joanna to choose from. She picked the white one with the pattern of pink flowers and the collar of pink lace. The dress matched Samantha's pink hat perfectly. I helped Joanna ease the baby, now a light shade of lilac, into the dress. The family then posed for pictures all together, with Joanna holding Samantha in the center, flanked by Dave and Ryan, then the broader family. They created a beautiful tableau.

The noise in the hallway picked up as nurses began arriving for the day shift. As the photographer prepared to leave, Abigail came back into the room.

"How's it going?" she asked.

I looked at Joanna, who had a contented smile on her very tired face. "Good, I think," I said.

Joanna nodded affirmatively.

"Ready to make the Memory Box?" asked Abigail.

"I think so. Joanna, can we borrow Samantha again? Time for foot prints."

Dave brought the baby over to us and Abigail got to work. She put Samantha's tiny hands and feet first onto a black ink card then onto special commemorative paper making a smudge-free print. Next she gathered all the things from her crib—the pacifier she never got to use, bulb syringe, thermometer, hospital logo T-shirt, and the miniature yellow plastic bottle of baby shampoo—and put them all into the special box.

Shift change came and the extended family went home, one of the grandmas towing a very sleepy Ryan out of the room by the hand. Abigail went back to the NICU to give a report to the daytime nursing crew. Finally, I was left with just Joanna, Dave, and the baby.

"Would you like to see her head?" I asked. "I can take off her hat and show you what anencephaly looks like..."

"Yes, we're ready."

I carefully removed Samantha's pink hat with my right hand, and sat her forward, supporting her chin in my left hand. Once the back of her head was exposed, Joanna said, "Oh, it's not that bad. She's still our perfect baby and we'll always love her." She looked up at Dave, who smiled sadly in agreement.

It is a hard thing to enter the world and leave it all on the same day. Samantha completed her short journey through life surrounded by those who loved and mourned her, leaving sweet memories and wistful tears in her wake.

***

Notes:

Samantha was born with anencephaly. About 3,000 babies are born every year in the United States with either anencephaly or spina bifida, both serious birth defects resulting from incomplete closure of the skull or spine, respectively, during prenatal life. While anencephaly is uniformly fatal, many infants born with spina bifida survive. Myelomeningocele is the most severe form; affected children may have multiple complex medical problems. The annual cost for medical and surgical care for people with spina bifida is more than $200 million. According to data from the CDC, lifetime care for a single child born with this condition was estimated to be $460,923 in 2009 (http://www.cdc.gov/ncbddd/spinabifida/data.html).

Dietary deficiency of folic acid, a B vitamin, is known to play an important role in the genesis of both anencephaly and spina bifida (also called neural tube defects). In 1998, a national campaign was begun to educate women on the importance of folic acid. The incidence of these congenital malformations can be decreased by 50-70 percent if a woman capable of becoming pregnant takes 400 micrograms of folic acid daily, starting at least one month before conception. The recommended daily amount of folic acid can be obtained by either taking a multi-vitamin daily (most will have 100 percent of the daily value of folic acid, check the label) or eating one bowl of fortified cereal every day. Such cereals include Raisin Bran, All-Bran, Special K, both instant and regular Quaker Oatmeal, and many others (again, read the labels to ensure the product provides 100 percent of the daily value of folic acid). Foods rich in folic acid include orange juice, asparagus, broccoli, peas, lentils, and melons. Read more on the CDC's website (http://www.cdc.gov/ncbddd/folicacid/data.html) or the March of Dimes' website (http://www.marchofdimes.com/pregnancy/folicacid.html).

The March of Dimes, whose mission it is to improve the health of all babies and to prevent prematurity, has been an important partner in the campaign to educate women about the role of folic acid in attaining a healthy pregnancy outcome. This campaign has reduced the number of infants born yearly with a neural tube defect by about 1,000. Established by President Franklin Roosevelt in 1938 with a mission to defeat polio, the March of Dimes does more than any other volunteer organization in the United States to advocate for healthy pregnancies and healthy babies. The March of Dimes' web address is www.marchofdimes.com.

Samantha's parents were offered palliative care, also known as end-of-life care or comfort care. Previously, many in society thought parents could not cope with the death of their infant. These parents' experiences were often similar to Joanna's, in that doctors did not allow them to see their newborns.

However, it has been shown that parents can effectively handle the death of an infant, and palliative care has moved into the NICU. Brosig et al. discuss factors that parents have indicated helped them cope with the loss of their baby. (Brosig C. L., R. L. Pierucci et al. 2007. "Infant End-of-Life Care: the Parents' Perspective." *Journal of Perinatology 27*(8): 510-516.) Bhatia describes the development of palliative care, and conditions in which it should be considered for newborns. (Bhatia J. 2006. "Palliative Care in the Fetus and Newborn." *Journal of Perinatology 26*(Suppl 1*)*: S24-S26.) Two other authors put forth guidelines for provision of palliative care for dying neonates. (De Lisle-Porter M. and A. M. Podruchny. 2009. "The Dying Neonate: Family-Centered End-of-Life Care." *Neonatal Network 28*(2): 75-83. Also *see* Pierucci R. L., R. S. Kirby, S. R. Leuthner. 2001. "End-of-Life Care for Neonates and Infants: The Experience and Effects of a Palliative Care Consultation Service." *Pediatrics 108*(3): 653-660.)

Joanna and Dave needed some guidance in how to talk with their son Ryan about Samantha's death. An excellent resource for talking with children about death is Earl Grollman's book, *Talking About Death: A Dialogue Between Parent and Child* (1991. Boston: Beacon Press).

Now I Lay Me Down to Sleep is an organization of more than 3,000 volunteer photographers worldwide founded by Cheryl Haggard and Sandy Puc in 2005. The photographers create sensitive images for families who have lost babies to critical illness or stillbirth. They provide an invaluable service that enables parents to bond with and honor their infants, and to heal from their loss through the memories that are created. They can be found on the internet at www.nowilaymedowntosleep.org.

Chapter 16

Saving Baby Jacob: Jacob Jenner

Numerous diplomas and plaques cover the wall of my office, certifying that I have been completely and successfully trained as a neonatologist. And over the years, I have learned the subtle points, the intricacies, the unwritten rules, and the nuances of taking care of babies.

However, one day I found myself asking the question, *Why do I feel so incredibly stupid?* What did I miss on Jacob Jenner? Why couldn't I figure out the cause of his sudden turn for the worse, when just a few hours earlier he had looked fine?

Jacob was a garden-variety premie, a cute little boy with a pixie face born at thirty-two weeks. His teenage mother, Shelly, sported ratty bleached blonde hair, a pierced tongue, and a tattoo of a butterfly on her shoulder. Her boyfriend and Jacob's father, Jason, typically wore baggy pants that hung a good six inches below his narrow waist.

One afternoon when he was several weeks old, the healthy-appearing baby slurped down a bottle of formula. An hour later, he looked dramatically different. Everything was okay until it was suddenly *not at all okay*. I could immediately see his condition was quite advanced when I arrived at his bedside. A sharp pang of fear rose in me as I recognized a formidable enemy. I wondered if I had time to stop its progression before it resulted in Jacob's death. It was too early to know which way things would go—toward death or toward life. But one thing was certain: it would be a pitched and hard-fought battle.

Jacob had wiggled around, quite robust and pink, two days earlier when a nurse practitioner had asked me to examine him, although his belly was noticeably protuberant. Abdominal distension in premature babies is always concerning because it can be the precursor to necrotizing enterocolitis, a type of intestinal inflammation also known as NEC. But Jacob did not have any worrisome signs of NEC at the time: he was not spitting up, he did not have green gooey bile in his stomach, and his stools were not bloody. Although he couldn't tell me how he felt and whether he hurt anywhere, he did not wince or cry at all when I softly pressed my fingers into his pregnant-appearing belly. I ordered an abdominal x-ray and ultrasound as I went off call that day. I left it to the doctor taking my place, Dr. Sondheim, to figure out what to do with the results.

A day later when I returned to take the second twenty-four-hour shift in my stretch of three every-other-night calls, I thought nothing of it when Dr. Sondheim reported to me in morning rounds that Jacob had been stable through the night. But as his illness took hold later that afternoon with the speed of an unrepentant wildfire, I faced the possibility of his impending demise. As I wondered what I had missed two days before that allowed Jacob to become so sick, so fast, I felt completely responsible.

His abdomen was even more swollen than before, and the skin overlying it was shiny and taut. Worst of all, his gut was silent. I could not hear a single healthy squiggle or gurgle with my stethoscope. Jacob looked pasty and his breathing appeared labored. He furrowed his brow with effort until I intubated him and placed him on the ventilator. He quickly ceased his struggle and went to sleep, and let the machine do all the breathing for him. An x-ray of his abdomen confirmed my fears: if an untrained observer had tried to guess what they saw in his abdomen, they might have thought it was ten big, fat sausages.

As I kept my vigil near his bedside, his parents wandered in and out of his room; whenever they returned, they reeked of cigarette smoke. Shelly held a wad of tissue to her red nose; Jason crammed the buds of his iPod in his ears, and then stuffed his hands in his pockets.

"He'll be okay, won't he?" Shelly asked, standing back from his isolette.

"We've both got to hope he will be. I'm going to do my very best for him," was all I could say. "And don't be afraid to touch him. It could help him feel better."

Shelly turned away, crying. "I can't stand seeing him this way. He looks so awful." I wanted her boyfriend to hug her or *do something* to make her feel better, but he didn't. Jason's head bobbed to an invisible melody on his iPod.

I shook my head in agreement, and left the room as Jacob's bedside nurse put her arm around Shelly.

Through the afternoon I wrote orders non-stop, took a bathroom break for the first time all day at 4 p.m., grabbed a Snickers bar and a banana for dinner, and finally pulled away from Jacob's bedside by about 11 p.m. Jacob looked worse by the hour, and so did I. Exhaustion, both mental and physical, was setting in.

I escaped into my call room and immediately felt calmed by its soothing low light and the white noise made by the hospital air conditioning system. I slipped under the covers of the bed for a nap, but sleep never came. Instead, I got up and tended to Jacob, and set a new personal record for the number of orders written on a single patient in a twenty-four-hour period: antibiotics, blood tests, x-rays, more x-rays, surgical consultation, pain medication, ventilator changes, transfusions, continuous IV drips to maintain his sagging blood pressure, diuretics to help him pee, more blood tests, more ventilator changes. Taking care of Jacob was exactly the reason I always told people who asked if our NICU was busy that it did not matter how many babies we had at any one time. It only took one to keep me up all night.

From midnight on, I silently prayed for my replacement to arrive the next morning while Jacob was still alive. Luckily, Jacob made it through the night; I turned over his care to Dr. Jed Handler, another partner in my medical practice, when he arrived the next morning. I was optimistic that Dr. Handler could help Jacob pull through. If anyone could, I was confident it was Jed, a no-nonsense, get-the-work-done kind of doctor.

That morning, Jacob's x-ray finally demonstrated tiny bubbles in the walls of his intestines, the dreaded pneumatosis intestinalis. This definitely clinched the diagnosis of NEC. I knew I had been fooling myself to even guess it was anything else over the last twenty-four hours. Sitting at the electronic radiology viewing station near the doctors' desk in the NICU with Dr. Handler and Dr. Stuart McDermott, the surgeon, I pulled out my retrospectoscope.

The retrospectoscope is a sophisticated medical instrument doctors are first taught how to use in medical school. Although not a real instrument, it is the term used when applying 20-20 hindsight to our actions. We doctors hone our skills in its use in morbidity and mortality meetings during our medical training. The retrospectoscope allows the user—and others—to look back on a situation that turned out badly and to magically illuminate what went wrong. It suddenly becomes clear what could have been done differently to avoid the patient's complication or death.

With the retrospectoscope, a doctor is granted the power to see every flaw in his or her thinking: to notice every time she missed a seemingly insignificant but ultimately critical detail, to understand each time her judgment was wrong, and to see every other choice that could have been made to keep the patient alive. Use of this valuable instrument has decimated many a young physician's ego and shattered the confidence of legions more.

"Man," I said to my colleagues, "if you ever start to think you are smart in this profession, you are dead."

"Yeah," said Dr. McDermott. He leaned back in his chair and let loose a belly laugh. "Just do that, and someone will come along with an ax and hit you across the legs and fell you like a gigantic pine tree. *Timber!!!*" I cringed as I reconstructed the image he painted.

"Hey," he went on, "shit happens. And how could you have known that it was going to turn out like this?"

I knew he was right, but as a salve, his words did not do much to diminish my discomfort. This was one of many times I felt woefully incapable of explaining to anyone who asked why this particular baby was now so sick. "I wish I was smart enough to know the answer to that," I would often say, and I meant it.

What I really wished was to be able to find the "black box" for this baby and for every other sick baby, the box that contained all the data about the baby's individual body systems, how they interacted, what went wrong in which area first, and how it all cascaded tumultuously into their illness. But babies don't have black boxes. We have to reconstruct them in our minds.

Nurses, patients, and family members often assume that every doctor knows exactly what is wrong with every single patient and how they are going to fix it. Part of every neonatologist's job should be to be point out gaps in medical knowledge, explain the difference between the art and the science of practicing medicine, and cautiously temper the expectations that ever-hopeful parents have with the realities of their baby's condition.

Unfortunately, there is no cookbook with recipes dictating "two parts science, one part art, and one really good guess" for this patient, and "one cup science, two cups of art, a dash of love and a strong prayer" for that patient. There is no step-by-step instruction manual for arriving at a correct diagnosis and no *Medicine For Dummies.* Physicians write their own books as they practice.

I left the NICU feeling completely spent. As I swiped my electronic identification badge to pass through the NICU's heavy security doors, two nurses chatted gaily as they entered for their shifts. I resisted a strong urge to warn them to turn around and walk back out if they wanted to continue to enjoy their day. Instead, I let them walk headfirst and unaware into the pressure cooker I was leaving. That is just the way working in the NICU was. They were used to it. They would adapt quickly.

Before I headed home, I passed through the doctors' lounge. A TV news announcer droned on in the background about the most recent dismal report of economic indicators. I suppressed my desire to grab one of the frosted donuts on the tray already half picked-over, knowing that a donut, even one with luscious-looking chocolate frosting, would be a cheap fix for what ailed me. Instead, I grabbed a cup of watered-down decaf from the coffee machine. I sipped the barely warm liquid as I walked to the parking garage.

Driving home on that grey, drizzly day in December, the weather matched my mood. As I passed barren, fallow fields, I felt compelled to grade myself: B- for missing Jacob's diagnosis the first day, A for keeping him alive to this point, C for managing my feelings about his case, and A+ for passing on the donuts.

Suddenly, an almost irresistible urge to cry welled up in me from nowhere. There is a lot of pain we doctors try to forget, especially the pain of recognizing our limitations, real or imagined.

***

When my alarm jangled early the next morning, a sense of dread enveloped me like a thick fog. It was easy to trace it back to my thoughts about Jacob and whether he would still be in the NICU when I arrived.

During the morning ritual of sign-out rounds, in which the patients were handed off from one doctor to another, I was amazed and happy to hear that Jacob was still alive. I kept my happiness in check, though, because I knew that the fight was not over yet. I could not get too excited about our team's success in saving his life until his survival seemed assured. At least I could be cautiously optimistic.

Dr. Sonya Sondheim had been off for a few days. She was stunned and saddened to learn how sick Jacob was. I had told her to check results of Jacob's x-ray and ultrasound a few days before he became really ill. After rounds, it surprised me when Sonya confided in me. The words rattled out of her in a voice even more high-pitched than usual.

"I feel horrible. I must have missed something the day you told me to check his x-rays. I can't believe he got so sick."

"But I thought he got sick because *I* missed something," I declared.

I guessed Sonya was just as accomplished at using the retrospectoscope as I was, and just as good at conjuring up guilty feelings.

She took her turn at caring for Jacob and the other NICU babies for the next twenty-four hours. The following day it was my turn again, my third on-call in five nights.

In morning sign-out rounds, Dr. Sondheim lamented the fact that Jacob was now faring less well than ever. "And his parents did not even come in at all yesterday. Not once." Dr. Sondheim's voice advertised her indignation.

I recognized this unfortunate syndrome: acute stress disorder, the precursor to post-traumatic stress syndrome, had invaded the parents' lives. The sicker their baby got, the less they visited, unable to take in any more bad news. It was simply too frightening.

After rounds, I headed straight for Jacob's room, with one of the nurse practitioners by my side. The baby had been placed in isolation when the lab identified a dangerous strain of bacteria growing in his bloodstream. We donned yellow-paper gowns and blue surgical masks, foamed our hands with alcohol rub, then struggled to pull on ill-fitting plastic gloves. Safely protected from him so that we would not pick up the renegade bacterium from his skin and transfer it to our other patients, we entered his room.

Jacob's belly was now enormous, as tense as a drum, and shiny red. Tiny wormlike veins decorated its upper border. Although heavily sedated, Jacob grimaced when I touched his belly. I felt sad when he drew his legs up in pain.

"I'm sorry, sweetie pie. I'm so sorry you are hurting," I whispered to Jacob.

"We need to get Dr. McDermott on the phone," I instructed the nurse practitioner. "This baby has peritonitis and needs to go to the operating room. He has probably perforated."

Shortly, an xray of the baby's abdomen confirmed that an intestinal perforation had occurred. Within thirty minutes, the surgeon waltzed into the NICU, singing a Broadway show tune loudly enough for anyone to hear. After seeing Jacob and his xray, he agreed with my assessment that the baby needed prompt surgery. He left the NICU to make preparations, humming.

With Jacob's appearance and lab values continuing to deteriorate, chances were good that some of his intestines were dead, their contents leaking out into his abdomen to worsen his infection. He could only get better if the dead bowel was removed, and at this point waiting even a couple of hours could mean the difference between life and death.

The nurse practitioner quickly ordered some blood and platelets to be on hold for the operating room. This type of surgery was usually a messy affair. Finally, I called Jacob's parents. Shelly did not answer her cell phone, but luckily Jason did.

"I'm sorry to keep giving you bad news," I started. "But, Jacob needs to go to the operating room. The surgeon and I think that the infection in his belly has progressed to the point that some of his intestines have perforated and need to be removed in order for him to get well."

"When do you think that might be?" asked Dad.

"Now," I replied.

"Now? As in...*right now*?"

"We need to take him down just as soon as we can. How soon can you and Shelly get here?"

After a pause, I heard a muffled version of Jason talking with Shelly in the background. "We'll be over as soon as we can."

In the meantime, I addressed another problem. Jacob needed a central line, a reliable IV threaded into one of the large veins near his heart. When I pressed his spongy limbs, I realized it would be extremely difficult to find a single vein where this could be done easily. His entire body, including his arms and legs where IVs might be started, was too swollen. I asked Jerry, a nurse who was a wizard at locating invisible veins, to take on the challenge.

"I'll give it a go," he replied, and forty-five minutes later, the rest of the nurses and I crowded around Jacob's room to give Jerry a standing ovation for getting the line in.

"You saved the day," I cheered. "Bless you." Although Jerry's smile was covered by his surgical face mask, I could see it in his eyes: He adored being adored.

The next time I looked up from Jacob's chart, Jason and Shelly were standing beside their baby, Jason's hands stuffed ever deeper into his pockets. Shelly's bright red eyes were ringed with a thick layer of black mascara; ghoulish rivulets ran down her cheeks. She looked as if she had lost ten pounds since I last saw her several days earlier. Her arms were wrapped tightly around a pillow and blanket she had brought from home.

"Give Jacob a kiss," I said. "After you talk with the surgeon, we'll be taking him downstairs."

Shelly bent down and awkwardly planted a kiss on Jacob's forehead. Jason stood stiffly at her side.

Before long, Jacob was on the operating room table two stories below ground level, his tiny body dwarfed under the gigantic overhead spotlight that reminded me so much of a bug's compound eye. Dr. McDermott painted his belly with antiseptic then covered it up with the same size blue-paper drape used on adults to create a sterile field. The only part of the baby's body I could see was a three by four inch square of his abdomen, and soon this had a long cut across the middle of it, which oozed bright red blood.

As soon as the surgeon sliced through the baby's thin skin, so many intestines popped out that it looked as if it would be impossible to ever squeeze them back into the baby's abdominal cavity. The intestines were bloated purple tubes filled with air, and some areas were nearly black. A putrid stench, the smell of dead gut and stool that had seeped out of the ruptured intestine, spread through the air, replacing the medicinal scent of the operating room. Dr. McDermott added to the olfactory sewage by using a cautery instrument to singe some bleeding tissue, and the repugnant smell of burning flesh penetrated my surgical mask.

I wondered what Dr. McDermott thought. Would this be a case like the one I saw years earlier when the surgeon opened the baby, deemed it hopeless because the entire intestine was gangrenous, and stitched the baby back up without doing anything?

The surgeon deftly pulled the entire length of the small and large bowel out through the incision, working quickly. He slid the intestines gently through his gloved fingers from top to bottom, and carefully considered which areas he could save and which were already gone. Most of the gut had that in-between look …not perfectly pink and healthy but not black and dead. If he cut too much out of the dusky area, he would create short gut syndrome; Jacob would never be able to digest enough food to survive. If he did not cut out enough, the smoldering infection would progress and Jacob would need to revisit the operating room in a couple of days.

Dr. McDermott identified the spot where the perforation occurred and cut back to healthy pink tissue five to six inches above and below it. He also created an ostomy, which would give Jacob's intestines the best chance to heal. As he worked on Jacob's distended intestines, they deflated like a balloon losing air, making it easier to replace them in his belly once surgery was completed.

The tension in my neck melted as I realized Jacob had a chance.

Before we left the operating room, Dr. McDermott asked, "Who wants to sing Christmas carols?" He launched into a spirited rendition of *Joy to the World* in a soaring tenor.

I joined him, and tried to find the harmonic line in the song while he carried the melody. The operating room crew, still trying to move Jacob from the table on which surgery was performed back to the transport isolette, watched us with hidden smiles as we concluded with *Oh Holy Night.*

While Dr. McDermott went to dictate his operative note, I went to the surgery waiting room to talk with Jacob's parents. I did not see them in the crowded room, but I thought I saw Shelly's white blanket on one of the couches. A closer look revealed sneakers sticking out from under the blanket; I recognized them as Jason's. The blanket was pulled up, nearly covering his face. However, the hair sprouting from under the blanket looked familiar.

"Excuse me, Jason?" I gently tapped on the spot where it seemed his shoulder should be.

"Huh?" he asked, pulling the blanket down to reveal his face. Sleep had made his eyes puffy. He took a few seconds to process the situation, and then said, "Oh."

"We're done with surgery. Jacob did well. The surgeon had to take out some of his intestines, but I think he's got a good chance now. The next forty-eight hours will be critical. He'll be up in the NICU in a few minutes and you can come see him."

I left the room and ran into Shelly in the hallway. She had just come back into the building and stopped to wipe the dampness from her shoes. She clutched her usual crumpled pack of cigarettes with fingers made purple by the cold.

"Jacob did great," I told her. "He's probably back up in the NICU by now. Come on up and see him."

As I scribbled post-op orders on Jacob's chart, Shelly and Jason entered his room. Jason took the corner spot and let out an exasperated sigh, and Shelly stood with her back to him, lines creasing her face.

"Come closer, if you want," Jacob's nurse encouraged her. "You can hold his hand. I think he'd like that actually."

After she studied her baby, who had a new white gauze bandage stretching across his mid-section, Shelly finally took a deep breath and picked up his limp little hand in hers, and eked out a weak smile. Jacob was snowed with pain medication and did not respond.

***

During the next week, Shelly and Jason did not visit Jacob a single time. The nurses recorded two late night phone calls from Shelly. At the end of the week, as Jacob improved and came off the ventilator, Mary, our social worker, got involved. She reported in morning rounds that she had finally reached Shelly, who had promised she would visit that afternoon.

Shelly arrived at 5:30 in the afternoon. Jacob's nurse called to alert me: "Better get over here quick, 'cause she might not stay for long."

I entered Jacob's room and noticed he was resting comfortably on his tummy in his isolette, his knees bent so as to tuck his legs under him. I smiled when I saw his little diapered bottom thrust up in the air, as this was a sign of health. However, I became alarmed when I saw Shelly. Gaunt and disheveled, she had a bruise under one eye with purple, green and yellow tones mixed together.

"Where's Jason?" I asked.

Matter-of-factly, Shelly answered, "We broke up. He couldn't take it anymore."

"I'm sorry to hear that. Are you okay?"

"Yeah, I'm okay. I was going to dump him anyway after this was all over. But after he went crazy and busted all the chairs in our apartment against the wall—and did this…"

she said, pointing to her eye. "He just made it easier for me. He's been cheating on me with at least one other girl that I know about, and who knows, probably more. I can't stand him." The content of her words was loaded with emotion but none of that came across in her voice. And no tears, this time.

"Wow. That's a lot for you to handle right now. Who do you have to help you with Jacob when he goes home? He's getting so much better. I think it's safe to say he will be going home in the not-too-distant future."

"I don't know," Shelly replied. "My mom left my dad a couple of years ago. I have no clue where she even is. And my dad's always all boozed up… I have a sister who lives a couple of hours away. That's why I was living with Jason, just so I would be with *someone*. I had to move back in with my dad when I kicked Jason out. Couldn't pay the rent."

"Oh gosh, I'm sorry for all your troubles. Sounds like you could use some help figuring things out. I'll let Mary, the social worker who called you, know about this. Can you come sometime tomorrow between 8 and 5 to meet with her?"

"I don't have a car and I hardly have any money for the bus. I don't know…"

"Can your dad bring you?" I sensed that Shelly would cry if she could, but she had already used up all her tears before coming in.

"I'll ask my neighbor for a ride. I'll find a way to come back." Her response was half-hearted.

"Okay. And Mary will be able to get you bus tokens and meal tickets. We'll do whatever we can to help you." I put my arm around her shoulder—the one with the butterfly tattoo—and gave her a motherly hug.

We had saved Jacob; he was going to be fine. The medical realities of getting him out of the hospital would be simple, compared to what had already taken place. But stabilizing his family situation so that he could go home would be the biggest challenge facing our team. I was grateful to have a social worker on our team who could take the time to sort this all out.

Mary did meet with Shelly, after she finally showed up the fourth time they scheduled an appointment. In spite of all the help and encouragement Mary offered, Shelly's visitation continued to be spotty and her stays brief. Even when Jacob was well enough to be held, Shelly declined the nurses' offer to hold him and feed him. She did not want to come anywhere close to his ostomy bag, and startled visibly each time a monitor alarm went off.

"Are you *sure* he's okay?" she asked, over and over, trembling with anxiety.

"I'm worried about this baby going home with this mom," Melissa, a nurse who took care of Jacob for many days, told me one day.

"She's just not bonding with him. He's going home on an apnea monitor and his ostomy bags need to be changed and all. Those things will be hard for her to take care of. Last time I talked to her about discharge, she did not even have formula or any diapers yet.

"How's she going to take care of him?"

It was simple for me to guess how she would answer her own question: *She won't be able to.*

"Well, Shelly's had a tough go of things, hasn't she? She doesn't have too many resources, psychological or otherwise, to help her care for Jacob," I said. "She's been through a lot of trauma and may even have a bit of post-traumatic stress syndrome. We'll have to create a support system for her with home nursing visits and social work follow-up. Mary is on the case. We'll just keep trying to work with mom as best we can, and hope the support services we put in place will enable her to pull things together."

"Yeah, but Jacob needs a *real* mom who loves him to pieces, like I do." Melissa was the only twenty-something nurse in the NICU who was married and did not already have a baby of her own, although everyone knew she and her husband wanted one. She often took Jacob out of his crib just to cuddle him close to her breast. As she stroked the baby fine hair at the nape of his neck, she tipped her head down to reach his and to inhale his scent.

"Melissa, you keep loving him while he's here and hopefully it will last him a good long while."

Shelly's visits remained infrequent, but when she did come, the nurses spent extra time helping her learn Jacob's cues. Mary asked the state's social service agency to put a "family preservation" plan into place to ensure Shelly would have support when she took Jacob home. A home health nurse would visit twice weekly for the first few months. We gave Shelly a brand new car seat when she could not come up with the cash for one. She purchased formula with vouchers from a state program. Volunteers donated diapers and clothes.

Our staff set a final schedule for Shelly's visits. During two nights in our family room, she slept near Jacob's crib and woke up every three hours to give him his bottle. She learned how to change his ostomy bag, administer his medications, and respond to monitor alarms. Although she handled him tentatively, she got the job done. Her confidence seemed to be increasing.

The day of Jacob's discharge, Melissa crossed the NICU to speak to me in hushed tones. "Dr. Hall, I still don't feel comfortable sending Jacob home with *her*."

I looked up from my computer screen. "It's hard to feel really good about it, isn't it?" I agreed. "But she's demonstrated she can meet his needs; we'll have to hope she can handle everything once she gets him home."

Shelly wasn't the first teenage mother to take home a high-risk NICU graduate. Although her own family hadn't provided Shelly with much of a foundation, I had to trust that the social services we had put in place to support her would be enough to get her and Jacob through his first critical year of life and beyond.

***

Notes:

Necrotizing enterocolitis (NEC), the condition which affected Jacob, occurs in approximately 7 percent of babies with birth weights between 500 and 1,500 grams. The causation of NEC is not well understood although it is almost certainly multifactorial, resulting from a combination of genetic factors, immaturity, a heightened inflammatory response, and abnormal microbial colonization of the gut. Up to 30 percent of babies who develop NEC may die, and those who require surgery are at somewhat higher risk than those who do not. The inflammatory cascade set off by NEC affects not only the intestine, but other more distant organs, including the brain. NEC may be responsible for serious, long-term neurodevelopmental delays, and even microcephaly, in 25 percent of survivors. (Neu J. and A. W. Walker. 2011. "Necrotizing Enterocolitis." *New England Journal of Medicine 364*(3): 255-264.)

Fortunately, when Jacob required surgery to treat his necrotizing enterocolitis, he was not left with "short gut syndrome" (length of small intestinal less than 75 cm.), as up to 20 percent of babies with NEC who undergo surgical resection are. In this condition, the remaining absorptive surface of the intestine does not allow enough digestion to take place to enable growth and survival. Babies with short gut must, therefore, receive either long-term IV nutrition in order to grow, or an intestinal transplant. Those who are forced to remain on IV nutrition (also known as TPN, or total parenteral nutrition) often encounter numerous complications such as liver damage from the elements in the IV nutrition, and bloodstream infection from prolonged dependence on an indwelling central IV line. In spite of these difficulties, babies with short gut syndrome now have survival rates as high as 80-94 percent.

Management of short gut syndrome and its complications, including liver disease, recurrent sepsis, and lack of venous access, are thoroughly discussed in a review article by Hwang and Shulman. Intestinal transplant is also described. (Hwang S.T. and R. J. Shulman. 2002. "Update on Management and Treatment of Short Gut." *Clinics in Perinatology 29*(1): 181-195.) The cost of caring for children with NEC is considerable, though; as much as $500 million to $1 billion is spent each year in the United States. (Neu and Walker, *op cit.*)

NICU parents have to find a delicate balance between fear and hope, quite a difficult task. In Jerome Groopman's book, *The Anatomy of Hope* (2004. New York: Pocket Books), the author talks about how hope can help people deal with frightening information so as to be able to make decisions without being panicked. However, if fear overwhelms hope, decision-making is made infinitely more difficult.

Parents whose infants are in the NICU can experience high levels of psychological distress, and this can lead to parental post-traumatic stress disorder as seemed to happen with Shelly. This, coupled with the potential for negative outcomes in their infants, suggests the importance of preparing parents for psychological reactions they may have while their infant remains hospitalized in the NICU. (Shaw R. J., R. S. Bernard, T. Deblois et al. 2009. "The Relationship Between Acute Stress Disorder and Posttraumatic Stress Disorder in the Neonatal Intensive Care Unit." *Psychosomatics 50*: 131-137.) Interpretation of the results of this scientific study are accessible in the lay press as well. (Tarkan L. 2009. "For Parents on NICU, Trauma May Last." *The New York Times*, August 25.)

A particular problem for teen parents like Shelly and Jason is that they may not understand the severity of their baby's illness. One study showed that teens whose babies were in the NICU often underestimated the nature of their infant's illness, even when the health problems were critical and/or lethal. Teens' comprehension of how sick their infant was tended to be worse when a physician had spoken with them, compared with other health care providers, likely because physicians do not do a good enough job of breaking down complicated medical information into terms an adolescent might understand. Also, teens remained reluctant to ask questions that might help them better understand their infant's condition. (Boss R. D., P. K. Donohue, R. M. Arnold. 2010. "Adolescent Mothers in the NICU: How Much Do They Understand?" *Journal of Perinatology 30*(4): 286-290.) Clearly, there is room for improvement when it comes to the NICU team's communication with teenagers who are also parents.

Shelly was at high risk to abuse or neglect her baby by virtue of the fact that she was a teenage parent with poor social support. For a detailed discussion on this topic, see "When Children Have Children," Facts for Families # 31, July, 2004, found on the website of the American Academy of Child and Adolescent Psychiatry at www.aacap.org. Lack of effective bonding with her baby further increased Shelly's risk. Our job in the NICU was to do what we could to promote her engagement with and bonding to her baby, and to help her maximize her supports so that social isolation after discharge would not heighten her risk even more.

Chapter 17

Who is the Victim? Tiffany Calkins

Tiffany Calkins' birth was a tense and ugly affair. I usually enjoyed the invigorating atmosphere and the joyous celebration of new life when I attended the delivery of a baby, but her birth was not to be one of those times.

As Rhonda Calkins was taken back to the operating room, she grabbed her belly and screamed in pain. "Get this baby out of me!" she wailed.

"Another druggie," the operating room nurse whispered to me in passing.

Here we go again, I thought. *How many times do I have to see this movie? Should I even hope it might have a different ending than usual tonight?*

The woman hardly lay still long enough for the nurses to get an IV in her, as she begged for pain medication. She shrieked; she writhed; she swore at everyone. The obstetrician and the anesthesiologist looked at each other over face masks drawn tight across their noses and cheeks, and a message passed between them. This lady was going down with general anesthesia.

"You are going to sleep now," the anesthesiologist told her. Silence spread through the operating room briefly, and then the chatter of the scrub nurse and the circulating nurses methodically doing their jobs filtered into my awareness.

"Grandma wants to come in, Dr. Sharp. Okay?" the circulating nurse asked.

The obstetrician did not take her eyes off the mother's belly, where she had already sliced through layers of skin and fat. She was down to the muscle, underneath which lay the peritoneum, then the intestines, and beneath that the uterus. "Okay," she said into the woman's belly.

The scrub nurse standing across from the obstetrician raised her eyebrows to indicate to the circulating nurse that permission had been granted. Soon, a woman who appeared to be about forty-years-old, wearing huge gold hoop earrings and tight blue jeans, teetered into the operating room on high heels behind the nurse. She was taken to a stool next to her daughter's head. *Must be weird*, I thought, *to sit next to your daughter and see her with eyes taped shut, a breathing tube coming out of her mouth, and her body disappearing behind a blue paper screen.*

Dr. Sharp pulled the scalpel blade lightly across the mother's beefy red, swollen uterus. When it gave in one spot, she abandoned the scalpel then poked her finger in through the opening and stretched it wider. The bag of waters surrounding the baby burst and fluid the color and consistency of crankcase oil splashed onto the operating room field. The obstetrician scooped dark purple clots of blood out of the opening in the uterus then stuck her gloved hand in and fished around for the baby. Her assistant directed the suction apparatus into the gaping wound, and it drained the bloody amniotic fluid. The fluid slurped and sloshed through the tubing and into a suction canister. Soon, at least half a liter of dark red blood filled the plastic container that sat on the floor.

The surgeon located the baby lying sideways at the top of the uterus, turned it and pulled it down and out, her fingers hooked under the baby's armpits for traction. Finally, there it was: a slimy small thing lying in a pool of blood on the mother's abdomen.

Dr. Sharp picked up the baby's crumpled form and cradled it against her sterile blue gown so she would not drop it. As she crossed the operating room to bring the baby to me, drops of blood marked her path like crumbs thrown behind by Hansel and Gretel. She set the baby down inside a large plastic bag up to its shoulders to prevent heat loss, and my team and I got to work.

"Twenty-six weeks. Abruption," she said, and then returned to her patient.

"Yeah, I noticed," I said.

A placental abruption means the placenta has torn away from the uterine wall. The baby's lifeline has been disconnected, and the baby is left without a supply of blood or oxygen. An abruption is a medical emergency because the baby's life—not the mother's—is in danger. One troubling cause is cocaine use by the mother.

I cleared the baby's airway of bloody secretions, and next applied a tiny green plastic mask attached to an oxygen source over her face, so I could give her some breaths to inflate her lungs. This jump-started her breathing and soon the baby moved around a little bit inside the bag and bleated like a lamb.

"How much does she weigh?" a loud voice intruded. There stood Grandma, video camera in hand.

"We haven't weighed her yet." I continued my work with the baby, assessed her breathing, listened to her heart, and pulled a standard-issue pink and blue striped cotton hat over her teacup-sized head. "Right now we're just trying to keep her warm, make sure she's breathing, and get her into the NICU," I said, when I assured myself that the baby's breathing was stable.

"Ma'am, could you turn off the video camera here in the operating room?" the circulating nurse asked her. "It's not allowed."

"All right, then." Grandma backed off and set her video camera down, but pulled out her cell phone and began to snap pictures. "When Rhonda called me tonight, I hadn't heard from her in more than six months. I did not even know she was pregnant and I certainly never heard about any doctor visits. What a surprise."

If Rhonda had gone for prenatal care, she could have been educated and counseled about her risk factors for poor pregnancy outcome, at least some of which she could have changed, had she wanted to. If she used cocaine, chances are that she also consumed alcohol, smoked cigarettes, and had poor nutrition. Each of these is an independent risk factor for giving birth to a baby who is either low birth weight and/or premature. Taken all together, they virtually ensure a baby will be born with problems, like the little baby my team and I were in the process of transferring from the warming table into the transport isolette.

Soon, we wheeled the baby down the hall as Grandma trailed behind, scrolling through the pictures on her phone. "Wait up!" she called, as we rushed forward. "Hey, I got some family here that want to see the baby. Hold on a minute while I get everybody."

My charge nurse rolled her eyes, but slowed her pace. We came to a brief stop in front of the waiting room, and a boisterous contingent of family members young and old stumbled out. "Oh, looky there. She's just adorable." So many cell phone cameras clicked it seemed like the baby was surrounded by paparazzi.

"Okay, we've got to go," the charge nurse announced.

As the night wore on, I transfused the Baby Calkins over and over again--six times in all. At first, I was disgusted. Then, I got downright angry, and by the end of the night I seethed. I went into the baby's room to look at her. The overhead light shone through the hard plastic shell of her isolette and I could almost see every threadlike vein through her translucent skin. She was surprisingly pink given her degree of anemia, perhaps because the top layer of her skin had broken down and now oozed bright red droplets. Puncture wounds dotted her arms and legs where the nurses had stuck her unsuccessfully for IVs, and deep purple bruises from delivery covered her head and trunk.

She looked like roadkill. It was hard not to turn away.

Grandma came in to visit the baby during the night and announced, "I just know this baby is gonna end up with me. Rhonda has five other kids, all by different guys, and I've got 'em all. She just doesn't seem to wanna stick around after she has 'em. Don't know how I'm gonna do it..." Grandma clucked her tongue while she shook her head, her earrings shimmering in the light.

I was too busy to engage in much conversation.

She brought several visitors into the room in pairs of two, and each time we had to tell them to keep the noise down: the baby was quite sick.

"But she's breathing, isn't she?" one asked.

"I have a cousin who had a twenty-five-weeker and he's four-years-old now. He's doin' just fine," another said.

"When do you think Rhonda will get to take her home?" asked the next.

Were all these people naïve, clueless, or deluded? I wondered. Did they really think a woman could give birth to a baby under any set of circumstances, at any time point in gestation, and the baby would be fine?

"Each baby is different," I explained. "It's too soon yet to tell how this baby's going to do," I added, although in my mind, it wasn't.

Many times a baby's disease process is not at all clear to me as it unfolds, but that night I had no question at all. The baby was in the throes of a massive intraventricular hemorrhage.

It was bad enough that the crack cocaine her mother smoked precipitated her premature birth. Once the cocaine entered mother's bloodstream, it caused her blood pressure to skyrocket. This caused the blood vessels behind the placenta, already bloated and stretched to their limit from pregnancy, to rupture. Blood seeped into a pocket behind the placenta. Under mounting pressure, the growing collection of blood pushed and pushed until it tore the placenta completely off the wall of her uterus where, only a few hours before, the baby had been safely encased.

The dose of cocaine the baby received across the placenta also caused her own blood pressure to rise to an alarming level. The increased pressure in her circulatory system in turn caused the fragile little blood vessels around the edge of her cerebral ventricles to burst. Now, I watched as her brain filled up with blood.

The baby's internal bleeding continued at a fast pace, and I could not get her blood count into the normal range in spite of back-to-back transfusions. When lab results failed to show any improvement with my efforts, I struggled to keep my professional demeanor in front of the nurses. Good thing Grandma had gone home for the night. The objectivity I had tried so hard to cultivate over the years escaped me. I had compassion for this baby, but when it came to her mother, my compassion was in short supply.

"Hey, little one," I told the baby before I left her room, "you did not get a fair shake at this thing called life, did you?"

I knew all about "blaming the victim," our society's tendency to blame poor and disadvantaged people for their plight in life. Maybe this baby's mother was a victim and I was unfairly blaming her for the troubles she encountered that may have led to her cocaine use. *Why did this mother use cocaine?* I wondered. Did she start using just to have fun with friends, or take a detour into the wrong crowd? Was she trying to erase an unpleasant memory, perhaps that of a molestation, a rape? Maybe cocaine transported her far away from a life of deprivation in the real world; quite possibly she had no job, no money. Or did her substance abuse mask mental illness?

She could have had a million reasons, but in my current frame of mind, I could not think of a single one to excuse her callous drug use during pregnancy. At that moment, all I wanted to do was hold her accountable. I had spent my entire career, both in social work and in medicine, helping people, trying to understand their situations, their motivations, the factors that led to their behavior. But tonight, I was completely fed up with trying to understand.

I was not sure I would be able to keep my emotions in check when I finally met the mother of the baby lying in front of me, this baby who was the face of collateral damage of a dangerous and destructive lifestyle. We would not meet that night, though, as she was in the Adult ICU after having lost so much blood at delivery.

The next morning, the baby's cranial ultrasound confirmed what I expected. The pictures on the radiology viewing station showed a brain that was soggy, spongy, and swollen with blood. All I could do was shake my head when I reviewed the films with my partner, Dr. Handler.

"Hope you have a better day than I did," I said, as I handed the on-call phone over to him.

"Yeah, right," he said.

***

When I got home, I slept soundly, and when I awoke, I took my kayak out on the lake behind my house. I dipped my yellow paddle into the calm green water in long strokes, and the boat slid forward under a pristine sky. A great blue heron streaked down the middle of the lake, its enormous wings flapping above me. I squealed and caught my breath when a fish jumped in front of my bow, and I smiled as I watched white-tailed bunnies hop in easy, regular strides across the lush lawns of early summer.

When I arrived at the hospital the following day, I learned that Tiffany had died the night before. Dr. Handler told me how her mother had held her infant daughter and bawled when her heart rate went down to zero. Grandma had bawled, too.

I thought long and hard about Tiffany. I had performed her resuscitation well, made the correct diagnosis, and given the necessary transfusions. Sometimes, modern medicine cannot fix what ails our patients, I had to admit. Many people do not understand or accept that reality, though. They are cavalier when making life choices—and even thoughtlessly ignore any possible consequences of their actions—yet, they still hold on to the unreasonable expectation that doctors can fix any condition or illness that they may bring on themselves.

I hoped the loss of Rhonda Calkins' baby would force her to take a look at her life and the choices she had made, and try to do things differently in the future.

Notes:

Immediately after Tiffany was born, she was placed in a plastic bag to help maintain her body temperature. Although temperature control has long been known to be important in improving the survival of low birth-weight infants, in the past decade researchers have shown that placing very immature babies in plastic bags at birth can minimize heat loss. This practice lessens serious complications experienced by premature babies while also contributing to their improved survival. (Watkinson M. 2006. "Temperature Control of Premature Infants in the Delivery Room." *Clinics in Perinatology 33*(1): 43-53.)

Maternal cocaine use is a risk factor for intraventricular hemorrhage in already-fragile premature infants. Tiffany did not survive, but if she had, chances are her development would have been impaired, not only from the effects of the intraventricular hemorrhage she suffered, but also from the direct effects of exposure to cocaine. (Singer L., T. Tamashita, S. Hawkins et al. 1994. "Increased Incidence of Intraventricular Hemorrhage and Developmental Delay in Cocaine-Exposed Very Low Birth Weight Infants." *The Journal of Pediatrics 124*(5 Pt 1): 765-771. Also *see* Singer L., R. Arent, K. Farkas et al. 1997. "Relationship of Prenatal Cocaine Exposure and Maternal Postpartum Psychological Distress to Child Developmental Outcome." *Development and Psychopathology 9*(3): 473-489.) The multitude of medical and environmental risk factors (such as unstable home lives) to which children of cocaine-using mothers are exposed also contribute to their poor developmental outcome. (Tronick E. Z. and M. Beeghly. 1999. "Prenatal Cocaine Exposure, Child Development, and the Compromising Effects of Cumulative Risk." *Clinics in Perinatology 26*(1): 151-172.)

I was unaware of the particular factors in Rhonda Calkins' life that may have led to her cocaine use. Her use of cocaine could simply have been a poorly conceived coping response to stresses in her life. The association of maternal psychosocial stresses, including the experience of racial discrimination during pregnancy or throughout a woman's life, with delivery of low birth weight and premature infants, is well documented. Sometimes stress is linked to preterm birth through the pathway of maternal engagement in high-risk behaviors such as drug use. Dr. Michael Lu has written extensively on the relationship between differential experiences of African-American and white women both during pregnancy and across the lifespan, and how these different life experiences contribute to racial disparities in birth outcomes. To learn more about the "life-course perspective" model Dr. Lu espouses to reduce racial disparities, please see Appendix 2 at the end of the book. (Lu M. C., M. Kotelchuck, V. Hogan et al. 2010. "Closing the Black-White Gap in Birth Outcomes: A Life-Course Approach." *Ethnicity and Disease 20*(1 Suppl 2*)*: S2-62-S2-76.)

Chapter 18

The Lucky Twin: Emma Masterson

Fourteen-month-old Emma Masterson, clad only in her diaper, sat smiling, her little legs stretched out in front of her, on the smooth, white-paper sheet drawn over the exam table in the follow-up clinic. Her mother stood close by, guarding her so she would not make a move and tumble off the table.

I remembered Emma's parents well from her long stay in the NICU, especially the day Emma was born. Dr. Kent had been in charge that day, and I had worked quietly and steadily with our other patients as he attended her delivery and handled her admission. I had examined baby after baby, written copious notes, completed all my orders, and then gone to lunch. When I returned, he was still working with the same baby and seemed to be in constant conversation with her nurse.

"What's going on?" I finally asked him, wondering what sort of challenge had been occupying him all morning. The baby had been born around 9 a.m. and it was now 1 p.m.

"The baby's had a low blood sugar since birth, and I haven't been able to get it into the normal range yet." Dr. Kent was the most steady, level-headed doctor I had ever known. He never lost his cool in high-stress situations. On his shift, things always seemed to be under control, a testament to his calm demeanor. But now his face appeared flushed and I could sense in his voice the pressure he felt.

"What have you done to correct it?" I asked, wondering if he needed any help brainstorming solutions.

"I started out running IV fluids of 10 percent dextrose at the normal rate, and each time the blood sugar's been low, I've gone up on either the rate or the concentration of sugar. I had to place an umbilical catheter when I got up to 16 percent dextrose, since I could not give that in a peripheral IV. Now I'm up to 20 percent at nearly twice the normal rate of fluids. And still her blood sugar is only 10. The highest I've gotten since birth is a 15."

I cringed. The blood sugar should have been closer to 40.

"With each change, I expected it to come up, like it usually does," he continued.

"And why wouldn't you? Sounds like you've been following the standard protocol."

I wondered, as I am sure Dr. Kent did too, why this baby was not responding to normal measures. After Emma's umbilical cord had been clamped and cut at birth, the glucose her mother generously provided abruptly ceased. It became Emma's job alone to produce and regulate glucose within her own body, a task at which she was failing miserably. Most babies did well when IV glucose was started.

"Any seizures?" I asked.

"Not yet. She's been jittery, but no seizures." Dr. Kent wiped a light tracing of sweat from his brow.

A prolonged low blood sugar can cause seizures, and later, brain damage. Ninety percent of all the glucose in the body is consumed by the brain. When its supply of this high-octane fuel is in short supply, the brain can short-circuit into seizures. The baby had a serious problem that had to be corrected as soon as possible. Brain cells could be dying with each passing moment.

Now I understood why Dr. Kent had stayed so close to the baby all morning, and I was glad he had given her his singular attention. He was the kind of doctor I would want if my child were in distress. His attention to detail and conscientious work ethic served our patients well.

"What's the baby's problem? Is it an infant of a diabetic mother?" I asked, following him into the baby's room. With the recent surge in maternal obesity, more and more mothers were being diagnosed with gestational diabetes, and their babies were always larger than average. Although diabetic mothers fight to control high blood sugars, their babies actually suffer from the reverse, low blood sugars. I expected, then, to see a robust and chubby baby—the typical appearance of an infant of a diabetic mother—but what I saw instead was the exact opposite.

The baby, Emma, was a scrawny little thing who looked to be an emaciated two pounds at best. Her skin sagged on her diminutive frame and her disproportionately large head appeared to be nearly bald, with only a few sparse tufts of hair pasted on top. She looked like the pictures of babies born in sub-Saharan Africa countries, the ones in magazine advertisements whose woeful eyes urgently beseech readers for monetary donations to save their lives. Her parents sat by her isolette waiting for good news.

"Nancy and Chris, this is Dr. Hall," said Dr. Kent. "I'm just showing her your baby. Do you mind if we talk about her for a minute?"

"No, go right ahead," said Nancy. She shifted her weight uncomfortably on the hard chair.

"What's her gestational age?" I asked Dr. Kent.

"She's thirty-two weeks, growth-restricted. Small for gestational age. She was a twin. Her twin died *in utero* at twenty-five weeks. She made it this far, which is good."

I turned to her parents. "I'm sorry to hear about your loss. What a bit of bad luck." Turning back to Dr. Kent, I asked, "What happened?"

"Twin-to-twin transfusion syndrome. This baby was the donor; the recipient died of heart failure. At twenty-five weeks, the obstetricians did not want to deliver this one unless they had to, and she seemed to stabilize after the twin died. Then, today she was in some distress, so the obstetrician elected to deliver her before it was too late." Although Dr. Kent was discussing the medical details in front of Emma's parents, I was sure by now they had learned about them from their obstetrician and probably from Dr. Kent earlier in the day.

Emma and her identical twin sister had been connected *in utero* by blood vessels that snaked through the placenta they shared. Emma pumped blood across one of the arteries coiling through her umbilical cord into a pool in the placenta, where it was immediately picked up by a vein feeding through her twin's cord and into her circulation. Emma's continuous donation of blood left her anemic; her twin gained so much blood that her heart could not keep up with the demands to pump it all around. Typical for this syndrome, Emma grew poorly, and now had few internal resources to maintain her blood sugar.

I did not envy the obstetrician's position any more than I envied Dr. Kent's. It takes enormous skill to decide when a fetus is in such dire straits that risking all the complications of prematurity is a better choice than risking a stillbirth. In this family's case, I could easily see how the decision would be weighted toward delivery, given that they had already lost one baby. Emma's parents must have been confronted with a wide range of emotions since the sudden death of the first twin.

"You've been through a lot," I said to the parents, and they nodded, faces somber yet trusting. "Well, with everything Dr. Kent's doing, Emma's blood sugar should be normal soon."

"We're really praying for that," said Chris. "We want her to come home with us so much."

I nodded, sensing his worry that his hopes for Emma were just out of his reach.

"We know you do," said Dr. Kent softly, and he and I left the room.

"Jeez, that's a tough one," I said to him. "I hope things straighten around before too long. What was her hematocrit? Did she need a transfusion?"

"Blood count was okay, not great, but okay. I guess once the other twin died and this one did not have to donate to her anymore, it gradually came up. Breathing's good, oxygen level is fine."

"At least you don't have those problems, too. What's your next move?" I asked him. "Hydrocortisone?"

Hydrocortisone is a form of cortisol; it helps regulate glucose metabolism throughout the body. Because it's a steroid with many potentially harmful side effects, it is not a first-line treatment for hypoglycemia (low blood sugar); giving glucose is.

"Yeah. I've already ordered it after speaking with the endocrinologist. It should come up from the pharmacy any minute."

Emma's nurse came out of her room. "Dr. Kent, the baby's legs are twitching; the movements don't stop when I put my hand on her. I think it's a seizure."

We all plunged back into her room and watched as the arms and legs of the small baby in front of us jumped as though they were reacting to jolts of low-voltage electrical current. Her parents now stood at her bedside; Chris had his arm on Nancy's shoulder as she held a tissue in front of her nose.

"Darn it. I was hoping this wouldn't happen. Time for Phenobarbital," Dr. Kent said. Knowing him as well as I did, I suspected he was upset with himself, even though he'd worked feverishly all morning to prevent this situation.

"Will she be okay?" Chris asked.

"I hope so. We're gonna keep doing everything we can for her," Dr. Kent answered.

The hydrocortisone did the trick with Emma's blood sugar—almost instantly—and Phenobarbital stopped the seizures. Dr. Kent spent the rest of the day and night adjusting the glucose infusion. Trying to tightly regulate Emma's blood sugar in the normal range turned out to be a difficult balancing act. I was pleased to hear of her improvement the next morning.

Often hydrocortisone is needed only on a short-term basis, as a baby's body adjusts after birth. When Emma's blood sugar had been stable for several weeks, we tried tapering off the hydrocortisone, but her blood sugar dropped into the danger zone once it was stopped.

"Just start it back up," directed the endocrinologist. "In the meantime, let's do more tests to figure out why she's still having trouble."

A test to see whether Emma's body could produce cortisol in response to the usual stimulus was abnormal; the endocrinologist was uncertain whether her body would ultimately regain the ability to regulate this hormonal pathway. Sometimes growth restriction causes long-lasting changes in many of the body's organs. She would have to go home on the hydrocortisone.

As Emma improved, her parents gradually relaxed into the daily rhythm of the NICU. "What's her weight today?" was always the first question either of them asked each day when they came to visit. After all, she had to double her birth weight—and then some—before she would be allowed to go home.

Up ten grams was the answer one day; down five grams was the answer the next.

"Why is she having such trouble gaining weight?" Nancy asked me one day. "Will she ever reach normal size for her age?" Her frustration with the "two steps forward, one step backward" pattern was evident, as Emma entered her third week in the NICU.

"Some babies who are born small for their age eat well and catch up to normal size by a year of age. Others stay small and never achieve normal height, for reasons we don't completely understand. Babies born the earliest and with the lowest birth weight are the least likely to catch up. Emma may be in this group. Her head is growing well; that's good news."

We measured each baby's head circumference weekly. Poor head growth in a baby born already small was a worrisome sign; they were more likely to be plagued with cognitive and developmental delays.

"Can't you do anything more to help her gain?"

"Believe me, we're trying. It's our top priority. She's already on really high calorie milk, and she'll need to go home taking these extra calories as well."

"So I can't breast feed her when she's ready?"

"A couple of times a day you can, but so far she's showing us she needs the extra calories to maintain her weight, much less grow well."

Nancy's smile sagged. I felt guilty depriving her of the one job a mother has a biological imperative to do: nurse her baby.

"Keep pumping, and we'll add even more calories to fortify your breast milk; she can take it through a bottle for about half of her feedings, to give her that extra boost. Breast milk is definitely best. Helps her immune system. And studies have shown, breast fed babies have higher IQs than formula fed babies."

"I know. Nursing is something I've planned to do ever since I found out I was pregnant. I was wondering how I would manage to nurse two, but now with just the one..."

Nancy's sentence trailed off as the memory of her lost baby invaded her thoughts. I wondered how often she reminisced over the plans she had made for the two identical babies she was supposed to have, and I realized how intently she had her hopes pinned on Emma.

***

Several weeks later, I talked with Nancy and Chris again. As I entered the room, Emma was snuggled up to Nancy and was nursing avidly. I watched as the four-and-a-half pound slip of a baby rhythmically sucked at her mother's breast, jaw moving up and down, eyes wide open, concentrating so hard. "Looks like she's doing great," I said.

"Yes, she's quite the little nurser. Surprised me," Nancy said. "I did not think she'd be so strong."

"We're really happy with her progress," said Chris, beaming. "We're finally starting to believe we may actually get to take her home."

"Of course you are going to take her home. But before you do, I want to discuss the results of the MRI scan of her brain. We looked for evidence that the hypoglycemia she experienced could have caused brain damage. The scan's definitely not normal, but it doesn't have the pattern of injury we'd see if hypoglycemia were the cause; the changes are very minor. I think the best thing to do is to take her home and treat her like a normal baby. Just have fun with her. Enjoy her. Love her."

Emma persevered with her feeding, cradled in Nancy's arms. With her right hand, Nancy gently rubbed back and forth over the top of Emma's head; I imagined she enjoyed the feel of the delicate fuzz under her fingertips.

"We've arranged for an early intervention specialist to come to your home twice a week, to make sure she has any help she needs reaching her developmental milestones. We'll follow her closely in our clinic. She's still at high risk for developmental problems, but your focus should be on all the good things she's doing. The more you interact with her, the better she'll respond. I can see she'll thrive with all the love you two have to give her."

"Yes, we do love her," Nancy said, kissing the fingers of her right hand and transferring the kiss onto the baby's head. "She gets twice as much love as the usual baby."

Chris smiled. It looked as though he and Nancy were in sync.

***

Emma had gone home with her parents a short time later, and now she awaited me in the clinic exam room.

I knocked twice then slowly pushed the door open, expecting Emma might be sitting or crawling on the floor on the other side of the door. However, when I entered, Emma, now fourteen-months-old, was sitting on the exam table wearing only a diaper. The first thing I noticed was her million dollar smile; the second thing was how her frame had filled out a bit more.

"Hey there. How are you guys?" I asked Nancy and Chris. "Hi, Emma."

Emma looked up at me from her perch and invited me into her world.

"What a happy baby."

"Yes, she's a joy," replied Nancy proudly.

Chris whispered to Emma, "Say 'hi' to Dr. Hall."

"Ga-ga," came the reply, although I wasn't bold enough to believe it was actually directed at me.

"How's she been doing? I see from her growth chart that she's been gaining weight steadily now. That's excellent."

"Yeah, she's doing great. We are so thrilled."

"Tell me what's going on with her."

"Well, she's babbling a lot, she can sit up very well, she does the army crawl all over the place…"

"The army crawl? You mean, she crawls on her stomach like a soldier sneaking up in battle?"

"That's right. Her left side isn't as strong as her right so she doesn't use that arm as well, and she kind of drags her left leg behind her. But she gets around, make no mistake about that."

I sat next to the little girl who still did not have too much hair on her head. Her bright eyes radiated a contagious energy and enthusiasm as they met mine without fear. A toothy grin stretched nearly from one ear to another.

I held up a small red block in front of her, enticing her to take it. She easily reached for it with her right hand and swiped it from mine, as her left arm rested by her side. I recovered the block, and then held it far to her left side. Her eyes followed the bright red object, and slowly, haltingly, she lifted her left arm. Not as well as her right, not with the same strength or coordination, but she did lift it. Eventually she batted the red block out of my hand and it tumbled to the floor.

"I can see the weakness you are talking about, but she sure can use that left arm."

"Oh yes, she can," said Nancy. "She just needs lots of encouragement."

"Well, you are just the folks to give it to her."

Chris nodded. "And we have the help of the therapists who come to our house twice a week. What a blessing that's been. Thanks for putting that in place."

"Hey, no problem. Early interventions services do wonders," I said. "Now, let's see what she can do when you put her on her feet."

"Upsy daisy," said Nancy, lifting Emma off the table and lowering her gently to the floor.

The good-natured infant kept her smile solidly in place as she struggled to steady herself on her two bare feet, her socks having been removed with the rest of her clothes in anticipation of her exam. Her legs met in a scissored position and her toes were pointed like a little ballerina's, making it impossible for her to balance. She wobbled from side to side while Nancy steadied her, but she wasn't yet ready or able to take any steps.

"She's got some work to do," I said. "But I think she'll get there."

"We're sure she will. We're just gonna keep on practicing and practicing. We do all the exercises the therapist shows us, and she's made so much progress."

Nancy's voice reflected what I sensed was her immense pride at how far Emma had come from her beginnings as a frail newborn whose very existence was threatened.

"Can you pop her up here to the exam table again?" I asked. "I'll make a quick check of her heart and lungs." I had trouble placing my stethoscope on Emma's chest, because she kept grasping it and pushing it back with her right hand. Eventually, I convinced myself her heart and lungs sounded normal, and I turned on the otoscope's bright light to look in her ears. Wiggling it in front of her eyes, I waited until she fixed her vision on it, and next slowly drew it across her line of sight, forcing her to turn her head. When she'd turned far enough, I quickly moved in to examine her eardrum, always a challenging maneuver with any toddler. Unlike most toddlers, Emma did not cry; she sat still and complied with my exam.

"Wow, she's amazing," I said, after finishing my survey of her small body. "She looks fantastic." It seemed as though Nancy and Chris had transmitted a gene for resilience to their daughter.

"We agree 100 percent," said Nancy. "She's our lucky twin."

"Lucky, indeed. In more ways than one."

"How do you think Emma developed cerebral palsy?" she asked me.

I had been waiting for this question; now it did not seem like such a troublesome one. Nancy and Chris were clearly thrilled with their daughter in every respect, and they did not see her muscle weakness—her cerebral palsy—as an insurmountable problem. Neither did I.

"Emma had so many things going on around her birth that could have contributed. First, she is a surviving twin. We know that when one twin dies during pregnancy, the other twin faces a higher than average risk of cerebral palsy. Secondly, she was born with growth restriction. When the brain has not grown well in the womb, there is a higher chance for long-term developmental problems. And then, of course, she had the low blood sugar, although hypoglycemia doesn't usually cause cerebral palsy unless it continues for days. We made sure that did not happen.

"So, it is difficult—probably impossible—to pin it down to one thing."

What seemed most important to me now was not Emma's past, or even how she came to have cerebral palsy, but her future. And her future looked bright, with parents who adored her at her side.

"We were just curious," Nancy said. "Not that it matters. Emma's doing great and we're just thrilled with her. We're really grateful we have her."

"Well, you two are doing a wonderful job. She is the happiest child I have seen in a long, long time."

The image of an ebullient and curious Emma, and her contented and joyful parents, buoyed my spirits for the rest of the day, and for days afterward. I realized yet again that when the NICU team gives babies their all, and when parents rise to the challenges facing them and do their absolute best, miracles can occur. Emma would never be defined by the label, or even the words, "cerebral palsy." The words that defined her were Happy, Determined, and Loved.

Notes:

Emma and her twin who did not survive had undergone twin-to-twin transfusion syndrome, which only occurs in identical, or monozygotic, twins because they share a layer of placenta (called the chorion) that other twins do not. Complications occur in many of the pregnancies and in many of the twins with this syndrome in spite of optimal medical management. Good explanations on twin-to-twin transfusion syndrome, as well as many medical references about it, can be found at www.tttsfoundation.org.

I was thrilled that Nancy wanted to provide breast milk for Emma. Human milk can ordinarily serve as a complete source of babies' nutrition during their first six months of life. The benefits of breastfeeding are widely documented, and include a decrease in the occurrence of respiratory and gastrointestinal infections, as well as lower rates of type I diabetes mellitus, childhood leukemia, atopic dermatitis,

SIDS, and childhood obesity. (Duijts L., V. W. V. Jaddoe, A. Hofman, H. A. Moll. 2010. "Prolonged and Exclusive Breastfeeding Reduces the Risk of Infectious Diseases in Infancy." *Pediatrics 126*(1): e15-e25.)

Giving breast milk to premature infants is particularly important, as it is easier for them to digest than cow's milk formula, it decreases the risk of necrotizing enterocolitis, and it boosts their developing immune systems. (Schanler R. J. 2007. "Evaluation of the Evidence to Support Current Recommendations to Meet the Needs of Premature Infants: The Role of Human Milk." *American Journal of Clinical Nutrition 85*(2): 625S-628S.) Premature infants may require fortification of breast milk with higher calories and specific nutrients (protein, carbohydrate, calcium, phosphate, vitamins, and trace minerals) to ensure adequate growth; fortification may also contribute to improved mineralization of their bones. (Kuschel C. A. and J. E. Harding. "Multicomponent Fortified Human Milk for Promoting Growth in Preterm Infants." *Cochrane Database of Systematic Reviews* 2004;1:Art. No.:CD000343. DOI: 10.1002/14651858. CD000343.pub2. Accessed April 4, 2011 at http://www2. cochrane.org/reviews/en/ab000343.html.)

While 75 percent of U.S. mothers start out breastfeeding, only about 13 percent of them are still exclusively breastfeeding their infants at six months of age. If 90 percent of mothers could reach this goal, $13 billion in health care and other costs could be saved yearly, largely by preventing both the acute and chronic medical conditions that breastfeeding protects against. (Bartick M. and A. Reinhold. 2010. "The Burden of Suboptimal Breastfeeding in the United States: A Pediatric Cost Analysis." *Pediatrics 125*(5): e1048-e1056.)

Recognizing our nation's breastfeeding rates are suboptimal, in 2011, the U.S. Surgeon General issued a "Call to Action to Support Breastfeeding." This report, which details numerous ways in which individuals, communities and employers can promote breastfeeding, can be found at www.surgeongeneral.gov/topics/breastfeeding/index.html. Other resources on the topic of breastfeeding can be found at www.womenshealth.gov/breastfeeding or at www.cdc.gov /breastfeeding.

Cerebral palsy, which affects two to three children in 1,000, results from either a brain injury or some other disruption in normal brain development; it is a disorder affecting a child's movement, balance, and posture. Premature babies, such as Emma, are far more likely than term babies to develop cerebral palsy, often because they develop intraventricular hemorrhage or periventricular leukomalacia. Other causes of cerebral palsy include infections during pregnancy, severe jaundice, lack of adequate oxygen during fetal life, and severe difficulty (asphyxia) during delivery. Sometimes, a specific cause is not determined. Children with cerebral palsy may have other central nervous system problems such as mental retardation, learning disabilities, seizures, and/or problems with speech, vision, or hearing. Read more about cerebral palsy on the March of Dimes website at http://www.marchofdimes. com/baby/birthdefects_cerebralpalsy.html.

The entire 2006 issue of *Clinics in Perinatology 33*(2), June, is devoted to examination of "Perinatal Causes of Cerebral Palsy." Individual articles examine associations between cerebral palsy and preterm birth, intrauterine growth, multiple pregnancies, and other topics.

Afterword

I have been privileged throughout my career to have shared moments of incredible and inspiring intimacy with many families like Emma and her devoted parents. I have been challenged to give babies the best start possible in their lives, and if things did not go well, I have seen a million different reasons for "how babies got that way." Some of the reasons were based in medical conditions and circumstances; some of them derived more from the social environment in which the baby was born or to which the baby returned after birth. In many, if not most, instances, a complex combination of factors coalesced into creating each baby.

I have also seen how parents' internal resources and external support systems play a huge role in how they cope with and survive their own NICU experiences. The critically important role that health professionals play in providing NICU parents with understandable information about their child's condition, as well as with emotional support, has become more apparent to me over time.

I have loved being a part of the process that ensures a child gets a healthy start in life. Having parents who deeply love their children as my partners in the journey has been a joy that has made the painful parts of my job—seeing both babies and parents suffer—worth it. Finding hope in every situation, and helping parents to do so also, has been the most important part of my role as a neonatologist. I have done it all for the love of babies, and I plan to continue.

Appendix A

Specific Advice for Parents of Infants in the Neonatal Intensive Care Unit

Gather as much support for yourselves as possible. Have grandparents, aunts, uncles, and friends of you and your baby help you out, emotionally and physically. Let people bring you meals, drive you to appointments, and babysit for your other children. Now is not the time to be Super Mom or Wonder Woman.

Use your NICU's social worker. He or she will have invaluable resources for you and your family and will offer emotional support as well as help with logistical and financial concerns. Stay on the lookout for postpartum depression, and ask for help if you are experiencing symptoms. Also ask for help if you are having trouble coping with the stress of having a sick child or with the NICU environment.

Find out as much information about your baby's specific condition as you can. Talk with your baby's nurses and doctors. Ask for information to read and for trusted internet sites on which to do your own research. Stay current with what the NICU team is thinking. Do not hesitate to ask to speak with your baby's doctors and nurses, and by all means, ask questions if you do not understand something.

Be aware that when doctors quote statistics and give you a negative prognosis, it is their job to inform you of all the possibilities so you can make an informed decision about what is right for you and your family. If you disagree with your baby's health care team, you can ask to speak with a representative from the hospital's Ethics Committee.

Always remember that you are your baby's parent. Get as involved as possible, as early as is possible. Visit often. Take the baby's temperature and change its diapers. Give the baby a bath, when it is safe to do so, and feed the baby. The NICU staff does not want to take your place in your baby's heart, and never will.

Try to find and hold on to hope. It may make all the difference for you and your baby.

Appendix B

More Information about Prematurity and Other Causes of NICU Admission

Ten percent of all babies born in the United States are admitted to a Neonatal Intensive Care Unit, most often as the result of premature birth.[1] We have more NICUs and more neonatologists per person than perhaps anywhere else in the world. For example, we have twice as many neonatologists and three times as many neonatal intensive care beds as the United Kingdom, when these numbers are compared for the same number of live births. Yet, our birth weight-specific survival rates do not even match, much less exceed, those in the United Kingdom.[2] In fact, our infant survival statistics fare poorly in comparison with thirty-two countries in the world, and they have been getting worse since 1960.[3]

Yes, the United States' infant mortality rate, the rate at which babies die in the first year of life, ranks thirty-third among nations worldwide. Five babies die for every 1,000 who are born alive. On this vital statistic, which could be interpreted as a measure of how we care for our most vulnerable citizens, we fall behind the Czech Republic, Slovenia, Estonia, Greece, Hungary, Poland, Slovakia, and even Cuba, as well as all the wealthy, developed countries of

Europe. Japan has the lowest rate of infant deaths in the world: at 1.8 deaths per 1,000 live births, their rate is less than half of ours.[4]

Our survival statistics look even more dismal when we break our population into racial groups. An African-American infant has double the chance of dying during his or her first year of life compared with a Caucasian infant;[5] in fact, his or her chance of dying is equal to that of an infant born in a developing country, such as one in Africa.

With all of our neonatologists and NICUs, why are our infant survival statistics not better?

Our infant survival statistics are not better because we are approaching the problem of infant mortality backwards. Instead of spending large sums of money to care for premature babies *after* they are born, we would do better to allocate our precious health care dollars to providing preconception and prenatal services to women. The desired result would be to prevent some of the preterm births, because they are strongly related to rates of both neonatal mortality (death in the first twenty-eight days of life) and infant mortality.[6] Prematurity is the second leading cause of infant mortality in the United States, and the leading cause worldwide.

Preterm births occur far too commonly in the United States. American mothers give birth to nearly half a million of the 13 million infants born prematurely worldwide every year. While one in ten babies is born early around the world, the ratio here is one in eight births, and among African Americans, one in six.[7] The corresponding number in both Ireland and Finland is one in eighteen.[8]

While racial disparities figure prominently in our nation's high preterm birth rate, another group with higher than average rates of prematurity is our teenage mothers (14.5 percent versus a population average of 12.7 percent).[9] Four hundred thousand teenagers, half of whom are seventeen-years-old or less, give birth each year in the United States.[10] Our teen-pregnancy rate is twice that of any other advanced country, and nearly ten times as high as Japan's.[11] Babies born to teens are also more likely to be preterm or to have a low birth weight than babies born to mothers older than twenty.

In addition, consequences of teen pregnancy are far-reaching. For the young mothers, they include being a single parent, living in poverty, and depending on welfare, and failing to continue education beyond high school. Their children are more likely to be victims of child abuse and neglect, to have worse physical health, and to have a higher a rate of incarceration when they become adults than children born to mothers who delay childbearing.[12] Costs to society are substantial as well: About $4 billion a year is spent providing public benefits to support the health and welfare of teen parents and their children.[13]

The economic burden preterm births place on the U.S. economy is staggering. In 2006, the Institute of Medicine reported that the United States spends $26 billion every year as a consequence of this serious public health problem, or $51,600 per infant born prematurely.[14] Survivors are prone to developing significant long-term developmental disabilities, including cognitive disorders or learning disabilities in 25-50 percent and cerebral palsy in 5-15 percent.[15] The cost of treating these and other complications of prematurity, which may last a lifetime, is hefty, too; more than $35 billion is spent for treatment of cerebral palsy annually.[16]

Although public policy initiatives to reduce preterm births have been in place for decades in the United States, the rate of prematurity actually increased 36 percent between 1984 and 2006.[17] The preterm birth rate has only recently declined marginally, from 12.8 percent in 2006 to 12.3 percent in 2008.[18] Although it is too early to know whether this is a definite trend, it is positive news, because it means that about 20,000 fewer babies were born prematurely in the more recent years, than if rates had stayed at the higher level.

What are the factors underlying our high preterm birth rates and correspondingly poor survival rates for infants?

Several medical factors associated with the increase in preterm births, particularly among Caucasian women, are older maternal age and the rise in pregnancies with "multiples" such as twins and triplets. When women delay childbearing, their fertility declines, and it becomes increasingly necessary for them to use ovulation-inducing medications or assisted reproductive technologies, such as in vitro fertilization, to get pregnant.[19] These methods predispose to becoming pregnant with multiples, which are born early more often than singletons.

Also fueling the rise in preterm births is the growing number of late preterm infants (thirty-four to thirty-six weeks gestation); their numbers have increased 25 percent since 1990.[20] Some of the increase in late preterm births can be attributed to the rise in Cesarean section deliveries in recent years; a number of these may be early deliveries, which are not medically justified.[21]

Many other medical conditions that contribute to prematurity are more likely to be found in African-American and other socially disadvantaged women than in Caucasian women. These include maternal urinary tract infections and genital infections,[22,23] periodontal disease,[24] poor nutrition,[25,26] clotting abnormalities,[27,28] and genetic predispositions.[29]

Dr. Emile Papiernik stated that the vast majority of preterm births are "closely related to social class," noting that although both medical and social factors are involved, spontaneous preterm birth is largely a "social disease."[30]

Exposure to racism[31] and the maternal experience of stress[32] are two risk factors known to be associated with preterm birth; these are hard to quantify. Several authorities have argued that a woman's ability to bear a healthy baby is jeopardized if she has experienced stress caused by racism over the course of her life. The stress can change the "early programming" of her body, or it can disrupt her body's adaptive systems ("cumulative wear and tear"), and lead to a decline in her health that worsens her chance for a favorable pregnancy outcome.[33,34]

Two social issues undoubtedly contribute to the racial disparities in preterm birth and infant mortality: the higher poverty rate in African Americans compared with Caucasians (20 percent versus 10 percent),[35] and the higher number of African Americans compared with Caucasians who are among the 45 million people in this country who lack health insurance (43 percent versus 24 percent).[36,37] These societal conditions may work together to limit access of African-American women to prenatal care. One measure of the importance of early prenatal care is a recent finding that women, regardless of their ethnicity, who do not receive any prenatal care are twice as likely to have infants with cerebral palsy compared with women who do have early prenatal care.[38]

However, the racial gap in access to prenatal care has actually narrowed substantially over the past decade. Currently, 95 percent of African-American women receive prenatal care at some time during their pregnancy.[39] Although access to care has improved, racial differences in pregnancy outcomes have not.

Dr. Michael Lu stated, "To expect prenatal care, in less than nine months, to reverse the lifelong, cumulative impact of social inequality on the health of African-American mothers, may be expecting too much of prenatal care."[40]

Public health initiatives to prevent preterm birth and improve neonatal and infant survival were described in the *Healthy People 2010 Report*, published by the U.S. Department of Health and Human Services in 2000. The goal outlined in the report was to achieve a reduction in the rate of preterm birth from more than 12 percent nationally to 7.6 percent.[41] In 2008, the March of Dimes recognized the nation's collective failure to even come close to reaching this mark, and issued its first *Premature Birth Report Card*.[42] The United States earned a "D," and no individual states were awarded "A's." The March of Dimes has therefore extended the Prematurity Campaign it launched in 2003 to the year 2020.

What can be done to reduce the rate of preterm births? Nothing short of major societal change is needed, which may take decades to accomplish. We can learn from the countries of Europe, especially Scandinavia. Their numerous social programs supporting pregnant women have been instrumental in achieving their low rates of both preterm birth and neonatal/infant mortality. In many of these countries, prenatal care is comprehensive and free. Paid maternity leave begins six-to-twelve weeks before birth, with a specific goal of minimizing preterm births. Mothers can also take sick leave, whether paid or not, from their jobs after birth. Subsidized housing and other social supports are also provided for the more vulnerable populations of women in these societies.[43]

Here in the United States, Dr. Michael Lu argues that instead of focusing only on improving access to care and on specific risk factors that predispose to preterm birth, a much broader "life-course approach" is needed to try to reach the goal of minimizing racial disparities. This would require improving African-American women's access to health care throughout their lives, including care before, during and between pregnancies. For Dr. Lu's model to be successful, it will be imperative to change both family and community systems as well, by encouraging greater involvement of fathers, supporting working mothers, improving educational outcomes, and reducing poverty.[44]

Prematurity is certainly not the only diagnosis of newborns admitted to Neonatal Intensive Care Units. Babies with birth defects and babies who have low birth weights, even though they are not premature, are two other major groups.

About 3 percent of all babies born in the United States have birth defects; the rate is twice as high in preterm infants compared with term infants. [45] Congenital heart defects are among the most common, occurring in 0.5-1 percent of those born. Most birth defects are the result of a combination of genetic and environmental influences. Others are caused by maternal behaviors, which could potentially be changed (so-called "modifiable risk factors"), such as drinking alcohol, smoking cigarettes, using illegal drugs such as cocaine, and taking certain prescription medications. Sometimes absence of a specific nutrient, such as folic acid, is implicated as a cause of specific birth defects.[46]

Women who give birth to babies with low birth weights (less than 2,500 grams or five-pounds eight-ounces) have many of the same risk factors for poor pregnancy outcome that women who give birth early do, namely use of cigarettes, alcohol, and illegal drugs.[47,48,49] Poor nutrition and young age at conception are two additional risk factors.[50,51]

The cost of caring for babies born to mothers with modifiable risk factors is enormous. The total spent for medical expenses of infants exposed to cocaine during pregnancy is more than $500 million annually, while the costs of caring for infants born to mothers who smoke cigarettes was estimated to be $1.4 billion in 1995.[52]

Preventing prematurity and improving outcomes for all infants born in the United States is something we can do. It will take a major shift in our thinking, away from "blaming the victim" to providing a basic level of health care and social support to even the poorest and most vulnerable among us. It will take time and money. Such expenditures will be worth it, though, when our up-front spending for health care and social services results in lower birth rates of preterm and low birth weight babies, and those with congenital anomalies. If this occurs, our very expensive after-the-fact treatment of these stressed infants will no longer be necessary. Our newest and youngest members of society will gain a healthier start in life, and this will enable them to become more productive contributors to our society as they grow. Families will be happier.

References for Appendix B

1. March of Dimes Helps: The NICU Family Support Program at http://www.marchofdimes.com/prematurity/21579.asp.
2. Thompson L. A., D. C Goodman, G. A. Little. 2002. "Is More Neonatal Intensive Care Always Better? Insights From a Cross-National Comparison of Reproductive Care." *Pediatrics 109*(6): 1036-1043.
3. Nordquist C. "US Infant Survival Rates Lower Than Most Developed Nations." 2006. *Medical News Today*, May 9.
4. Ibid.
5. "U.S. Infant Mortality Rate Decline Stalls, Racial Disparities Remain, CDC Data Indicate." At http://www.medicalnewstoday.com/articles/116767.php.
6. MacDorman M. F. and T. J. Mathews. 2009. "Behind International Rankings of Infant Mortality: How the United States Compares with Europe." *NCHS Data Brief, No. 23*; November.
7. Martin J. A., B. E. Hamilton, P. D. Sutton et al. 2006. "Births: Final Data for 2004." *National Vital Statistics Report 55*(1): 1-101.
8. MacDorman and Mathews, Op cit., #6.
9. March of Dimes. Fact Sheets on Teenage Pregnancy, at http://www.marchofdimes.com/professionals/14332_1159.asp.
10. Ibid.
11. Hoffman S. D. and R. Maynard, Editors. *Kids Having Kids: Costs and Social Consequences of Teen Pregnancy*. Urban

Institute Press. Accessed April 4, 2011 at http://www.urban.org/books/kidshavingkids.

12. Ibid.

13. Ibid.

14. Institute of Medicine. 2006. *Preterm Birth: Causes, Consequences, and Prevention.* National Academies Press, Washington, D.C. July 13, at www.nap.edu.

15. Medical News, Products and Information. 2009. *Neonatology Today*. March, p. 7, at www.neonatologytoday.net.

16. Ibid.

17. Martin J. A., B. E. Hamilton, P. D. Sutton et al. 2009. "Births: Final Data for 2006." *National Vital Statistics 1. Reports 57:* 7. Hyattsville, MD: National Center for Health Statistics.

18. Reinberg S. "Preterm Birth Rates Declining, U.S. Report Shows." Accessed April 4, 2011 at http://www.healthfinder.gov/news/newsstory.aspx?docID =638986.

19. Wilson E. E. 2005. "Assisted Reproductive Technologies and Multiple Gestations." *Clinics in Perinatology 32(*2): 315-328.

20. Martin and Hamilton, Op cit, #17.

21. Bettegowda V. R., T. Dias, M. J. Davidoff et al. 2008. "The Relationship Between Cesarean Delivery and Gestational Age Among US Singleton Births." *Clinics in Perinatology 35*(2): 309-324.

22. Wadhwa P. D., J. F. Culhane, V. Rauh et al. 2001. "Stress, Infection and Preterm Birth: A Biobehavioural Perspective." *Paediatric Perinatology Epidemiology 15*(Supplement 2): 17-29.

23. Kramer M. S., L. Goulet, J. Lydon et al. 2001. "Socio-economic Disparities in Preterm Birth: Causal Pathways and Mechanisms." *Paediatric Perinatology Epidemiology 15*(Supplement 2): 104-123.

24. Lieff S., K. A. Boggess, A. P. Murtha et al. 2004. "The Oral Conditions and Pregnancy Study: Periodontal Status of a Cohort of Pregnant Women." *Journal of Periodontology 75*(1): 116-126.

25. Fiscella K. 2004. "Racial Disparity in Infant and Maternal Mortality: Confluence of Infection, and Microvascular Dysfunction." *Maternal and Child Health Journal 8*(2): 45-54.

26. Olsen S. F., N. J. Secher. 2002. "Low Consumption of Seafood in Early Pregnancy as a Risk Factor for Preterm Delivery: Prospective Cohort Study." *British Medical Journal 324* (7335): 447.

27. Lockwood C. J. and E. Kuczynski. 1999. "Markers of Risk for Preterm Delivery." *Journal of Perinatal Medicine 27*(1): 5-20.

28. Rosen T., E. Kuczynski, L. M. O'Neill et al. 2001. "Plasma Levels of Thrombin-Antithrombin Complexes Predict Preterm Premature Rupture of the Fetal Membranes." *Journal of Maternal Fetal Medicine 10*(5): 297-300.

29. Wang X., B. Zuckerman, G. Kaufman et al. 2001. "Molecular Epidemiology of Preterm Delivery: Methodology and Challenges." *Paediatric Perinatal Epidemiology 15* (Supplement 2): 63-77.

30. Papiernik E. 2004. Quoted in U. Snyder. Editor, "Preterm Birth as a Social Disease." *Medscape Pediatrics*, May/June. Accessed April 4, 2011 at http://www.me dscape.com/viewarticle/48173.

31. Rich-Edwards J., N. Krieger, J. Majzoub et al. 2001. "Maternal Experiences of Racism and Violence as Predictors of Preterm Birth: Rationale and Study Design." *Paediatric Perinatal Epidemiology 15*(Supplement 2): 124-135.

32. Collins J. W., Jr., R. J. David, R. Symons et al. 2000. "Low-income African-American Mothers' Perception of

Exposure to Racial Discrimination and Infant Birth Weight." *Epidemiology 11*(3): 337-339.

33. Lu M. C., M. Kotelchuck, V. Hogan et al. 2010. "Closing the Black-White Gap in Birth Outcomes: A Life-Course Approach." *Ethnicity and Disease 20*(1 Suppl 2): S2-62-76.

34. Burris H. H. and J. W. Collins, Jr. 2010. "Race and Preterm Birth—The Case for Epigenetic Inquiry." *Ethnicity and Disease 20*(3): 296-299.

35. *Income Inequality: Millions Left Behind.* Third Edition. 2004. Americans for Democratic Action, Inc. Washington, D.C. February. Accessed April 4, 2011 at http://www.inequality.org/incineqada.pdf.

36. U.S Census Bureau, Table 6: 2008. "People Without Health Insurance Coverage by Selected Characteristics: 2006 and 2007," August. Accessed April 4, 2011 at http://gfretwell.com/ftp/medicalinsurance/censusuninsured.pdf.

37. Snyder U. 2004. "Preterm Birth as a Social Disease." *Medscape Pediatrics*, May/June. Accessed April 4, 2011 at http://www.medscape.com/viewarticle/481732 .

38. Wu Y. W., G. Xing, E. Fuentes-Afflick et al. 2011. "Racial, Ethnic and Socioeconomic Disparities in the Prevalence of Cerebral Palsy." *Pediatrics 127*(3): e674-e681.

39. Lu et al, Op cit, #33.

40. Ibid.

41. Office of Population Affairs, U.S. Department of Health and Human Services. 2001. "Healthy People 2010–Reproductive Health," October. Accessed April 4, 2011 at http://www.hhs.gov/opa/pubs/hp2010_rh.html.

42. March of Dimes. 2008. "Nation Gets a "D" as March of Dimes Releases Premature Birth Report Card." Press Release November 12. Accessed April 4, 2011 at http://www.marchofdimes.com/aboutus/22684_42538.asp.

43. Williams B. C. 1994. "Social Approaches to Lowering Infant Mortality: Lessons from the European Experience." *Journal of Public Health Policy 15*(1): 18-25.

44. Lu et al, Op cit, #33.

45. Honein M. A., R. S. Kirby, R. E. Meyer et al. 2009. "Association Between Major Birth Defects and Preterm Birth." *Maternal and Child Health Journal. 13*(2): 164-75.

46. Centers for Disease Control and Prevention. "Basic Facts about Birth Defects." Accessed April 4, 2011 at: http://www.cdc.gov/ncbddd/birthdefects/facts.html.

47. American College of Obstetricians and Gynecologists (ACOG). 2000. "Intrauterine Growth Restriction." *ACOG Practice Bulletin*, Number 12, January.

48. Berghella V. 2007. "Prevention of Recurrent Fetal Growth Restriction." *Obstetrics and Gynecology 110*(4): 904-912.

49. U.S. Department of Health and Human Services. 2004. "The Health Consequences of Smoking: A Report of the Surgeon General." Centers for Disease Control and Prevention, Office on Smoking and Health, May.

50. Goldenberg R. L. and J. F. Culhane. 2007. "Low Birth Weight in the United States." *American Journal of Clinical Nutrition* (Supplement): 584S-590S.

51. Berghella, Op cit, # 48.

52. Hoffman et al, Op cit, # 11.

Glossary

Abruption: See Placental abruption.

Anencephaly: A birth defect in which a part of the brain and skull do not develop, caused by failure of the embryonic neural tube to close.

Apnea: Pause in breathing, which may lead to drop in heart rate (bradycardia) or drop in oxygen saturation (desaturation).

Blood gas: A blood test to determine the blood's acid-base status including pH and levels of carbon dioxide and oxygen; usually performed on arterial blood.

Bradycardia: Low heart rate. Often occurs after apnea (pause in breathing).

Bronchopulmonary dysplasia (BPD), also known as Chronic Lung Disease (CLD): A lung disease found primarily in premature infants, many of whom have been on mechanical ventilators. BPD is characterized by scarring and inflammation of the lungs. Babies may need to go home on oxygen if they have BPD.

Cardioversion: A method to treat an abnormal heart rhythm by providing an electrical shock to the heart. Paddles are applied to the patient's chest, and an electrical current, which is discharged through them, travels to the heart to "reset" its pacemaker.

Cerebral palsy (CP): A group of non-progressive disorders that primarily affect movement, balance, and posture; results from damage to the part of the brain controlling muscle tone.

Chronic Lung Disease (CLD): See Bronchopulmonary dysplasia.

Code Pink: A resuscitation procedure performed when a baby's heart rate is dangerously low or the baby is not breathing; similar to a Code Blue in an adult patient.

Continuous Positive Airway Pressure (CPAP): A form of respiratory support in which positive pressure is applied to an infant's airways usually through nasal prongs.

CPR: Cardiopulmonary Resuscitation. Emergency first aid procedure provided to patients with cardiac or respiratory arrest (cessation of heart function or cessation of breathing).

Creatinine: A blood test measuring kidney function.

Deep hypothermic circulatory arrest: A procedure used during open heart surgery to bring the heart to a stop by significantly cooling the patient's core temperature to a desired range.

Denial of pregnancy: A psychological condition in which some women deny—even to themselves—that they are pregnant.

Dialysis: A procedure used in kidney failure to cleanse the patient's blood of waste products.

Digoxin: A common medication used to slow an abnormally fast heart rate. It is also used to treat congestive heart failure.

Down Syndrome (Trisomy 21): A genetic condition in which a person has three copies of the twenty-first chromosome, for a total of forty-seven chromosomes instead of the usual forty-six. People with Down syndrome have characteristic physical features as well as developmental disabilities.

DNR: Do Not Resuscitate: Orders written to direct that a patient not receive life-sustaining treatment in the case of a cardiac or respiratory arrest. Orders can be individualized for each patient.

Eclampsia: The condition of preeclampsia (pregnancy-induced hypertension) when it progresses to the point of causing seizures in the pregnant woman.

Epinephrine: A naturally occurring hormone, which is given as a medication, to increase heart rate and raise blood pressure. It is a drug commonly used during a Code Blue or Code Pink resuscitation procedure.

Exchange transfusion: Procedure usually performed to remove bilirubin from baby's blood stream when bilirubin is so high as to lead to kernicterus if not treated. The baby's blood is removed, a little at a time, and replaced with blood from a blood bank.

Gastrostomy tube (G-tube): A feeding tube, which is placed through the skin and stomach wall directly into the stomach.

Gestational age: The age of the embryo, fetus, or infant as calculated from the first day of the mother's last menstrual cycle; measured in weeks of pregnancy.

Gestational diabetes: Diabetes (high blood sugar) diagnosed during pregnancy; it may persist after pregnancy or only occur during pregnancy.

Hematocrit: A blood test measuring the proportion of red blood cells in whole blood.

Hemangioma: An abnormal overgrowth (non-cancerous tumor) of blood vessels, most frequently occurring in the skin but can be found in internal organs.

Home monitor (home apnea monitor): A small, portable machine, which can be used in the home. It is used to alert caregivers when a baby's heart rate or breathing is lower than normal.

Hydrocortisone (cortisol): A steroid hormone released in response to stress; produced by the adrenal glands.

Hyperbilirubinemia: An elevated serum bilirubin, can be due to many causes, most commonly due to immaturity of the enzymes in the liver, which process bilirubin. Hyperbilirubinemia may also be known as *jaundice.*

Hypoglycemia: Low blood sugar.

Intraventricular hemorrhage (IVH): Bleeding into the brain, often into or near the ventricular system where spinal fluid is produced.

Isolette (Incubator): A temperature-controlled environment for an infant.

Jaundice: Yellow-orange color of skin resulting from hyperbilirubinemia of any cause.

Kangaroo care: Skin-to-skin contact between a parent and infant (usually a premature infant); promotes bonding, temperature control, and growth.

Kernicterus: A form of brain damage in newborns, often caused by severe hyperbilirubinemia (jaundice); can have many different causes.

Lidocaine: A medication used to treat abnormal heart rhythms.

Mosaic (referring to chromosomes): A person has some cells with abnormal genetic or chromosomal makeup and some cells that are normal.

Necrotizing enterocolitis (NEC): A gastrointestinal disease usually affecting premature infants; intestinal tissue becomes inflamed and possibly infected, and may become necrotic (dead).

Neonatologist: A pediatrician specializing in the care of sick and premature infants. The training for neonatologists is three years beyond the usual training for general pediatrics.

NICU (Neonatal Intensive Care Unit): A specially designated unit in a hospital for the care of premature or sick infants.

Oxygen saturation: A measure of how much oxygen the blood is carrying; usually measured with a small probe around a baby's hand or foot called a pulse oximeter.

Palliative care ("comfort care"): Care to improve the quality of life, but not produce a cure, for a patient with a serious or fatal illness.

Pediatric Intensive Care Unit (PICU): A specially designated unit in a hospital for the care of children with critical and life-threatening conditions.

Phenobarbital: A medication used to control seizures.

Phototherapy: A type of light treatment used to treat hyperbilirubinemia.

Placental abruption: A complication of pregnancy in which the placenta separates from the wall of the uterus prior to delivery; usually a medical emergency.

Preeclampsia (also known as pregnancy-induced hypertension or toxemia): A disorder of pregnancy causing hypertension in the pregnant mother; may also cause swelling and large amount of protein in the urine.

Post-hemorrhagic hydrocephalus: An abnormal build-up of cerebrospinal fluid in the ventricles of the brain, resulting from an intraventricular hemorrhage.

Postpartum depression: A form of clinical depression occurring in a woman within weeks to a year after she gives birth.

Pulse oximeter: A non-invasive way to measure oxygen saturation.

RespiGam®: Respiratory syncytial virus immune globulin; a preparation of antibodies to RSV given to infants at risk of acquiring this infection to bolster their immunity.

Respiratory syncytial virus (RSV): A virus common in young children less than five-years-old that causes a respiratory tract infection manifested as a wheezing-type illness (bronchiolitis). It is often more serious in former premature infants or those with chronic lung or heart problems.

Retinopathy of prematurity (ROP): An eye disease affecting premature infants in which the blood vessels in the retina do not develop normally. It can lead to blindness from retinal detachment.

Retrospectoscope: An imaginary instrument, which allows the user to look back in time and see mistakes that were made.

Rh incompatibility: A type of blood group incompatibility in which mother has Rh-negative blood type and the baby in her womb has Rh-positive blood type. This incompatibility leads to a breakdown of the fetus' blood cells and subsequently to hyperbilirubinemia.

RhoGam®: A shot providing passive immunization (antibodies) to the Rh-blood factor; given to women who are Rh-negative during pregnancy (usually at the twenty-eighth week) so their bodies will not form their own antibodies to Rh. Prevents Rh isoimmunization.

Small for gestational age (SGA): Baby whose birth weight is less than the 10th percentile for gestational age.

Supraventricular tachycardia (SVT): An abnormally fast heart rhythm originating in the upper chamber (atrium) of the heart.

Surfactant (Pulmonary surfactant): A substance produced by the lungs to enable the alveoli (individual air sacs) to expand by lowering their surface tension.

Synagis® (Palivizumab): A monoclonal antibody against respiratory syncytial virus; given monthly during the RSV season by intramuscular injection to babies at risk to prevent them from acquiring this infection.

Toxemia: See preeclampsia.

Trisomy 18 (also called Edward syndrome): A genetic condition in which a person has three copies of the eighteenth chromosome, for a total of forty-seven chromosomes instead of the usual forty-six. People with Trisomy 18 have characteristic physical features as well as severe developmental disabilities; they frequently do not survive past one year of age.

Trisomy 21: See Down Syndrome.

Twin-to-twin transfusion syndrome: A complication of pregnancy in which one twin transfers blood to another through abnormal blood vessel connections in a shared placenta.

Vasa previa: A complication of pregnancy in which the fetal blood vessels are within the fetal membranes instead of within the umbilical cord; they can also grow across the cervix and can rupture, causing hemorrhage, during labor.

Ventricular fibrillation: A life-threatening abnormality in heart rhythm resulting from disorganized electrical impulses; the heart's contractions are not coordinated, and cardiac output falls leading to inadequate circulation.

Ventricular septal defect (VSD): A congenital abnormality of the heart in which there is an opening between the two lower chambers of the heart, the ventricles.

Ventriculoperitoneal shunt (VP shunt): A surgical procedure to relieve hydrocephalus; involves placing a catheter in the ventricle of the brain to drain cerebrospinal fluid into the peritoneal (abdominal) cavity, thereby relieving excessive pressure in the brain.

Questions for Reading Groups

1. The costs to care for a premature baby, such as Jacob Jenner, in the newborn period alone may be half a million dollars or more, and lifetime costs can be far greater. If "rationing" were to be instituted in the U.S. health care system, do you think it should be applied to any aspects of NICU care, and if so, how?

2. The United States has one of the highest rates of premature birth of any developed country in the world. Did you find that any of the stories shed light on why this is so? Did reading the stories give you any ideas for how premature birth could be prevented?

3. The technology to save babies' lives has improved greatly over time. In the story about Josi, some neonatologists' opinions that "because we can (save lives), we should (save them all)" was voiced. Can you think of any situations in which technology should not be applied to save a baby's life?

4. Jaxon and Jacob are babies who were born prematurely to teenage mothers. After reading their stories, how do you think teen pregnancies could be better prevented, or how could teen mothers be better supported?

5. The stories about Samantha and Grace demonstrated how far both medical professionals and the public have come in their willingness to talk openly about babies born with birth defects, instead of shunning them as being "abnormal" and not worthy of care. How do you think that societal change came about, and does it need to go further? Do you know individuals who went through an experience

where they felt as if they could not talk about their child who had a birth defect? How did it affect them?

6. The lower age limit for resuscitation of babies has continually dropped over the years, and now even babies born as early as the twenty-third or twenty-fourth week out of a normal forty-week gestation (such as Josi and Devon) may survive. It seems that current techniques in medicine may have reached their limits, and the next step to lower the gestational age at which babies can survive might be to go to creation of an artificial womb, in which embryos or fetuses could be nurtured in aquatic chemical environments outside the uterus. Already researchers are working to develop this possibility. Is this a positive and desirable step? Why?

7. Jésus and Tiffany are two babies who began their lives under the influence of maternal drugs. What do you think are reasonable criteria drug-using mothers should meet to take their babies home with them? Why?

8. Since a doctor's prognosis about an individual baby's outcome may be wrong, do you think doctors should share their opinions about a baby's prognosis with the parents? Under what circumstances should they, and when should they not? What duty do they have to inform parents of possible consequences of their choices for ongoing care of their babies?

9. Neonatologists work long hours in a high-stress environment, often twenty-four hours or more at a time, as in the stories about Preston and Devon. Do you think their work hours should be limited? Why?

10. In Charlie's story, the topic of "informed consent" was brought up. Do you agree that doctors should inform patients/parents about all possible complications, no matter how remote? Or, is their duty limited to informing patients/parents of major, more common complications?

What would you want to be told if you were undergoing an invasive procedure or operation?

11. Were there any stories in which you thought the doctors and/or nurses should have responded to a baby's family differently, and why?

12. Was there any baby you found you had particular empathy for? What was it about the baby's story that resonated with you?

13. What was the most surprising thing you learned from reading this book?

14. Grace's mother held on to hope that her daughter would live a reasonably normal life even when evidence suggested otherwise. Oliver Wendell Holmes said to "beware how you take away hope from another human being." How should a health care professional best walk the fine line between hope and reality when a patient is facing difficult circumstances? Have you ever had an experience in which holding on to hope made a difference in your life?

Acknowledgements

I have many people to thank for their support and encouragement as I wrote this book and followed the path toward its publication, starting with my two daughters, who have always cheered me on. Numerous people read all or a good part of the manuscript and provided critical commentary as well as helpful suggestions for its improvement: Mandy and Ben Gramkow, Mary and Rob Evans, Art and Gail Long, Kori and Doug Bigge, Judy Schaefer, Margaret Lyddon, Mary Brink, Martha Hagedorn-Krass, Chris Moody, Jane Jones, Lori Bentley Law, Becky Mitchell, Diana Hockley, Sheila Dalton, Caroline Kellems, Patti Anne Yaeger, Nadine Gallo, Dan Lake, Alan Miles, Scott Eberhart, and Vladimir Lange. I especially thank Angela and Anthony Decker for their assistance.

I am grateful for the friendship of Nancy and Joel Hamlin, who provided me with a wonderful place to spend time writing, and encouraged me to do just that. Special thanks to Vicki Forman for her early vote of confidence and her unflagging optimism about the importance of this book, and to Deb Discenza for also being a champion of the project. Greg Johnson provided support early on as well. Thanks are also in order for Editors Alice Rosengard, who helped me refine and sharpen the book's focus in the early stages of my writing, and Alice Heiserman, who applied her precision with words and form to the task of copy editing the finished manuscript. In addition, I greatly appreciate my publisher, Sol Nasisi of WorldMaker Media, for his unbridled enthusiasm for the book.

I owe a tremendous debt of gratitude to the families whose babies formed the basis for these stories. These and many other parents welcomed me into their lives and allowed me to share some of their most intimate moments. For me, this has been the most treasured privilege of being a physician.

As a neonatologist, my job has been made infinitely easier by the NICU staff members with whom I have worked. I have the utmost respect for the professionalism, dedication, courage, and heart of each and every one of the doctors, nurses, social workers, and all others who give of themselves on a daily basis to provide care in the NICU.

I have spent a lot of time in the trenches with many fine physicians over the years, some of whom have helped make me the physician I am today while becoming dear friends along the way. They include Drs. Robert T. Hall, Kayt Klein Havens, Cynthia Ewing, George Emerson, Maha Amr, Kendra Gorlitsky, Kirsten Evans, Robert Sidlinger, Maria Navarro, and Heather Morgan. And finally, thanks to Dr. Keith Brodie for first suggesting that I consider going to medical school. I am grateful he planted the seed in my mind that eventually germinated and blossomed into a wonderful career.

Sue Lyddon Hall, M.D.
April 2011

About the Author

Dr. Sue Hall earned a B.A. in psychology from Stanford University, a Master's in Social Work from Boston University, and an M.D. degree from the University of Missouri at Kansas City. She was a practicing social worker prior to embarking on her twenty-five-year career as a neonatologist. Formerly an Associate Clinical Professor of Pediatrics at UCLA's David Geffen School of Medicine, Dr. Hall is now in a private practice of neonatology.

Dr. Hall, who lives in the Midwest, has two daughters, now both adults. She is an enthusiastic sailor in her free time. She also enjoys reading and speaking to groups about health care issues of our most vulnerable children.

To learn more, please visit the author's website, www.suehallmd.com.

Made in the USA
Lexington, KY
01 September 2011